Open access edition supported by the National Endowment for the Humanities /
Andrew W. Mellon Foundation Humanities Open Book Program.

© 2019 Johns Hopkins University Press
Published 2019

Johns Hopkins University Press
2715 North Charles Street
Baltimore, Maryland 21218-4363
www.press.jhu.edu

ISBN-13: 978-1-4214-3499-5 (open access)
ISBN-10: 1-4214-3499-7 (open access)

ISBN-13: 978-1-4214-3497-1 (pbk. : alk. paper)
ISBN-10: 1-4214-3497-0 (pbk. : alk. paper)

ISBN-13: 978-1-4214-3498-8 (electronic)
ISBN-10: 1-4214-3498-9 (electronic)

This page supersedes the copyright page included in the original publication of this work.

THE DRAMA OF LANGUAGE

Essays on Goethe and Kleist

Sigurd Burckhardt

THE DRAMA OF LANGUAGE
Essays on Goethe and Kleist

The Johns Hopkins Press *Baltimore and London*

Contents

Foreword

SIGURD BURCKHARDT planned to return to the study of Goethe and Kleist once he completed his sequence of essays on Shakespeare. (Those of the latter which had been previously published or were ready for publication have been collected as *Shakespearean Meanings* [Princeton University Press, 1969].) He spoke at times of developing the essays on Goethe and Kleist he had already published and of perhaps, as a kind of ironic metaphor for the theoretical aspects of the enterprise, introducing a collection of them with an essay on Karl Kraus. For his abiding faith was in the capacity of language, in the hands of a master of theater, to say, with ultimate clarity, economy, and finality, precisely what it meant—and so saying, to furnish the only possible means of human communion. He pretended—or seemed to be pretending—to see this proposition as one of simple common sense. Thus, at moments of high exuberant argument, he claimed that his faith in this proposition meant that he was the only "true" positivist left among his generation's scholar-critics and that, were he a theorist constructing an apologia for his positivism, he would be driven to write it in a Kraussian mode. His particular passion, dedication, and commitment (his "Prussianism" was too much with him, he would say) did not allow him ever to write in that Kraussian mode, although he occasionally talked in it. And a perspicacious reader may detect the mode immanent in his work —detect it as a force that enabled Burckhardt (for a time at least) to live and work and prosper in a world increasingly unable to sense his abiding faith, much less to subscribe to it.

The essays on Goethe and Kleist collected here all demonstrate that faith. We have put as an essay introductory to them one more general but, we think, altogether relevant. Keeping in mind those readers like the second named below, whose German is small tending to less, we have supplied literal translations of the passages from Goethe and Kleist, upon the understanding of which Burckhardt's interpretations crucially depend. The title for the collection is our invention. We suspect that Burckhardt at the outset might have found it too rhetorical for his "positivistic" tastes but that we might in the end have persuaded him that the rhetoric was honorably deserved. The title then is our tribute to him—small thanks for these and other essays of his, and for the man himself.

With the exception of the last, all essays here collected have been previously published. Original publications are as follows:

"Of Order, Abstraction, and Language," *Yale Review*, LIII (1964), 533–50. © 1964 Yale University Press.

"Sprache als Gestalt in Goethes *Prometheus* and *Pandora*," *Euphorion*, L (1956), 162–65. © 1956 Carl Winter Universitätsverlag, Heidelberg.

"Die Stimme der Wahrheit und der Menschlichkeit: Goethes *Iphigenie*," *Monatshefte*, XLVIII (1956), 49–71. © 1956 by the Regents of the University of Wisconsin.

"The Consistency of *Tasso*," *Journal of English and Germanic Philology*, LVII (1958), 394–402.

"*Die natürliche Tochter*: Goethes *Iphigenie in Aulis?*," *Germanisch-Romanische Monatsschrift*, X (1960), 12–34. © 1960 Carl Winter Universitätsverlag, Heidelberg.

"*Egmont* and *Prinz Friedrich von Homburg*: Expostulation and Reply," *German Quarterly*, XXXVI (1963), 112–19.

"Heinrich von Kleist: The Poet as Prussian," *Centennial Review*, VIII (1964), 435–52.

We are grateful to the publishers and editors concerned for allowing us to reprint the essays here.

Particular gratitude is owing to the Committee on Research of the University of California, San Diego, for generous grants which made preparation of this edition possible; to Earl Wasserman, of The Johns Hopkins University, who suggested that we prepare it; to Dagmar Barnouw who helped with the proofs; and, above all, to Lillian Reed Atkins who made all the translations.

BERNHARD BLUME

ROY HARVEY PEARCE

THE DRAMA OF LANGUAGE
Essays on Goethe and Kleist

Introduction:
Of Order, Abstraction, and Language

THE NOTION I want to pursue sprang from my dissatisfaction with *Doctor Zhivago*—more specifically with the opposite and complementary futilities of the two men who love Lara: Zhivago himself and Antipov-Strelnikov, the idealist who turns into a ruthless Red general and finally commits suicide. In the end Pasternak casts his vote for the title hero, who, though he has retreated as entirely into himself as it is possible for a man to do, seems thereby to have preserved something which, in the novel's world, only withdrawal can preserve—his heart. While of Antipov we read: "He had two characteristic features, two passions: an unusual power of clear and logical reasoning, and a great moral purity and sense of justice; he was ardent and honorable. But ... if he were really to do good, he would have needed, in addition to his principles, a heart capable of violating them—a heart which knows only of particular, not of general cases, and which achieves greatness in little actions." Pasternak makes the dichotomy between principles and heart, between particular and general cases, appear final; and we assent only too readily. But is there not, in the last resort, some evasion concealed in the dichotomy, some sentimentality?

As generalizations go, I think it is a safe one that the modern mind distrusts abstractions, even while it is busily inventing more abstractions to feel threatened by. By intellectual temper, if not by philosophical persuasion, we are nominalists; we feel that not only the reality but the truth of a thing inheres in its individuality, and that the act of abstraction lessens this reality and as likely as not violates this truth. The road to deception and self-deception—we not only feel but observe—is paved with abstractions, while the path of truth leads toward the particular.

Up to a point, this nominalist distrust is healthy; but if we follow it to the end, it leads to chaos. Particulars are infinitely numerous; they cannot be ordered except as they are grouped in classes, and every classification entails abstraction. A language that would avoid all abstraction would have to consist entirely of proper names; even our simplest common nouns are already abstractions of a high order. A proper-name language would allow things simply to be "there," would not violate their individuality. But by the same token it would leave them beyond ordering, beyond meaning, beyond truth.

There can be no truth without abstraction; every assertion of which I can meaningfully say: "That is true," or: "That is not true," involves some ordering of experience, some classification of the infinity of things and events. Hence, if by "real" we mean what today we commonly seem to mean—the uniquely individual—we are mistaken in thinking that "truth" and "reality" are all but synonyms. We would do better to think of them as antonyms; but still more precisely: Truth is purchased at the expense of the reality—i.e., the particularity—of the things we talk about. And the more encompassing the truth, the greater the expense. A minute truth—that is, one that provides very little ordering of reality, such as: "Johnny is playing in the garden," or: "Caesar was murdered in 44 B.C." —will cost little in abstraction; whereas a large truth—say, "Every noun carries an existence claim"—costs a great deal.

By the same token, there is no meaning without abstraction. Things that are simply "there" have no meaning, though they have undeniable reality. Nor—as I use the term—do proper names have meaning, though obviously they have a referent. Proper names leave their bearers unrelated and unique; things can be related only by classificatory—i.e., by abstracting—terms. Hence the quest for a thing's, or a word's, meaning is the quest for that more general term or set of terms by which the thing can be related to others. Whether I search for the meaning of a word or for the meaning of my life, I am doing the same thing: I am looking for something under which I can subsume the otherwise unrelated and meaningless particular so as to place it, at the cost of some of its particularity, in a larger order.

I take it that truth, order, meaning are things we value; why, then, are we afraid to pay their price in abstraction? That the abstraction may be a false one explains at most part of this fear—and I think by far the less significant part. More important is our sense that once things are subsumed under an abstract term they seem to lose their identity and become interchangeable. The more we care about things, the more we insist on their having proper names. And since we care most about ourselves, we resent most fiercely the attempt to classify *us*. We are sure that there is more to us than any set of classifying terms, no matter how complete, can possibly exhaust—that there is, at the core, that ineffable, unique, "real" self which wants to be known and understood "just as it is," in its undiminished particularity. We dream of a kind of nominalist paradise, where there is complete individuality without chaos, complete relatedness without reference—where we can be "simply ourselves" and still live in what we vaguely call "harmony" or "organic order," as though we were tones or flowers rather than men. Oddly—this is the paradox of all such paradisal thinking—we fancy that only then can our lives be really "meaningful." But though it may be possible for tones and flowers to be "simply there," it isn't possible for man. Man, who demands meaning, for that very reason cannot have it in the paradisal sense; he cannot have harmony but must have order. The Fall was a fall from the Eden of proper names into the world of common nouns.

We probably recognize nominalist dreaming for what it is; but its indirect effects are not so readily recognized—and are more pervasive. In literature, for example, the equivalent of the thing itself, the unviolated particular, is the "symbol," as that term has come to be understood since the early nineteenth century. A symbol, as distinct from a metaphor, rests on the paradoxical faith that a thing can be quite itself and still, somehow, have meaning, or at least "significance." But the results of this faith prove the opposite. Symbolic readings of poetry tend to abound with death symbols, Christ symbols, sexual symbols, and the like; the result is an archetypal fuzziness, a lack of concreteness and particularity, which makes poems so interpreted all sound vaguely the same. Meaning cannot be kept out; if it is not openly admitted by the door of metaphor, it will seep in as a symbolic fog.

A metaphor, demanding to be analyzed, implicitly acknowledges the separateness of being and meaning and so accepts the challenge of abstraction. Not that metaphors do not also court a danger: the danger of being mere ornaments, pseudo-concrete signs for an abstraction rather than incarnations of it. But I would rather take my risk with a metaphoric than with a symbolic reading of poetry, because meaning commits me to ordering, while being commits me to nothing but "empathy." A mixed metaphor is a fault; but there can be no such thing as a mixed symbol, and I wouldn't know how to find fault even with mixed smybols in the plural, any more than I could with a growth of wild flowers. A true metaphor not only signifies but defines the abstraction implicit in it; it gives outline and specificity, it *embodies*. Whereas a symbol, by pretending to be the ineffable "thing in itself," is likely to dismiss me, unguided and unballasted, into the intense inane of "experience."

Within its sphere, then, the metaphor pays tribute to our fallen estate; it does not evade the problem of meaning and abstraction, but confronts it. Though it too is born of the mistrust of mere abstraction, it does not chase the illusion of the particular as the sole bearer of truth. To paraphrase Oscar Wilde: nominalism is the unspeakable in pursuit of the incomprehensible—a modern form of mysticism. In fact, it is—with its divergent but sibling literary offspring, symbolism and naturalism—simply a mysticism of the Many instead of the One. (I apologize for this cacophony of -isms, but I cannot well avoid it. There is no literary movement called "metaphorism," nor can there be.) Metaphor accepts the limits short of these mysticisms as the specifically human limits and tries to do within them the hard work of saving us from the desert of abstraction and the jungle of particularity.

The sure sign that metaphors are "human" in this sense is that they remain intimately bound to the given language with all its accidents and limitations and seek to transform them into opportunities. As every translator knows, metaphors are hardest, often impossible to render adequately in another language; symbols translate much more easily, and the more imagistic they are, the more easily are they rendered. Poetry is the least translatable of all modes of discourse, not because the poet surrounds his words with a vague aura of "rich connotation," but because he treats *all* the features of the language—its rhythms, sounds, and puns, as well as the concrete meanings buried in its abstractions—as metaphors. As we approach the limits of language—the all but total abstraction of mathematical signs and the all but total particularity of proper names—the obstacles to translation vanish; they increase to the degree that we submit to the language entrusted to us—that we treat its corporeality with the care due a carrier of meaning.

Translatability—interchangeability—is the corollary of abstraction and so of order and truth; an apple and a planet are interchangeable under the laws of gravitation. Hence, as classes become more embracing, interchangeability increases. But more important for my present purpose is the reverse: as interchangeability increases, so do classes. It is a chicken-egg question whether the principle of interchangeable parts is a response to the demands of mass production, mass culture, mass society or whether it creates them; obviously the causal relation is reciprocal, and we can read it either way. In any case, common linguistic usage registers the changes which this sort of abstraction causes in our thinking: the word "number" is rapidly losing ground to "statistic." "Here is a statistic on how many people voted in the election," the news commentator will say—and produce a number, the result of a simple count. This is not just a lapse into jargon; it testifies to the advances of interchangeability. Counting and numbering is of individual things and so implies handling; statistics are derived from classes and proceed by inference and extrapolation. As the statistical methods of sampling and extrapolating become more refined and sure, the counting of votes become more superfluous, though as a vestigial ceremony of popular sovereignty it will no doubt continue to be performed.

By now we feel so threatened by order—or rather by what we feel to be its corollaries, abstraction and interchangeability—that we find it difficult to remember that order used to be felt as one of the peculiar glories of creation. The chain of being and the golden ladder—now transformed into the chain of command and the organizational chart—were once matters, and metaphors, both of comfort and pride. Dante's *Divine Comedy* is a hymn to order—not of the organic kind, but insistently, almost metallically *wrought*. The startling—at least for us moderns startling—fact about it is that at the same time it is so richly concrete and individual. Almost miraculously, Dante manages to have the best of both worlds; in the totally ordered world he constructs for us, every inhabitant exists, in undiminished reality, within the sight of Him Whose eye is on the sparrow.

Unlike Dante, Homer does not set out to create a world—though he does; with the sublime parochialism of the Greeks, he trusts that one episode from one war will sustain and order the vast bulk of narrative—and it does. Olympus for him is not a dimension of the world, as the Paradiso is for Dante; the gods are mortals with death subtracted, so that they mirror men in an almost parodistic counterimage: their inconsequential, because "deathless," squabbles and jealousies turn into men's death agonies. The question of justice—the most powerful motive force behind the attempt to order by abstraction—is never seriously raised in any but the trader's sense of proper equivalents; Thersites, who does raise it as a modern might, is scourged out of the assembly as an ignoble scoundrel. What matters—with death as the ineluctable *terminus ad quem*—is nobility, an heroically ceremonial propriety of conduct, speech, and bearing. The epic's final and most moving scene—Priam's confrontation with Achilles, which for me ranks with Lear's recovery of Cordelia—arises from a point of ceremony, the treatment of Hector's body; the common humanity of Homer's heroes reveals itself in the common need to make grief and pain bearable, and in a measure meaningful, through nobly stylized enactment. Hence Homer's concreteness has none of the modern, anxiety-driven effort not to violate a thing's unique individuality; it is the concreteness of figures and actors in a sometimes wild, sometimes grave, and always noble rite.

Dante's concreteness is entirely different; it has some of the quality of a collection of lepidoptera carefully ordered by species, genus, and family (provided we are passionate lepidopterists and each specimen has its story). The analogy is inadequate, of course; but it does point up the fact that the classificatory instinct, so utterly lacking in Homer, is everywhere at work in the *Divine Comedy*, ordering everything between the triple mouth of Satan and the Trinity. And the informing principle of the vast classification is justice. But as Homer never raises the question of justice itself, so Dante never raises that of legitimate final authority, which to our minds is inseparable from it. The problem of God's own justice—of His right to order the world as He has—is settled in the line: "In His will is our peace." And Vanni Fucci—the Thersites, as it were, of the *Divine Comedy*—is last seen in the posture of obscene defiance.

The damned have their own, inverse hierarchy; a good deal of the dignity that seems to attach to all hierarchical ordering also belongs to them. Not that Dante wants to glorify sin (though in his contempt for the "neuter" souls he takes a step toward doing so); he certainly was no Romantic diabolist. But the sheer, metaphor-engendering force of the sins cannot but give them the dignity which all generative forces have; and beyond that is the fact that Hell is a fully articulated part of the divine order. The order itself is legitimate beyond question; and since to challenge its justice is unthinkable, Dante is not compelled to deny evil the noble attribute of substantial existence. I am not competent to speak of Dante's theology; but whatever it was, the poet knew better than to represent evil as privative.

A glance at *Paradise Lost* will be of help here. Anti-royalist and anti-episcopalist though he was, Milton knew of the dignity and differentiating concreteness possessed by creatures that are hierarchically ordered. The newly fallen angels still have some of the glory of their heavenly origin—and with it a measure of individuality. The palace they rear is a replica of the royal mansions of Heaven:

> The hasty multitude
> Admiring enter'd, and the work some praise
> And some the Architect: his hand was known
> In Heav'n by many a Towred structure high,
> Where Scepter'd Angels held their residence,
> And sat as Princes, whom the supreme King
> Exalted to such power, and gave to rule,
> Each in his Herarchie, the Orders bright.

So they begin; but when Satan returns to report on the success of his mission, though he opens in the old style—"Thrones, Dominations, Princedoms, Vertues, Powers"—he ends by speaking to a coiling "rout" of snakes: "for now were all transform'd / Alike, to Serpents." The point to note is not so much the hideousness as the undifferentiable *sameness* of these transformed spirits; they have merged into an abstractly uniform image of Evil.

This comes of having to justify the ways of God to men. Dante is not apologetic about classification; it is a happy achievement, warranty of order and truth. It is justified by the intolerability of its opposite:

> Oh, how hard it is to tell
> what a dense, wild and tangled wood this was,
> the thought of which renews my fear!
> So terrible it is that death is hardly worse.

Within the order everything falls into place, so that, far from doing violence to reality, it alone *gives* reality. Dante is completely untroubled by the neo-classical problem: how much individuality may safely be given to representative, ideal-typical figures? Happily he numbers the streaks on his tulips, because for him the ordering category is not something precarious and fragile, which might break under the burden of the concrete; it is something so unquestionably sure, good, and true that the more fully it is embodied the truer it appears.

Also, the order itself being timeless, it gives scope to the "histories" of the individuals it places; these histories, in fact, justify the individuals' placing within the eternal frame. For Milton, on the other hand, that frame *itself* demands justification; so that of necessity he tells, not histories but archetypal History. The shift prefigures nothing less than the historicism of a much later time—the nineteenth century's attempt to justify the ways of God to men. That Milton focuses the problem of ultimate justice on our first parents has more than only theological significance: the case (Latin for "fall") of Adam and Eve is the case of all cases and so, in the moral sphere, the class of all classes. Under it all future cases are subsumed, so that God's justice can be vindicated once and for all, in the most encompassing of abstractions.

The eighteenth century abounded with attempts to justify God's ways, but each attempt left the grand design rather worse than it found it, for the simple reason that the evils the apologist's ingenuity summoned up to explain away remained substantive and sensible, while the explanations were speculative and debatable. By the time Samuel Johnson finished with Soame Jenyns, it should have been clear that evil can never be explained away; the attempt is self-defeating. The last word on every such effort is Johnson's massively sane point about the supposed benefits of poverty: "Sir, all the arguments which are brought to represent poverty as no evil, show it to be evidently a great evil. You never find people labouring to convince you that you may live very happily upon a plentiful fortune."

The point is this: the so-called Age of Reason shows every sign of losing faith in the great ordering abstractions which it is so often maligned for having unduly relied on. (Tell me what a man insists on proving, and I'll tell you what he is unsure of.) And with the loss of faith went a loss of concreteness. There seems to be a law at work: abstractions—at least in the moral, the human sphere—will not abide question. They retreat to the next higher abstraction, until the end is reached, and then there is nothing. God, Reason, Nature, Idea, Historical Process—these are, in roughly chronological sequence, the chief ultimate abstractions we have "run through," with increasing speed, since we began to demand that any such abstraction must be able to present its credentials. None of them can.

Ferrero's principle of legitimacy holds in the intellectual as well as in the political realm: once God was dethroned, all the successors were usurpers, quickly recognized as such and toppled in turn. But in this process abstraction was by no means got rid of; on the contrary. When Pope, in the *Essay on Man*, proposed that "Whatever is, is right," he said something not very different, in theory, from Dante's "In His will is our peace." But in concrete substance, in metaphorical fact he was saying something altogether different. The need he and his age felt to justify God did not in the long run save God, but it reduced men and things to cases. Pope has abundance of what are called "specific details," but they are instances, cases in point; so that, as soon as they have made their point they are dismissed from the witness stand. Dante's line meant to him that, secure in it, he could attend—in pity, terror, wonder, indignation, and love—to whatever *was*. But when, in the *Essay on Man*, it turned into a proposition demanding proof, the world turned gray.

Perhaps we can say that the truth-yielding commerce between reality and ordering abstraction is mutually beneficial only as long as the legitimacy of the abstraction is not questioned; as soon as it is, the abstraction, to prove itself legitimate, will draw sustenance from the particulars and reduce them to cases—evidential instances instead of individual things. The abstraction will not thereby save itself, but neither, unfortunately, will its fall restore reality to its victims. For our overriding need of order will set up another abstraction, which—lacking legitimacy since it is manifestly our creature—will exact truly Napoleonic tributes in concreteness.

Legitimacy is a humpty-dumpty; there is no restoring it. When the Protestants challenged the authority of Holy Church, the Catholics cast doubt on the sufficiency of Holy Scripture; both sides won their point. When natural-right republicans denied the divine institution of monarchy, legitimists denied the validity of natural rights; when socialists called private property theft, liberals called public ownership tyranny. These are battles in which none can lose; what by now we have lost is our zest for them. Except where the ceremonial invocation of absolutes is demanded or the defense budget needs to be defended, we have stopped worrying about the legitimation of what we do and believe; who wants to be a true believer?

There would be nothing wrong with this if, as the psychoanalysts say, we could be happy with it. Why weep over lost absolutes, if they are worth having only as long as they aren't questioned? Is it not just a matter of cultural lag, of our rhetoric and moral reflexes not yet having caught up with the actual state of our intellectual affairs? The linguistic philosophers tell us—plausibly enough—that most concepts, especially of the larger, ordering kind, are "open," definable not by a limited set of necessary and sufficient criteria but only by usage. Psychologists show that someone who believes in absolutes tends to have an authoritarian personality structure. This is an age of great mobility; we must, and in time will, learn to think in terms of fields and functions instead of trying to locate ourselves by any fixed system of coordinates.

Perhaps so—*if* our malaise were that we aren't used yet to living without ordering abstractions. But our real trouble is the feeling that we are losing our identities. It is a mistake to think that the less we have of the first the more we are bound to have of the second. Consider the new Unabridged Webster, or rather the common speaker, who finds his authority so handsomely acknowledged in it. The makers of the Dictionary disclaim the role of lawgivers; they have simply recorded the words as they are actually used. But, like Dwight MacDonald, I doubt very much if the common speakers—and users of the dictionary—will be grateful for this deference to *vox populi*. They have an uneasy sense that often they aren't "right," and they consult the dictionary to discover what *is* right. If they find—as under the descriptivist dispensation they are increasingly likely to—that they are *vox dei* and what they are saying is "in the dictionary," they would *like* to feel that they have been right, but the most they do feel is that they haven't been wrong—a very different feeling. It's not a question of either looking facts in the face or joining the last outpost of spinster schoolmarms who fulfill themselves by "upholding standards." The real problem is whether on the principle that whatever is is right, things—words, in this case, but through them also the things they stand for—do not lose contour, concreteness, savor.

When T. S. Eliot, in *Murder in the Cathedral*, has the Knights address themselves directly to the audience to defend their murder of Thomas à Becket, I think he wants us to listen with Brutus' speech in our inner ear:

We beg you [the Knights plead] to give us your attention for a few moments. We know that you may be disposed to judge unfavourably of our action. . . . [But] you are Englishmen, and therefore will not judge anybody without hearing both sides of the case. . . . For that reason I shall do no more than introduce the other speakers, who, with their various abilities, and different points of view, will be able to lay before you the merits of this extremely complex problem.

The merits of this extremely complex problem aside, this is what has become of: "As Caesar lov'd me, I weep for him; as he was fortunate, I rejoice at it; as he was valiant, I honour him; but, as he was ambitious, I slew him." It's *our* merits that are at issue; by making the Knights speak in this fashion directly to us, Eliot tells us who *we* are (compared to the Roman rabble) that we should be so spoken to. It's not that the Knights' language is more abstract; Brutus has a fatal capacity for abstraction, for separating spirit from body and virtues from faults. It's not that the language is jargon, though of course it is that also. It is that the Knights, to escape from the jaws of Satan where Dante had put Brutus, are pleading for admission among us, the shapeless neuter souls:

> The heavens, to remain beautiful, drove them out,
>   nor would deep Hell receive them,
>   lest the wicked gain pride by comparison.
> They have no hope of death,
>   and their blind life is so debased
>   that they are envious of every other lot.

Nothing is easier, and more superfluous, than to scourge our time for being that of the organization man, the status seeker, and the other-directed inside dopester; self-flagellation is the fashion. And nothing is more futile than to mourn over dead divinities; statistics are here to stay. But I think it is important that we do not mistake the nature of what we feel threatened by. If I have brought Dante into the argument, it was not to preach a return to what is gone beyond recovery, but to make clear that it is not order and abstraction *as such* who are the enemy. The enemy is the abstraction that evades the responsibility of being one, the order that tries to persuade us of its non-existence.

   After Lara, in *Doctor Zhivago*, sees Antipov once more, she reports: "It was as if something abstract had crept into his face and made it colorless. As if a living human face had become the embodiment of a principle, the image of an idea." Lara's is the modern view, and it is too simple. Just what is this color-draining principle? It is a state that professes to seek the withering away of the state—i.e., an order that tries to make itself legitimate by declaring its own illegitimacy. Which means that its servants are from the outset absolved of coming to personal terms with it or of making it come to personal terms with them—in other words, truly to *embody* it. For "really" they do not serve the order; they serve its dissolution into an orderless utopia. Utopias are in bad repute with us—and rightly. But I am not sure the reason we have to fear them is always clearly understood. The reason is not—as most anti-utopias suggest—that utopias themselves are nightmares; it is that they rob the order within which we do live and act of moral content and us of moral responsibility for it. The utopian is not someone deludedly on the road to a hell which he thinks heaven; heaven or hell, he is someone who spends his life in motel rooms to get there.

An order which disowns itself is bad; one which is so fuzzily defined, so anxiously permissive that we cannot even strike out at it is no better. What makes the American rebels sound so oddly futile is not, or not always, the causes in whose name they defy the establishment; the difficulty is that their very cries are muffled and smothered in an enveloping fog of ready acceptance. Instead of being *épaté'd*, the bourgeois provide fellowships; short of flinging the paint at the spectators instead of at a canvas that is sure to be found at least "interesting," the trick simply cannot be turned. (And even that, I gather, has been tried and is now institutionalized as a "happening.") Beatniks are invited to Westchester house parties; Henry Miller writes for *Harper's Bazaar*; *Naked Lunch* is a best-seller even without the benefit of an obscenity trial. The gestures of social protest, unless they turn into actual crime, degenerate into twitches; they have no style, since there is no style for them to define themselves against. Some things may secretly frighten us, but we wouldn't be caught dead being scandalized.

If not in the world, at least in my argument, surely "The Second Coming" is at hand, Yeats's poem even the terror of which we have failed to live up to. It is truer than ever that the ceremony of innocence is lost and that the best lack all conviction; but I at least see no rough beast slouching toward Bethlehem. And is mere anarchy loosed upon the world? There is, it would seem, plenty of cohesion—or better, cohesiveness, since it is somewhat viscous. If the center cannot hold, the reason is that we have discovered how to do without one; like a homogeneous liquid, we are held together by surface tension. Having managed to make the Second World War give birth to an economic miracle rather than an apocalyptic beast, we are by way of learning to co-exist with "fusion." It is only the nostalgic hindsight of 1964 that detects a touch of wistfulness beneath Yeats's fearful hope?

The private little apocalypses which the existentialists prescribe I for one find futile or worse. In a misdirected rage against a misunderstood idea of order and abstraction, we are invited to strip ourselves of every attribute, every last predicate, and take the existential leap. As social beings we are told to become *engagés*, to invest our passion and energies not in enterprises we have first judged valuable and therefore chosen, but in such as we, by our choice and investment, first *make* valuable. To say that this is meaningless is, of course, no answer to the existentialist, since meaning is precisely what he wants, at least initially, to get rid of and what then, by the sovereignty of the naked "I am," he wants to *give*. I am not denying that the existentialist experience can be a very real one; except for the last step it is that of King Lear. But there is a vast difference between suffering an experience and advocating it as a road to salvation—and also between Lear and men of ordinary stature. Most of us are Gloucesters at best; and even Lear, after he has suffered through the insane agony of thinking that he alone can give meaning, wakes up to *find* it—in Cordelia. However genuine the experience may be for the few, the very few people capable of so much suffering—

> The oldest hath borne most; we that are young
> Shall never see so much, nor live so long—

I think it an arrogant fraud to cry it abroad as a recipe.

Where, then, is order to be had? Or how can we save ourselves from statistics—the only kind of ordering our nominalism seems to permit? (For statistics draws its insidious strength from the fact that it *appears* to leave the particular inviolate and yet to create order.) I have, of course, no general order to propose; and if I did, it would certainly not command the unquestioning assent such an order needs to be any good. But I think I can propose a paradigm case of what ordering other than statistics is still possible for us. I can propose language.

What strikes me as the falsity of the descriptivist view of language— the essentially statistical view taken by the new Unabridged Webster— is not that it refuses to dictate what is wrong and what is right usage but that it refuses responsibility for its dictation. In making the average speaker the arbiter of usage, it in effect puts the decision of rightness and wrongness into the mouths of those who take no, or almost no, responsibility for their decision—who are, in fact, not even aware that they are making one. In politics the voter, no matter how uninformed or irresponsible he may be, at least knows that when he casts his vote he is deciding something; but the votes which decide the meaning of what we say and hear are, under the descriptivist system, cast unthinkingly by the billion every day. This might be all right if language were a tool and nothing more; but language is also an ordered and ordering entity. It can, of course, be used badly, but it can also be ill-used. Which means that ideally every speaker should, with every utterance, feel a moral obligation not only to the man he speaks to, but also to the language he speaks *in*. Every sentence is a moral act in both these senses; formally to vest the authority over usage and meaning in those who are least aware of this twofold obligation seems to me perverse.

Like money, language is a medium of exchange; it is there to be used, mostly in a very prosaic fashion. But it differs from money in this: while money can be used badly, it cannot, in itself, be abused. Money is by definition interchangeable; that is why it has no moral identity, except for misers and numismatists. Since it is interchangeable, money is fully defined by usage or by the institutional form of usage—government control. Once words are felt to be of the same order as money, they go the same way. That is the point when we begin to talk like Eliot's Knights.

I am not so monomaniacal as to think that the root of all our troubles is linguistic, and that if only we learn to speak with care and responsibility, our problems will solve themselves. Nor do I suggest that what ails us is that most shapeless of abstractions: a failure of communication. When I propose language as a paradigm case, I mean no more than this: that properly looked at, it may rid us of our nominalist sentimentalities, clarify our nominalist confusions—and perhaps even point to ways of doing something about them. Language—more precisely, *our* language— is an order we are born into, which we cannot abandon, which we have very little prospect of changing in any basic way—in short, an order we are stuck with. Its very essence is that it abstracts; only thus can it order raw experience. If we fear and resent it as somehow violating our essential reality—our ineffably individual "truth"—we do not thereby escape from either order or abstraction; we only abandon them to the lowest, meanest level: statistics. And having done so, we are still stuck with language; in fact, we are mired in it. It's worse than useless to cry out against the "tyranny of words" or to punctuate a sullen silence with "Howls" against a homogenized civilization. Nor is there any point in fighting hopeless rearguard actions in defense of archaisms dear to teachers of grammar. But I believe there *is* point in our accepting our language as an entailed estate, given, inalienable, and entrusted to us for use, care, and improvement.

To the degree that we so accept it, we will discover in it, and through it, rich reserves of ordered particularity. Like the poets, we will learn to think of it as a mode of action that is necessarily public but at the same time assumes the sharp moral contours of private dealing. We will find that, in its parts and in its entirety, language is a structure of metaphors —of "concrete universals"—which permit and compel us to make the spirit answer to the letter, the letter to the spirit. We may not have the time or the skill fully to meet our obligation; but at least we will feel the shame of liars over words we render shapeless by ill-usage, over figures whose integrity we violate by mean employment, over sentences that we let soggily ooze toward a halt.

The great Jewish-Austrian satirist Karl Kraus (1874–1936) came as close to despairing of language as it is possible to come without lapsing into cries or incoherence. Since he worked entirely with, and within, the *body* of German, treating its words, phrases, and features as moral metaphors, he is rarely translatable; nor did he wish it otherwise, since this particular language was the only deity he served. But one passage of his does permit translation—for reasons that will be obvious from the passage itself. As he does most of the time, Kraus begins by quoting excerpts from a newspaper item (in brackets) and then comments:

[Dedication of the Social Center of the Austrian Political Society.... Councillor Dr. Friedrich Baron von Wieser gave the main address.... Among other things he said: "... The war has restored our faith in ourselves, and this faith will remain with us ... Phalanx ... Austria for the Austrians! ... and at home only those will have a voice who profess loyalty to the state. Those who do not feel drawn to the state by love and reverence will be kept down by the fear to which they are exiled by the force of the public conscience...." Among those present were noted: ... Landesberger ... District Councillor Stiglitz ... Imperial Councillor Berl ... Commercial Councillor Koffmann ... Neurath ... Herzfelder ...]
Thus the *Free Mind*, the enemy of censorship. But I am resolved, at war's end, to unlearn German as it is now spoken, to retreat before these masters of the German language into the language itself.... My talk will be in broken German; I will not give voice to the word that feels at home in their mouths, nor will I let it reach me.... Phalanx, I shall say, nix German; me no love Stiglitz, me no reverence Landesberger; me fear Neurath, yes, me fear; this faith us remain—me kept down—prices up—me fear, bad time come—big bad time—me go away to nigger—there no see Imperial Councillor, no see Berl, no see District Councillor, Commercial Councillor—me no more note present—no more hear—no more speak—me fear—fear—fear.

Kraus did continue to speak, to use the language as a whip upon its abusers. He was anything but genteel in his standards; he cared about the living language, the spoken idiom. But he could look at a sentence or phrase and discover in it—not behind it but in it—whatever fraudulence, callousness, meanness, or cowardice had gone into its making. Except for his language he had no "cause"; he scourged venal Jewish journalism and anti-Semitic vileness, Socialist hypocrisy and Capitalist greed, Internationalist mouthings and Blood-and-Soil barbarities. (And when it came to the point, as with the accession of the Nazis in 1933, he knew how to distinguish between all these and the degrees of their viciousness.) But he never struck at one in the name of the other; he struck at all in the name of the language they had abused.

When Voltaire despaired of metaphysical certainty, he advised each of us to cultivate his own garden. But then Voltaire was still sure of a good many things we are no longer sure of. Being sure of almost nothing, we have to *make* sure of what we have—in common. If we can no longer trust even the Cartesian "cogito, ergo sum," the last resort is not the existentialist one of deleting the "cogito" and retreating into the empty noise of "sum," but to recall that the most minimal and private assertion is still speech: a moral, social act presupposing another speaker, a shared order, and the possibility of rendering that order truer than it is. "Loquor, ergo es"—I speak, therefore you exist *as a hearer and speaker—* is a sentence which even he who tries to dispute must prove true in the very act of disputing.

1. Language as Form in Goethe's *Prometheus* and *Pandora*

> Ob man nun wohl, wie auch geschehn, bei diesem Gegenstande
> philosophische, ja religiöse Betrachtungen anstellen kann, so
> gehört er doch ganz eigentlich der Poesie.
>
> [Even though one may reflect in philosophic, indeed religious,
> terms on this subject, as has happened, it still belongs quite
> literally to poetry.]
>
> *Dichtung und Wahrheit*, Book XV

ANDORA is a favorite daughter with me to whom I intend to give a strange dower"—Goethe writes thus to K. F. v. Reinhard (June 22, 1808), but then changes his mind and instead of "intend" puts a passive "am compelled."[1] The correction startles us. Again and again the accoutrements—that is, the language—of the play have been called "masterly"; even Goethe himself remarked in another place, "how intentionally this was undertaken and carried out."[2] Conversely, "compelled" seems to characterize exactly the verbal creativity of the young author of *Prometheus*; language, pushed forth by forces that were hardly subjected to "intentional" management and control, still bubbled up for him like a fountain. What "compelled" Goethe to bring into the world a child which again and again he characterizes by epithets like "strange," "abstruse," "mysterious" and which he recommends to the benevolence of his friends, as though it could not count on such a reception without his intercession? And how can he have meant it, when he speaks of the so very forced language of the late work in a manner which brings it close to the entirely different language of his youth? It may be rewarding to pursue these questions a bit, especially as it is a matter here of one of Goethe's "vital *idées fixes*" that he himself relegates expressly to the realm of poetry.

Textual criticism today leans to the assumption that the famous ode of defiance of Prometheus must have originated before the dramatic fragment—that the ode gave birth to the fragment and not, as Goethe believed thirty-seven years later, the fragment to the ode.[3] However that may be, it is significant that such a lyrical utterance could be fitted into the drama without constraint or break; in its frame it does not at all seem an "interpolation," but simply dramatic monologue. The whole play is maintained in this ode-like language, which bubbles forth without

16

impediment, without strict versification, without distinction between speech and song. At one place, to be sure, there are indications of the inner contradictions which are hidden behind its Titanic bravado—in the declaration to Minerva:

> Und du bist meinem Geist
> Was er sich selbst ist;
> Sind von Anbeginn
> Mir deine Worte Himmelslicht gewesen!
> Immer als wenn meine Seele spräche zu sich selbst,
> Sie sich eröffnete
> Und mitgeborne Harmonieen
> In ihr erklängen aus sich selbst.
> Das waren deine Worte.
> So war ich selbst nicht selbst,
> Und eine Gottheit sprach,
> Wenn ich zu reden wähnte,
> Und wähnt' ich eine Gottheit spreche,
> Sprach ich selbst.[4]   (ll. 100–113)

[And you are to my spirit what it is to itself; your words were my celestial light from the beginning, always as though my soul were speaking to itself, as though it would open up its heart and innate harmonies would resound of themselves in it! That is what your words were. Thus I myself was not myself, and a deity spoke when I imagined I spoke, and if I imagined a deity were speaking, I myself was speaking.]

The claim of Promethean language—of magically fusing subject and utterance—rests therefore on the feeling of identity with the deity. This is however no obvious certainty and cannot be one as long as it is not also expressed; it should and must be first created verbally, be "claimed." And we perceive the rage with which language here revolts against its own nature: therefore the desperate subjunctives and the double "imagined"; therefore the monomanic repetitions of "myself" and finally even the denial of this self in "Thus I myself was not myself." This is no song of triumph, no matter how much it strives to comport itself as such; here Goethe wrestles with the word face on, and it conquers him. Otherwise the claim of identity lends his language "innate harmonies." Gods speak in this way; for them, everything—even the word—is direct creation, and is thus directly true and self-justified.

Pandora also makes mention of the word at a significant point, in the closing promise of Eos:

> Gleich vom Himmel
> Senket Wort und Tat sich segnend nieder,
> Gabe senkt sich, ungeahnet vormals.   (ll. 1058–60)

[Word and deed alike descend as blessing from heaven, a gift descends—once unimagined.]

We might now suppose that—whatever it may lack in the play—unhappy humanity has word and deed in sufficiency, for the two Titans are respectively the very essence of word and deed. But the deeds of the Prometheans, the words of Epimetheus, are branded here by Eos as provisional, since true word, true deed, is actually just promised. We naturally have a premonition—it could only have become completely clear in the unwritten second part of *Pandora*—that the solution of the riddle is to be sought in the singular verb, that the divine gift was to make unnecessary the choice with which Faust in translating the Bible already saw himself faced. But in what sense is the language of the first part, that is, human speech, only provisional?

One thing is apparent: the harmonies of *Pandora* are anything but "innate." We know that during its composition Goethe commissioned Riemer to prepare regular reports on Greek metrics; but even without this there could be no doubt that the language forms of the pageant are "preconceived" in an extremely high degree. They lay no claim to directness but to the exact opposite: they push forward and force our attention before it can turn to the subject matter. It is perhaps going too far, if we describe them simply as "unnatural"; such judgments depend too often on habits which the poet possibly wishes to break or at least ease. A six-foot iambic line (although called "long-tailed" by Goethe himself) is, in absolute terms, certainly as "natural" as the more familiar blank verse. But we may safely take Goethe at his word when he describes the form of the play as "strange." Samuel Johnson once remarked that eternal efforts to present poverty as an advantage just prove that it is a great evil, and that nobody bothers to convince us of the advantages of wealth. The same is true of the numerous attempts to present the language of *Pandora* as not at all so unnatural as it "appears." No worse critical service could be rendered Goethe's intentions. When we scan

Mühend versenkt ängstlich der Sinn
Sich in die Nacht, suchet umsonst
Nach der Gestalt   (ll. 789–91)

[Toiling and fearful, the mind subsides in the night, and seeks in vain the shape.]

then we do well to feel this kind of metre as an act of violence and to incorporate it as such in our interpretation of the whole. And if, "toiling" and "fearful," we try to follow a construction like

Wer säh' den Saum an, zeigte sich der Fuss im Schritt,
Beweglich, wie die Hand, erwidernd Liebesdruck (ll. 643–44)

[Who would look at the hem, if he saw the striding foot as lissom as a hand responding to loving pressure],

then we will certainly be more just to Goethe if we do not attempt to explain away the "inter-wedging"[5] of this syntax. What should first strike our eye, or, rather, our ear most emphatically, is how the corpus of language becomes autonomous. *Pandora* does not invite us to a direct sharing and identification with those acting and speaking; it places language as a barrier between them and us. We feel as though we were under water; we see things, but we always see also the water in its own movement.

This opalescence does not seem to me sufficiently explained by the entirely justified reference to the baroque-allegorical character of the pageant—much less appraised.[6] Goethe's turning to allegory certainly does not mean that he regarded this as a form of representation superior in itself, but rather that he found in it a device for treating significant meanings which he wished to express just in this play. Thus we are helped little by the concept of "allegorical"; we must pursue the specific verbal effects which *here* make up the content of the concept. Let us begin with the conduct of dialogue in *Prometheus* and *Pandora*. In doing so we must be sure to bear in mind that it is a question of two different genres, and that drama and pageant are subject to diverse formal laws. Still, the pageant also has plainly dramatic components and aspects; the figures are entangled with one another in the action and by their behavior impel it to its catastrophic ending. Indeed, from the point of view of action, *Pandora* is essentially "more dramatic" than *Prometheus*. But the linguistic relationship of the figures to each other lets none of this be felt. In *Prometheus* the figures address one another quite directly and take the very word "out of one another's mouths." Formally regarded, the dialogue is genuine exchange; the utterances are given repeatedly in fragments which are not completed syntactically until they have been responded to:

PROMETHEUS: Und dafür hatten sie Gehorsam meiner Kindheit,
Den armen Sprössling zu bilden
Dahin, dorthin, nach dem Wind ihrer Grillen.
MERKURIUS: Und schützten dich.
PROMETHEUS: Wovor? Vor Gefahren
Die *sie* fürchteten. (ll. 18–23)

[PROMETHEUS: And for that they had the obedience of my childhood, to
                mould their poor offspring this way, that way, according
                to the wind of their whims.
MERCURY: And they protected you.
PROMETHEUS: From what? From dangers that *they* feared.]

At almost no point can one begin to quote without some sort of syntacti-
cal thread being severed. The very beginning of the whole work posits a
preceding dialogue, and through the raising of the curtain we do not
become witnesses of an incipient action, but fellow hearers of a con-
tinuing conversation.

   In *Pandora* the dialogue—if one can at all call it such—is of an entirely
different mould. The public is, to be sure, directly addressed only once—
by Elpore; but this stepping out of the frame, which would bring *Prometheus* out of joint, represents here in no way an absolute break. It is
rather an expressive gesture for the inner state of affairs of the play,
which does not at all allow for a frame that encompasses all its figures.
(We shall see that it is more than that.) For these speak to be sure, but
with whom do they communicate? *Prometheus* opens with: "I will not!
Tell them that!"—the pageant, on the other hand, opens with a long
address to nobody other than perhaps "the vigorous age of youth." It is
not even a genuine monologue, like Iphigenia's for instance, in which
the speaker gives voice to his thoughts; rather, Epimetheus steps as
speaker as it were out of himself:

   Ein solch Behagen, ferne bleibt's dem Alten, mir.   (l. 6)

   [Such delight, it is remote from an old man, from me.]

Iphigenia would have said, "Such delight is remote from me"; the young
Prometheus would have complained vehemently. But Epimetheus as
speaker stands off to the side, and introduces himself to himself. (As he
also repeatedly sets forth and presents other things out of their contexts;
the typical sentence form of *Pandora* breaks apart subject and verb, word
and deed: "But the paths of men, they are not to be illuminated.") Yet
this is not enough: Goethe appears not to want to leave anything at all
to our immediate apprehension. As Phileros appears, we hear from
Epimetheus:

   Was aber hör' ich? Knarrend öffnen sich so früh
   Des Bruders Thore. Wacht er schon, der Thätige? ...
   Nicht so! Ein eilend leiser Tritt bewegt sich her,
   Mit frohem Tonmass herzerhebenden Gesangs.   (ll. 28–35)

[But what do I hear? Gratingly, my brother's gates open so early. Is he already awake, the man of action? ... But no! A hurrying light step approaches with joyous measure of heartwarming song.]

This is of course not lack of expository skill, but conscious calculation. Everything is presented to us in the cloak of the word and really exists only in it; we are not permitted direct apperception.

To be sure, the figures do speak with each other; if this were not so, even a pageant play would be impossible. Still, the few utterances in dialogue are just as self-contained as those of *Prometheus* are open at both ends. Epimetheus and Phileros meet:

EPIMETHEUS: Wie tönet mir ein mächt'ger Hymnus durch die Nacht!
PHILEROS: Wen treff' ich schon, wen treff' ich noch den Wachenden?
(ll. 56–57)

[EPIMETHEUS: I hear how a mighty hymn resounds through the night!
PHILEROS: Whom should I be meeting, whom do I meet who is still awake?]

Not question and answer, but question juxtaposed harshly against question; in this kind of dialogue the answer is repeatedly lacking. Let it not be said that here we have to do with that classistic stichomythia which in its stylized limitation of conversation creates also a certain distance between the speakers. For in the first place, the stichomythias here have become the almost exclusive form of dialogue; and more important, they are essentially different from those, for example, of *Iphigenie*. Let us take them at comparable points. Epimeleia, pursued by Phileros with unsheathed axe, seeks protection with her father:

EPIMELEIA: Weh! Mord und Tod! Weh, Mörder! Ai! Ai! Hülfe mir!
PHILEROS: Vergebens! Gleich ergreif' ich dein geflochtnes Haar.[7]
EPIMELEIA: Im Nacken, weh! den Hauch des Mörders fühl' ich schon.
PHILEROS: Verruchte! Fühl' im Nacken gleich das scharfe Beil!
EPIMETHEUS: Her! Schuldig, Tochter, oder schuldlos rett' ich dich.
EPIMELEIA: O Vater du! Ist doch ein Vater stets ein Gott!
(ll. 408–13)

[EPIMELEIA: Woe! Murder and death! Woe, murderer! Oh! Oh! Help me!
PHILEROS: In vain! I shall seize your plaited hair immediately.
EPIMELEIA: On my neck, woe, I already feel the murderer's breath!
PHILEROS: Villainess! Feel at once the sharp axe on your neck!
EPIMETHEUS: This way! Guilty, daughter, or guiltless, I will save you.
EPIMELEIA: O my father! A father is indeed always a god!]

Opposed to this passage, three lines from *Iphigenie*:

OREST: Will er die Rückkehr friedlich uns gewähren?
IPHIGENIE: Dein blinkend Schwert verbietet mir die Antwort.
OREST: So sprich! Du siehst, ich horche deinen Worten.
                                    (*steckt das Schwert ein*)
                                              (WA 10, 88)

[ORESTES: Does he intend to let us return in peace?
IPHIGENIA: Your gleaming sword forbids my answering.
ORESTES: Then speak! You see, I heed your words (sheathes his
              sword).]

The difference is striking: in *Iphigenie* the figures listen and answer even
when they maintain they cannot; the powerful word forces the sword
into its sheath. In *Pandora* all talk past one another; only the raw force
of Prometheus—the "grip of his strong fist"—calls a halt to the axe. Thus
it is not the stichomythia which brings forth this talking past one
another, still less any intention on the part of Goethe to be "classical."[8]
At this point—as also at many others in the play—the language works
against the normal relationships of the figures and for this reason makes
them seem incomplete and chaotic.

But in one scene the nature of the conversation changes basically.
Suddenly, in the dream dialogue between Epimetheus and Elpore, everything sounds intimate and familiar. We can imagine that we have
almost been transposed back to *Prometheus*:

EPIMETHEUS: Nicht unbekannt bewegt sie sich herauf
              Die schlanke, holde, niedliche Gestalt.
              Bist du's Elpore?
ELPORE: Teurer Vater, ja!
              Die Stirne dir zu kühlen weh' ich her!
EPIMETHEUS: Tritt näher, komm!
ELPORE: Das ist mir nicht erlaubt.
EPIMETHEUS: Nur näher!
ELPORE: So denn?
EPIMETHEUS: So! Noch näher!
ELPORE: So?
EPIMETHEUS: Ich kenne dich nicht mehr.
ELPORE: Das dacht' ich wohl.
                                              (ll. 325–31)

[EPIMETHEUS: Not unfamiliar, it approaches me, the slender, charming
              and delicate shape. Is it you, Elpore?
ELPORE: Dear father, yes! I waft my way to you to cool your brow!

EPIMETHEUS:	Step nearer, come!
ELPORE:	That is not permitted me.
EPIMETHEUS:	Come!
ELPORE:	Then thus?
EPIMETHEUS:	So! Nearer still!
ELPORE:	So?
EPIMETHEUS:	I do not recognize you any more.
ELPORE:	That is what I thought.]

Here communication, exchange, is carried to the extreme; in the three lines the speaker changes seven times. We might almost feel at ease in this informal blank verse, but—the scene is a dream and hope a teasing spectre that is fundamentally negated for us because it seems to offer itself in boundless, Philine-like affirmation. Exactly to the degree that Elpore *and the language* approximate "reality" and seem ready actually to communicate with us; in the very moment when we, in the strangeness and obscurity of the language, breathe a sigh of relief and want to embrace what is familiar—this last ceases to be recognizable. And in order that we not surrender to the enticing illusion that in this uncommunicative play at least we, the listeners, are the ones *directly* addressed, Goethe draws us into the play at this very point—in the dream scene, in the illusion standing before our eyes. It is as if he wanted to tell us: "If you believe you can apprehend all this directly, then you are sleeping and dreaming like Epimetheus."

The meaning of the classicistic accoutrements of *Pandora* can be understood from this vantage point. In *Iphigenie* Goethe was concerned with bringing *form* into relief, with shaping from the restless flicker and blind self-assertion of primitive times a language world that would make apperception possible. The young Titan gave recognition only to Minerva, who spoke *his* language—that is, only to himself. Examined for its actual content, his wholly communicative speech is therefore only soliloquy. How his conflict with the gods would have been settled in the completed drama, this remains unclear; but it seems hardly too much to assert that the play had to remain unfinished just because the language did not allow the shaping of a genuine conflict. Conversely, *Iphigenie* is based on a confrontation of autonomous human beings, who accordingly have to exist as such. Hence, they have need of a language which at the same time sets bounds and communicates. Whether this is classical in the true sense, I do not venture to say; for Goethe, in any case, it signified the classical. But a completely different intention underlies the language of *Pandora*.

As we know, Goethe says of it that it could well have blossomed along with *Die Wahlverwandtschaften* [*Elective Affinities*], since in it is expressed the same "painful feeling of renunciation."[9] Wilamowitz (who, in his mistaken humanistic-classical interpretation, so often sees the play in a more correct light than Petsch, for instance, who tries to domesticate it for us[10] points to the end and to the plan of the second part and boldly says, "Here Goethe errs." It is quite certain that Goethe, who as artist had to be concerned "with the form and meaning of the whole,"[11] can have meant by the "painful feeling of renunciation" not simply the tone and cast of the lyrical passages. Cassirer does partial justice to the truth when he speaks of Goethe's painful insight that perfection is forever denied the individual, that it can be realized only in collective endeavor into which the individual, serving and imperfect, must be integrated.[12] But the first to grasp the real spirit of the work is Hankamer, to whom all exegesis of Goethe's late work must remain deeply indebted. He says that Goethe, from the phenomenon of Napoleon and from his passion in old age for Minchen Herzlieb, became fully aware of the concept of the demonic, and that he, by his renunciation of this demonic compulsion, achieved the painfully ironic, aloof, and superior range of vision into the play of forces that hold sway over all activity, for purposes incomprehensible to us.[13]

Thus Hankamer correctly applies the word "jest"—Goethe used it referring to the classical sections of the Second Part of *Faust*—also to *Pandora*. For we must remember that Goethe clothes his work in an almost pedantically Greek garb. Wilamowitz reacted quite correctly; this is exaggeration, only it is not that of the imitator but that of the parodist. *Pandora* parodies the classical—that is, that which the Goethe of middle years had regarded as the essence of "the natural." He believed he had experienced in Greek art how the artist could grasp and mould the shapeless-chaotic sensual world in its true order. But if we have read aright the linguistic intentions of *Pandora*, then it is a bitter jest that just through so complete a taking-over of the Greek, of "the natural," "unnaturalness" is created here. The irony lies in the fact that by their Greek demeanor the figures who speak in this way, and the language itself, draw our attention forcefully to their subordination to the realm of art. If grapes had been painted in this style, no birds would attack them. We are not entitled to conclude that the parody means a rejection of the classical ideal of art; on the contrary, Pandora is its true embodiment. But its attainability, or at least its tenability, is *denied* here. In one sense, which we want to try to define more exactly, Goethe renounces in *Pandora* an ideal that at the time of *Iphigenie* still seemed to him capable of realization.

All irony—not only the corrosive romantic, but also that Goethean irony with the assistance of which much "that is pleasant" can be said—means disintegration, a break between utterance and object. The young Prometheus still believes unconditionally in the identity of both; the word is the creative movement of the mind, and Goethe makes us witness of such creativity when he lets us actually hear Prometheus create the word "death," which he in splendid high-handedness coins for the act of love. *Iphigenie* knows of the mediacy of language, since its meaning lies not least in the fact that unequivocalness develops out of the ambiguity of the divine oracle. Ironic break thus exists as possibility and permanent danger; but it is the role of the *act* of language to obviate this danger. Blessed straight-forwardness, which establishes peace and humanity, is created at two critical points by the truth being spoken. As far as he ventures, the human being can use expressive *means* according to his intended ideal, he can "tell the truth," that is, make the object visible in complete, unbroken clarity by means of a quite transparent language. But a fundamental irony like that of the language of *Pandora* implies that the poet no longer believes in this possibility; there has not only been a loss of integration between word and object, but what must be the same for the poet, a disintegration of the world. Whatever of the true, beautiful, and "pleasant" this language may reveal, it has renounced the eternally desirable ideal of complete transparency, of unflawed articulateness.

It is exciting to see over and over again how Goethe unerringly reaches for the correct linguistic and dramatic means—even if he wants to portray a vision of the world condemned to fragmentation by its inner contradictions. The stage setting of *Prometheus* is literally constructed before our eyes; at the beginning the world is hardly there, the stage is only the place where the Titan is. As creator, he is the single centre of force; all other persons, even the gods, exist only in relation to him. The world of *Iphigenie* is incomparably more complicated. What unifies it is, first, a stage setting already *provided*, the firmly integrated island world that enforces its claims and laws vigorously. The "classical unities" are no external stylistic rule for Goethe, but the generally valid dimensions of space and time only within which the manifold but also ordered human relationships become possible and meaningful. There are many centres of force and they are grouped variously; not only are Greeks opposed to barbarians, but also Orestes to Pylades, Thoas to Arkas, and Iphigenia to Thoas and Pylades. But the stage is the point of incidence for all of them; in its unified and definable space they can communicate with each other, even if not always in friendly fashion, and modify their relationship to one another and to this pre-established, but also change-able, world. An organically interwoven order has replaced the naive-egocentric order of *Prometheus*.

In *Pandora* the principle of order is something else again: neither monistic nor organic, but dialectic. It has—to use Blake's word—a "fearful symmetry." The stage set splits into two sides: that of fire and that of water, the irreconcilable elements.[14] The stage is completely "set" in the form of this polarity; it is neither created nor modified in its human meaning, but exists as immutable fact. Fire is and remains destructive; water, formless and unmouldable; and the attempt at rap-prochement can lead only to violence. This means, though, that this order—like all dialectical order—can only be given redemptive unity by a miracle. Thus *Pandora* is necessarily a miracle and redemption play, or was conceived as such, although it developed successfully only to the point of giving promise. This very circumstance alone should have for-bidden the grouping of the play with the "classical" works; it belongs to mysteries of the late period such as *Novelle, Die Wahlverwandtschaften*, and the Second Part of *Faust*.

Seen from the perspective of *Prometheus*, the world of *Pandora* is thus a product of disintegration (even the hero becomes dual). And world and language are not to be separated. In still another sense than that already discussed, the language too is a product of disintegration. *Prometheus* knows no distinction between speech and song, at most differ-ing oscillations within the same continuum. In *Iphigenie*, the solemnly regulated language of blank verse is that of human communication, and it governs the play throughout. When Orestes goes mad, it is put out of joint; for Iphigenia, it is on two occasions intensified for a brief period at the level of ode-like hymn. But only once is it completely suspended—in the "Song of the Fates." As in the songs of the harpist and of Mignon, here too a voice penetrates from darker levels of being,[15] although it cannot shatter the linguistic unity of the whole. What the play actually achieves is the silencing of this voice and the celebrating of ennobled human speech as something created though always threatened.

As we have said, *Pandora* is a pageant and thus closely related to opera; the frequent alternation of iambic trimeter and song-like interpo-lations must not surprise us. That the choruses always sing and that even the main characters shift to song now and then, we must regard as a premise of the form. But the form in itself affords no explanation of the fact that each of the main characters really has a private language. Yet not entirely: Prometheus and Epimetheus both speak in iambic trimeter. But Phileros and Epimeleia—aside from the short stichomythias—never do so. When Prometheus expels his son, Phileros "answers" with a poem in those rhymed anapests in which he always speaks:

PROMETHEUS: Jetzt lös' ich dich. Hinaus mit dir in's Weite fort!
Bereuen magst du oder dich bestrafen selbst.
PHILEROS: So glaubest du, Vater, nun sei es gethan?
Mit starrer Gesetzlichkeit stürmst du mich an.

(ll. 447–50)

[PROMETHEUS: I now release you. Out with you, off and away! You may repent or you may punish yourself.
PHILEROS: Then you believe, father, the matter is settled? You assail me with inflexible adjudication.]

And when Epimeleia is interrogated about his complicity, the final remnant of connection vanishes; she "answers" in her great elegy, in her own characteristic trochaic pentameters:

PROMETHEUS: Bist du beschämt? Gestehst du wessen er dich zeiht?
EPIMETHEUS: Bestürzt gewahr' ich seltsam uns Begegnendes.
EPIMELEIA: Einig, unverrückt, zusammenwandernd
Leuchten ewig sie herab, die Sterne ...   (ll. 489–92)

[PROMETHEUS: Are you ashamed? Do you confess to what he accuses you of?
EPIMETHEUS: Confounded, I perceive a strange thing happening to us.
EPIMELEIA: As one, steady and moving together, they shine down eternally, the stars ...]

A comparison with the pageant *Paläophron und Neoterpe* (1800), in many ways similar, shows that *this* kind of exchange is not at all peculiar to the genre but is, rather, intended to indicate disintegration. The incursion threatening in *Iphigenie* has ensued and makes accommodation impossible.

The course of the action underlines this. Wilamowitz found inexplicable the equanimity with which the fathers allow their children to depart in despair, and ascribed it to a long interruption during the writing of the play. But paternal indifference corresponds exactly with verbal logic. The fathers can hardly be moved, for they have not been addressed in their language. They react only to the crudest physical perceptions and to their common memories. (Also to the latter in very different manner, but at least in the same language.) Their exchange is completely devoted to the past, and—like the scene with Elpore—is clothed with unreality through the very fact that it takes place against the background of a great misfortune that occurs before our eyes. It takes the fiery glow of burning houses to recall the brothers to the present; the language does not achieve this.

The world of *Pandora* is seen as disintegrated also from another—conceptually, one might say, the most important—point of view: that of time. Nothing is more characteristic of the *Prometheus* fragment than the already mentioned equation of death with the act of love. In a grandiose, Wertherian if-clause, the young Titan crosses out true death, and with it time, from the list of our categories of experience; like space, time is also only a dimension of creation, not of the creator. In the pageant play, on the other hand, everything is experienced under aspects of time. And yet the remarkable thing about it is that "day and night are not decisively distinguished" for anyone. For Epimetheus the morning star is "precipitate; it were better if it stayed night forever." Prometheus vaunts his ability, by virtue of the fire stolen from heaven, to bring about the light of "day before the day." For Phileros, the moment of which he can ask no question represents the breaking point between past and future: "Whom should I be meeting, whom do I meet who is still awake?" Epimeleia, finally, weeps for the transitoriness of all earthly happiness, in the light of the eternal stars. Past, future, moment, and transitoriness—time thus has been broken up into its human-dialectical components; as such, it is suffered in sadness, unconsciously grasped, brutally overpowered, or paralyzingly lamented.

But above all this arches the bow of a quite different time: the divine time of Eos and of Helios, of starry glitter and brightness of the moon. Nothing daunted by its refraction in human experience, this time pursues its course—unswerving, and therefore filled with blessing. In the last analysis, time cannot be coerced; at the conclusion, its embodiment appears in the form of Eos and announces the new day, after the fire that was to force it into existence has created only burning houses and the red glow of an "abortive" dawn. Eos bestows no shallow consolation:

Erst verborgen, offenbar zu werden,
Offenbar, um wieder sich zu bergen   (ll. 1051–52)

[At first kept secret, in order to be revealed, revealed in order to be concealed once more.]

Divine time moves according to divine laws: if day must follow night, then night must in turn also follow day. But in view of what human arbitrariness has brought about, it is clear to us that the possibility of blessing lies exactly in the supra-human quality of time. "Time is the mercy of eternity," says Blake. To experience this grace as grace, instead of as curse or limitation to be overcome—this surely should be one of the gifts of the "divinely chosen hour."

In one sense, thus, *Pandora* is also a tragedy of human arbitrariness, of human usurpation. In the end Prometheus reproaches his family:

> Freilich fröhnt es nur dem heut'gen Tage,
> Gestrigen Ereignens denkt's nur selten;
> Was es litt, genoss, ihm ist's verloren.
> Selbst im Augenblicke greift es roh zu;
> Fasst, was ihm begegnet, eignet's an sich . . .   (ll. 1063–67)

[Indeed, they are enslaved to the present day and think but rarely of yesterday's occurrence; they have lost what they have suffered and enjoyed. Even within the moment they reach out crudely; they seize what comes their way and appropriate it for themselves . . .]

Thereby he harks back to the opening self-reproach of his brother:

> So bittre Mühe war dem Jüngling auferlegt,
> Dass ungeduldig in das Leben hingewandt
> Ich unbedachtsam Gegenwärtiges ergriff . . .   (ll. 13–15)

[Such bitter toil was imposed on the youth [i.e., me], that, impatiently turned in the direction of life, I heedlessly seized what was present . . .]

"What was present"—that is, Pandora—is the "divinely sent image of delight" that he "appropriated" with strong embrace. The smiths thus praise Prometheus for the theft of that other gift from heaven which then proves so fatal—fire; thus Phileros also heedlessly seizes the moment and is cruelly disappointed by it. A curse weighs upon such commandeering. The human being is forfeited to his theft, yet cannot retain it. Time, fire, "form"—all these divine gifts man has to take unto himself, if he intends to be human; but if he seizes them, they do not hold together. "Everything comes undone," like the wreath of Pandora, and in gathering we lose what is gathered.

It is not exactly that we should or could let the gathering go and wait for gifts in inactive passivity; love, the demonic Eros, in its mysterious way compels the blessing from above. However destructive he may be, with whatever indifference to beneficent ends and constructive tendencies he may reach out, Eros is still a creative basic force. Not only "the will of the gods," but also "life's peculiar, pure, unquenchable striving" brings Phileros back re-born. But his father's "wisdom and aspiration" are unavailing. If therefore the ruinous reaching out changes in the end to a blessing, this comes about through the working together of "inhu-

man" powers—in the sense that even the demonic which is withdrawn
from human control must be called inhuman.

But this means that the most human aspect of man—language—has
no share in this miracle. That the word is deed was for the young poet of
Prometheus a certainty hardly impugnable; that the word *can* and *must
become* deed was a profound human requirement for the poet of *Iphigenie*. It is the painful—to the poet as poet—hope of *Pandora* that the
play of forces will provide and allow their unification. The enormous
renunciation of the poet of *Iphigenie* is expressed in Epimeleia's "splendid" lines (we thank Goethe for the jesting epithet):

> Sternenglanz, ein liebereich Betheuern,
> Mondenschimmer, liebevoll Vertrauen,
> Schattentiefe, Sehnsucht wahrer Liebe ...   (ll. 524–26)

[Starry glitter, a protestation rich in love, brightness of the moon, loving
confidence, depth of shadows, the longing of true love ...]

The divine supra-world and demonic Eros stand side by side without
connection; *the mediating word is lacking*.[16] The powerful "gracious"
word, which, even if it is a "farewell," can change a tragedy into a work
of joy—in the pageant play, this human word no longer brings about a
connection; only hope for a miracle remains.

With this, so one might believe, the poet would have been completely
prevented from carrying on his craft. And yet: what we have tried to
present here with painstaking exegesis, the poet creates as it were in three
lines. Language can mould the action in valid forms and mirror in its
shape the disintegration of the world; as we have seen, it can transform
its own impotence into potent and unforgettable words. The language
of *Prometheus* undertook to create the world as image of the Titan-
creator of language, and fell mute for lack of an objective opposition.
Language in *Iphigenie* thought to be able to clarify the ambiguity of the
divine will and uncover the image of the godhead in the human being—
and seldom surely did a belief experience a finer justification; but in the
violent disturbances of the years 1805 to 1807 it was shattered by phenomena that it could not master. The language of *Pandora* intends to
be "nothing but" the reflection of an incomprehensible, "inhuman"
playing. Just for this reason Goethe is thus "compelled" to handle it so
arbitrarily; like the forces, he has to govern in sovereign fashion, so that
a copy of life may emerge from his absolute play. The copy is so real just
because it is so monstrously "artificial," so serious because it is so arbitrarily playful. Forced to renounce all claims to the original creativity of

Prometheus and to Iphigenia's humanistic ennoblement of man, the poet is freed.

And as though there were not enough ironies, Goethe even crowns them with a "jest." In *Prometheus*, Pandora is a creature, the daughter of a Titan; in the pageant play, she is the creature of the gods. The fragment closes with the defiant rejection of Zeus, *Pandora* with the counseling of pious submission:

Merke:
Was zu wünschen ist, ihr unten fühlt es;
Was zu geben sei, die wissen's droben.
Gross beginnet ihr Titanen; aber leiten
Zu dem ewig Guten, ewig Schönen,
Ist der Götter Werk; die lasst gewähren!   (ll. 1080–85)

[Take note: you here below feel what is desirable; they on high know what may be given. You Titans undertake great things; but the path leading to the eternally good, the eternally beautiful, is the work of the gods; let them have their way!]

A difference as great as possible divides the two works. However, even the late "Pandora" is of course Goethe's daughter and creature. The play not only *represents* her return; it *is* also her return within Goethe's creative work. And when Eos says:

Manches Gute ward gemein den Stunden;
Doch die gottgewählte, festlich werde diese!   (ll. 1046–47)

[Much that is good the hours shared; but let this hour, divinely appointed, be festive!]

then we remember that not only the hour *in* the play, but also that *of* the play is meant: *Pandora* indeed *is* not only a pageant, it also *represents* one. The poet, in being compelled to "demean" the work of language to a copy of creation, is in like manner compelled to "elevate" himself to a copy of the creator. Epimetheus was not to be raised to the gods until the second part; but Goethe is already among them. The "divinely appointed hour" is his own, the "divinely sent" creature is his own—"a father is indeed always a god." Point of departure and goal are thus, as in sailing around the world, the same point and yet two quite different points. The departing Titan *claimed* the identity of word and object, of poet and god; he who returns—shall we call him man or god? —*knows* it; knows what it means in the way of triumph and renunciation to have learned that language *is* what it *represents*. And if such a voyage appears hazardous to us in the audience, us "groundlings," if such language seems alien and unintelligible to us "down below," then we must simply bear in mind what Eros bids Prometheus take note of:

Was zu wünschen ist, ihr unten fühlt es;
Was zu geben sei, die wissen's droben

[you here below feel what is desirable; they on high know what may be given]

and we must not interfere with the Olympian poet in his sublime jests, with the hope that he will thus guide us to the eternally good and beautiful.

2. "The voice of truth and of humanity": Goethe's *Iphigenie*

RIEDRICH GUNDOLF[1] brilliantly explains why Goethe used a Greek world for his dramatization of pure humanity in *Iphigenie auf Tauris*. According to Gundolf, Greekness represented for Goethe a human quality transcending individuation; in the Greek world, Goethe's faith in human goodness as such, not yet undermined by historicism, found its concrete form, undistorted and undifferentiated by dress, rank or calling. However illuminating these views, one would like to have time and place in *Iphigenie* more specifically defined. The distinctive thing about Goethe, which is related to his conception of the symbol, is that he is really only understood when he is taken quite concretely, quite at his word. The "pure humanity" he so celebrates has come to have an almost unGoetheanly abstract ring; and though in Italy he still hoped to find the "protoplant" (*Urpflanze*), we must try to draw the line between prototype and ideal form somewhat more sharply than has been commonly done in the literature about Iphigenia. The land the heroine seeks "with her soul"—even more, the land on which she stands —ought to be somewhat more firmly fixed in time and space, so that it not evaporate into the realm of pure ideas. For even in his search for the protoplant, it is significant that Goethe hoped to grasp it as tangible substance. Accordingly, we feel slightly uneasy about Gundolf's spiritualization of the figure of Iphigenia.

A similar uneasiness is aroused by the interiorization of the dramatic action, by its almost lyrical resolution. Aristotle considered the action, or story (*mythos*), as the heart of drama—rightly, for the choice of dramatic form is only justified when its very uniqueness becomes the core symbol of the whole. The meaning of the work must find clear expression in the action, if anywhere; characterization and imagery may enrich or define it more exactly, but if they do not harmonize completely with the action then the drama is incomplete, its meaning ambiguous or even contradictory. This conception of the drama is surely not too rigid, at least as regards *Iphigenie* and Goethe's concern with its form. But if we measure the play by this Aristotelean standard, we discover a discrepancy between traditional interpretations of it and its action, a discrepancy

33

which must be considered either a blemish in the play or an error in interpretation. For the pure humanity of Iphigenia has thus far *not* been interpreted as the "single redeeming force"; the action is not resolved just in the moral sphere but also in that of objects and facts.

Goethe has clearly directed the action toward a peripeteia—the confession with which Iphigenia delivers up herself and those dearest to her to the magnanimity of Thoas. From this moment on, then, the final outcome should depend only upon how Thoas reacts. "Pure humanity" has now done its utmost—whether it wins or loses has nothing more to do with its essential nature. And yet, the king's hand is still on his sword when he says:

> So würden doch die Waffen zwischen uns
> Entscheiden müssen; Frieden seh' ich nicht.
> Sie sind gekommen, du bekennest selbst,
> Das heil'ge Bild der Göttin mir zu rauben.[2]   (ll. 2097–2100)

[Then arms would still have to decide between us; I do not see peace. They came, as you yourself admit, to rob me of the holy image of the goddess.]

With his submission to the moral claim of pure humanity the conflict is thus not yet resolved, inasmuch as it still contains a quite material component—the image of the goddess. A second peripeteia appears necessary in order to achieve the dénouement. Human frailty would seem to be only partially curable by means of pure humanity.

This second peripeteia has with justice aroused a negative reaction among critics, without however giving rise among them to any clearer interpretation. They have been baffled by the nonchalant way in which Orestes announces his saving discovery. He, who has just intended to steal the divine image, now explains the delusion under which he has labored as though he had long recognized it. Goethe could be said therefore to have minimized the dramatic effectiveness by sacrificing psychological realism. Was the structural weakness to be covered up in this way? Or is it possible that Iphigenia's confession is indeed the only, all-decisive peripeteia, that the turning point not only in the story but in the moral structure is here accomplished, and that the sacrifice of a dramatic element serves to deepen the meaning of the whole? Critics must pursue this question, for it is a matter here not only of a possible aesthetic blemish but at the same time of an obscurity. Form is meaning, and in the drama action is symbol.

We must ascertain, therefore, whether and in what sense subject matter and idea in *Iphigenie* coincide in mutual dependence; more concretely expressed, whether and how being Greek and being human, Iphigenia's confession and the actual situation explained by Orestes, as it were, fuse into the irreducible symbol, that whole which is the play itself. And as soon as we examine the conceptual world of the play from this point of view, we notice that one, really *the* basic concept—truth—is subjected to the contradictoriness that we want to trace. In the word itself this contradictoriness is expressed as ambiguity; to speak truth means two things—not to lie, and not to speak in error. Therefore the word, which Goethe places with almost mathematical exactness at the middle of the work (l. 1081 in 2174 lines) and to which he allots the dignity and weight of a full line—Orestes' "Between us/Let there be truth"—this word shows a dual commitment to two worlds, the moral and the factual, each of which, given single sway, would necessitate a tragic ending, but which united can bring salvation. Only because Iphigenia decides to tell the truth, and also because at the same time a truth comes to light, does all turn out well.

Complementary to the ambiguity of "truth" is that of the divine oracle. Nothing is more unjustified than Pylades' sturdy confidence: "The gods do not speak in words of double meaning." The oracle *is* ambiguous; and here again the rescue depends upon its becoming clear that the material component (the "image") and the spiritual (the "sister") find one another and fuse into a united whole.

But with this the crux of the action is revealed in its real form: in language. The action concerns word and meaning, statement and keeping silent, true and false speaking. That the word is not only outer shell, sign, and means of communication we have all been made conscious of through anthropology, linguistics, and with horrible clarity through the events of recent decades; poets have always known this. But what language is or can be, moreover what it must be in a really *human* community, probably hardly anyone has said so "very exactly" as the poet of *Iphigenie*. We must therefore question him; and our question will have two aspects, moral and factual: How does it happen that Iphigenia tells the truth (i.e., does not lie), and what is truth?

I

We ask: how does it happen?—for what we must recognize first is the developmental process that is completed in Iphigenia. Whatever the concept pure humanity may mean, its embodiment at the end of the play is an other than at the beginning. It is remarkable how rarely up until the third act Iphigenia's insensitivity has caused offense. For she is confronted with a perfectly clear moral problem; the decision is hers alone, whether the two shipwrecked strangers will be sacrificed or saved, indeed whether her own civilizing work will continue or will sink back into bloody barbarity. If she were not Iphigenia—that is, the figure whose purity and nobility Goethe has known how to present with such marvelous conviction—we might say that she was lying when she bewails her helplessness to Orestes:

> Doch verweigr' ich jene Pflicht,
> Wie sie der aufgebrachte König fordert,
> So wählt er eine meiner Jungfrau mir
> Zur Folgerin, und ich vermag alsdann
> Mit heissem Wunsch allein euch beizustehn.   (ll. 936–40)

[But if I refuse the duty that the aroused king demands, he will choose one of my maidens as my successor, and then I will be able to support you only with fervent wishing.]

But it is not so; she could accept Thoas' suit. Not that we wish to underrate the sacrifice that she would thus make—she would have to give up her most cherished hope. Still, we need only consider how Schiller, for example, would have treated such an emotional situation to find startling with what calm resignation, indeed lack of awareness, Iphigenia ignores the choice that faces her. No inner voice admonishes her that the lives of these unhappy men lie in *her* hand; she is ready, with no sense of conflict, to leave them to their fate. Her prayer is her only answer to so sharply posed a moral question (I, 4).

But this means that the choice does not exist for her, that the shape it takes has no real content for her. There is a great difference between this choice and the later one, which she recognizes and accepts as her own with a seriousness incomprehensible to a Pylades. Or again, a deep transformation must have taken place in her; or finally, she as well as the nature of the choice may have changed. Let us not be frightened by what may seem analytical pedantry—these points are raised by the work itself.

A choice is born of circumstances and conditioned by them; its real nature therefore is not to be sought in itself but in the tangle of relationships and conditions that produce it. What sort of a world does Goethe create here? Is it not—as odd as this may sound—the world of a language school? The whole play ends with the at last successful attempt to coax from a halting mouth an unaccustomed "gracious" word: "Farewell!" The laconic syllables of such speech are so redeeming because they break

through walls of distrustful and inimical silence—because they are a *first*
word. Right at the beginning we were told that Thoas was no orator:

Der Skythe setzt ins Reden keinen Vorzug,
Am wenigsten der König. Er . . .
Kennt nicht die Kunst, von weitem ein Gespräch
Nach seiner Absicht langsam fein zu lenken.   (ll. 164–68)

[The Scythian places no virtue in speech, least of all the king. He . . .
knows not the art of directing a conversation from afar slowly and delicately towards his goal.]

Moreover, it is not just the Scythian world that is silent; even Iphigenia
speaks reluctantly:

Vom alten Bande löset ungern sich
Die Zunge los, ein langverschwiegenes
Geheimnis endlich zu entdecken.   (ll. 300–302)

[My tongue frees itself reluctantly from an ancient bond, to reveal at last
a secret long concealed.]

Here the world of the play is characterized in one sentence. Speaking
repeatedly represents a painful, dangerous resolve; the real, dramatic
course of action is a continual struggle between utterance and silence.
And accordingly, expressions—that is, images—of speaking, hearing,
being silent dominate *Iphigenie* just as do animal images Shakespeare's
King Lear; we overlook the essential nature of the whole play if we do
not feel in every "Speak!" which urges statement, in every venturesome
"Listen!," the full weight of meaning that Goethe assigns them. What
bears, wolves, and snakes accomplish in *King Lear* is done here by ear,
mouth, tongue, voice, and allied concepts. Actually, they are not concepts but images in the fullest sense; the world of the drama is woven of
them.

Thus it is probably not alone the supra-historical human quality that
Goethe found in the Greek myth and wished to give form to. Language
plays a meaningful role in *Torquato Tasso* too, although in an entirely
different way. The princess says:

Ich höre gern dem Streit der Klugen zu,
Wenn um die Kräfte, die des Menschen Brust
So freundlich und so fürchterlich bewegen,
Mit Grazie die Rednerlippe spielt.   (ll. 125–28)

[I like to hear intelligent dispute, when the eloquent tongue gracefully
plays about the forces that stir the human breast so amicably and so
fearfully.]

This kind of speech is mastered possession. Here the tongue does not
need to struggle out of pre-human confinement; it is already a graceful
courtly sword, although suitable for a game more deadly than the princess as yet imagines. The Greekness of *Iphigenie* serves to bring before
us not so much a naked, abstract purity, as that early time before which
there was no language and in which language was first born. That is the
quite concrete meaning of this world, in the sense of a meaning valid at
a single point in time.

From this world now comes the first moral challenge to Iphigenia; she
is obliged to do a *deed*. But it is the "lamentable" fate of women to be
excluded from masculine activity and to have to obey. Arkas tries with a
sure feeling for the vital point to show Iphigenia that her life has not
been useless and that she has accomplished a great deal by means of
"gentle persuasion." But she repudiates his praise as undeserved, knowing what lies behind it: Instead of persuading, she should sacrifice herself unheard. Thus she defends herself against Thoas by calling on the
voice of the gods. As long and as well as she can, she tries to shift the
decision to the sphere of language, in which she feels she belongs and is
competent; she even goes so far as to reveal the fearfully kept secret of
her background and so for the first time to appear not only as mouthpiece of the deity but in her own person. But nothing helps; Thoas
remains deaf. He refuses to be persuaded and insists on his alternative of
acting, which is without real meaning for Iphigenia. As woman and
priestess, it is not for her to act but only to listen, to prophesy, and if she
finds no response then to suffer.

What frightens her away from the realm of action resounds first in
her genealogy of the house of Tantalus, second in the great dialogue
between Orestes and Pylades, and finally in the introduction to her confession. We have said that the world of the play is the world of language; but it rises from a darker underworld: the realm of action. What
it means for Iphigenia is compressed in her grave words: "the first deed."
It is fratricide, the deed of Cain, which is transmitted from generation to
generation in a series of "grave" and "monstrous" deeds of "minds confused." The genealogy of the Tantalean race and that of the deeds are
really identical; the same terrible necessity of biological transmission
obtains in both. Only occasionally is there a glimpse of another kind of
deed, especially in the heroic youthful dreams of Orestes and Pylades. But
these are dreams or poetic inventions, and no real link joins them to the

bloody chain which stretches from the past into the present. The "monstrous" deed is the real curse of the house of Tantalus. And however refreshing and reasonable Pylades' happy confidence may sound, the end of the fourth act gives it the lie; Iphigenia knows that redemption is not to be won by deceit and theft.

For this reason the first opportunity to prove her high morality passes her by without being comprehended; for it is not *her* morality. And yet, not only for this reason. We must glance back once again at her attempt to persuade Thoas. Is he only a stubborn barbarian? The answer is given in that often misunderstood exchange:

THOAS:	Es spricht kein Gott; es spricht dein eignes Herz.
IPHIGENIE:	Sie reden nur durch unser Herz zu uns.
THOAS:	Und hab' ich, sie zu hören, nicht das Recht?
IPHIGENIE:	Es überbraust der Sturm die zarte Stimme.
THOAS:	Die Priesterin vernimmt sie wohl allein?
IPHIGENIE:	Vor allen andern merke sie der Fürst. (ll. 493–98)

[THOAS:	There speaks no god; your own heart speaks.
IPHIGENIA:	They only speak to us through our heart.
THOAS:	And do I not have the right to hear them?
IPHIGENIA:	The tempest drowns out their gentle voice.
THOAS:	You think the priestess alone hears it?
IPHIGENIA:	May the sovereign perceive it before all others.]

"They only speak to us through our heart." This is certainly a bold statement of the religion of human goodness, but where does it lead? We will have opportunity later to point out the questionableness of an imagery in which against all laws of anatomy the heart is fitted out with ears and tongue. It is sufficient to say here that Thoas' answer is quite irrefutable and so remains unrefuted. Any one of us may claim to hear the voice of his heart and therefore of the gods; it is purely subjective and we are all subject to ourselves. To put it bluntly—for about this point there has been much sentimental nonsense written—an expression of aversion because of a wart on Thoas' nose would have much greater power of persuasion, and a much higher objective validity. But in this completely indecisive conflict about who perceives the true, divine language of the heart, Iphigenia's further attempts to open Thoas' ears for the voice of *his* heart collapse completely. He hears his own very clearly; he wants to hear from Iphigenia what higher authentication she has for hers. But she has none, since she considers the voice of her heart that of the gods and refuses to speak for herself.

This impersonality of speech characterizes her up until her meeting with Orestes. Never does she start her exchanges in the first person singular; in opening them, she speaks always only as priestess, "the One unknown," as hieratic We. Arkas feels the difference between what her speech actually is and what it would be were it personal:

> Vergebens harren wir schon Jahre lang
> Auf ein vertraulich Wort aus deiner Brust.
> . . . .
> Und wie mit Eisenbanden bleibt die Seele
> Ins Innerste des Busens dir geschmiedet.   (ll. 68–73)

[For years we have waited in vain for a confiding word from your breast ... And your soul remains bound as though with iron bands within the innermost recess of your bosom.]

But Iphigenia does not give in—at least not until the intuitively felt affinity with her brother wrests from her the promise: "Thou shalt know who I am." Still, we have noticed that in her confrontation with Thoas the process of becoming a person has already begun, though as yet hesitatingly and soon to be reversed; she reveals who she is. And her very first word is "Forth."[3] It indicates the path that she must follow: forth from the protection of consecrated anonymity into the risk of the individual consciousness; forth from the non-obligating language of the gods into the committed speech of human beings. In learning to speak as an individual, she becomes an individual.

Delineating this emergence in its entirety would mean quoting the whole work; we intend to limit ourselves to tracing it in her prayers.[4] Prayer is a speaking to the gods; in it, therefore, the progress must show clearly and verbally. Comparing Iphigenia's first prayer (ll. 43–53) with her last (ll. 1916–1919), we may make two observations: from the point of view of content we hardly dare characterize the last as a prayer (it has moreover been mistakenly understood as being addressed to Thoas); it is much more an ultimatum, whereas the first is still pious beseeching. Syntactically, however, both are stated as conditional clauses. The contrast of content, despite syntactic similarity, creates a harsh contradiction in the prayer which stands midway in the whole work and is immediately heard:

> Und ist dein Wille, da du hier mich bargst,
> Nunmehr vollendet, willst du mir durch ihn
> Und ihm durch mich die sel'ge Hilfe geben,
> So lös' ihn von den Banden jenes Fluchs,
> Dass nicht die teure Zeit der Rettung schwinde.   (ll. 1327–31)

[If what you intended by sheltering me here has now been achieved, and if you wish to grant restoring help to me through him (Orestes) and to him through me, then free him from the bonds of that curse, so that the precious moment for escape not be lost.]

Looked at carefully, this prayer is a negation of itself; if the condition were true, if the divine will had been fulfilled, the plea based upon it would hardly be capable of fulfillment, since it seeks a further manifestation of this will. If we compare it with the canonical prototype of such conditional praying—Christ's: "My Father, if it is possible, take this cup from me, but not as I wish but as You wish"—both its logical and, from the Christian point of view, religious enormity becomes clear to us: Iphigenia demands that the goddess confirm her abdication by means of a last voluntary act, so that from now on the human being can himself "grant restoring help." And yet, it is this prayer that is immediately fulfilled. Orestes is healed.

This means that Iphigenia has won her own emancipation by prayer; she now attains the independence she has demanded of herself, an independence which she did not at first understand but which in the end she has discovered within herself. The gods are in no way denied, yet their sphere is clearly set apart from the human, their moral responsibility clearly outlined. And thereby the conditions finally become true, verbally and logically—that is, negatively reversible. While in the first prayer Iphigenia's petition is still tied to a condition which does not make a condition at all but only represents another plea—and while in the central prayer plea and condition seem to contradict one another—at the end two if-clauses stand sharply separated, and inexorably consistent, side by side:

Ich werde grossem Vorwurf nicht entgehn,
Noch schwerem Übel, wenn es mir misslingt;

and with the "if" now in isolated emphasis:

Allein *Euch* leg' ich's auf die Kniee! Wenn
Ihr wahrhaft seid, wie ihr gepriesen werdet,
So zeigt's durch euren Beistand . . .   (ll. 1914–18)

[I shall not escape great reproach nor serious harm, if I do not succeed . . . However, I lay it on *your* knees! If you are truthful, as you are extolled for being, demonstrate it by your support.]

Even at the end of the fourth act Iphigenia had not dared let this conditional factor be completely voiced: "Save me,/ And save your image in my soul."[5] She still had demanded the saving deed from above, and therefore could not logically conclude that the gods were without responsibility. But now she takes the consequences of her own resolve fully upon herself and thus can make the gods responsible for the moral composition of the cosmic order, an order that joins resolution and results in a realm beyond human control. With this clarification, this separation of the divine and human spheres, the language becomes clear, so that it now will satisfy the claims of the most formal logic. These conditional clauses are negatively reversible. And in the language of prayer Iphigenia's coming forth is completed.

But we have not yet expressed the essential challenge to her—can she learn to make herself clearly understandable to *human beings*? Right from the beginning she has spoken voluntarily and without inhibition to herself, nature, the gods; but that is not true speech, not dialogue. The gods remain silent, nature sends only "hollow sounds" in reply to her sighs; and as soon as she confronts Arkas and Thoas, she takes shelter. But even for them she must come "forth"; what she herself had prepared the way for, when she revealed to Thoas her true identity, is fulfilled in the appearance of her brother and in the unavoidable necessity of acknowledging in *deed* her accursed family. Still as one speaking, but speaking in a wholly new sense.

Now suddenly the risk of speech appears to her in a new and much more frightening form. Formerly, as priestess, she had the choice between speaking and being silent, the really god-like choice between revelation and concealment. Now the situation has changed: she must choose between truth and falsehood. The first scene of the fourth act, in which she realizes this, may without hesitancy be placed among the greatest scenes in dramatic literature. Here Goethe combines the underlying urgency of a Hamlet monologue with the pathos of that sorrowful initiation to life that Ophelia succumbs to and is destroyed by. The scene begins with a joyous hymn to the friend who is now to replace the benevolent gods in this exposed human life. The words flow headlong in the direction of the concretely human, the name; and as soon as this is spoken, they become poetry, blank verse. And now there is a forward impetus: from gratitude to uneasy obedience to the painful "Woe!" that from the beginning lurked hidden in the flow of words. Only if we react to this cry of anguish quite physically will we do justice to it and to its cause: here the masculine element, the deed, plunges brutally into Iphigenia's virgin-pure world. Goethe lets us be witness of an initiation into womanhood.

"Woe betide the lie!" Swift's noble horses had no such word; Gulliver had to translate it for their paradisiac virtue as "saying what is not." How inconsiderable the difference between lying and being silent (not saying what is); and yet how radical for Iphigenia! The existence of the verb, the word of action, can no longer be denied, and thereupon the armor of negation is shifted into the realm of actuality. That is what the word "lie" means here. There has been disagreement as to how Orestes' cure is to be explained, whether as divine intervention or as the effect of his sister's purifying humanity. The essential point is that the recovery is just as conditional as was her prayer for it; Iphigenia has assumed the curse. Significantly, it is Orestes who offers the prayer of gratitude, not Iphigenia who was formerly so ready to pray. Her as yet unsullied soul now bears and experiences the curse of the Tantalean house and is enchained in the iron succession of cause and effect in which each act follows the other. Just as external circumstance and her own position previously conjoined to let her evade the moral challenge with which she is confronted, so now they unite in order to force ineluctably upon her this second challenge. She has come entirely into the realm of human values and the choice is, how she shall speak or what she shall say.

With incomparable skill Goethe has so fashioned the fourth act that Iphigenia's falling is really audible; she experiences in his own language the fall of her family. In reply to her disclosure in the first act Thoas observed: "A word of great import you calmly utter." Of course, she who thought herself exempted from the curse could still be calm. Now it is different: she herself learns what belonging to "the house of Tantalus" means. When Goethe took the trouble to recast the rhythmic prose of his drama as blank verse, he intended, or brought about in any case, more than a "more classic" form, which as such would in fact have added nothing but would have remained pure mannerism. In consequence, he created three clear levels of language. Now that Iphigenia's two hymns were distinguished for the first time from blank verse, and the Song of the Fates set apart more sharply than ever from blank verse, there arose three spheres of speech: the Olympian, the hymn proclaiming the essential being of the gods; the blank verse of human communication (also directed to the gods, as prayer); and, resounding from the underworld, the Song of the Fates. Iphigenia sings when she is "possessed"—not in the sense of being "deeply moved" (she is often so elsewhere) but in the literal sense: whenever she becomes the mouthpiece of a voice from above or below.[6] Orestes in his madness mixes two languages; he believes that he is communicating as a human being, but is actually speaking as a subject of the underworld. His madness lies in the very fact that he denies any borderline between the two and believes that he recognizes his essential quality as subjection to the dark forces. Iphigenia's pure humanity, as she now learns, does not lie in her exemption from the fall of her house, but in her being able to experience this fall without confusing spheres and languages, in being able to renounce those of the gods without plunging in despair to those of the underworld. As descendants of Tantalus, she and Orestes have ears for the voices from above and below (which are unheard by others); but only Iphigenia knows how or learns to separate these clearly from her own, human voice. She falls but she does not succumb; she knows whose song she is singing and at the very last moment prays that the Song of the Fates not become her own.[7]

And now begins in full earnest the struggle, the deadly nature of which she became aware of in the stichomythic skirmish with Arkas; her conversation with Thoas, against the background of a battle perhaps still being fought, is a true battle of words. First, the positions which have changed since the first act are made clear:

IPHIGENIE: Er [der König] aber schwebt durch seine Höhen ruhig,
               Ein unerreichter Gott, im Sturme fort.
THOAS: Die heil'ge Lippe tönt ein wildes Lied.
IPHIGENIE: Nicht Priesterin! nur Agamemnons Tochter. (ll. 1819–22)

[IPHIGENIA: But the king calmly soars on in the tempest through the
               heavens, a god unrivaled.
THOAS: From your holy lip a wild song sounds forth.
IPHIGENIA: Not priestess! only Agamemnon's daughter.]

Thoas is right; it is a wild song, an almost blasphemous echo of the first hymn as well as of the Song of the Fates, concerning a human being this time, the king. And aimed at him; Iphigenia no longer wishes to speak as priestess but as one human being to another. In despair she attempts to call on Thoas' humanity and to fight the battle on this general plane; but Thoas does not allow it. He knows that she who earlier seemed to adjust in comparatively resigned fashion to her sad duty is now taking a much more concrete, personal interest in the fate of the strangers. With sure instinct he therefore proceeds against this weak point. The first of his attacks Iphigenia seeks to repel in falling back on the barricade she once before could not maintain—the language of the heart:

Red' oder schweig' ich, immer kannst du wissen,
Was mir im Herzen ist and immer bleibt.   (ll. 1841–42)

[Whether I speak or am silent, you can always know what is in my heart and remains there.]

How touchingly pitiful this attempt at defense! This time Thoas does not need to expose it—she does it herself. This non-speech of the heart she has renounced forever, and so she brings forth what is pure non-sense: Thoas cannot possibly know what remains in her heart. The heart is no organ of speech and has no tongue; in order to be understood Iphigenia must come "forth" with *speech*. So Thoas presses forward again, this time not skirmishing but with the full force of "Say!":

Es scheint, der beiden Fremden Schicksal macht
Unmässig dich besorgt. Wer sind sie, sprich ... (ll. 1886–87)

[The fate of the two strangers seems to concern you excessively. Who they are, say ...]

In the face of this "Say!" there can be no more evasion; with it comes the real challenge to Iphigenia. She must say irrevocably: what is or is not.

Does she make a choice? Hardly. She attempts to say the "wily word" that Pylades has "put in her mouth," not her own words but those of cunning and calculation:

Sie sind—sie scheinen—für Griechen halt' ich sie. (l. 1889)

[They are—they seem—I believe them to be Greeks.]

But in this helplessly stammering line she—*her* language—celebrates her true and finest triumph; she breaks under the lie, she *cannot* lie. She has done her best to remain faithful to the moral resolve she made earlier:

Ich muss ihm folgen: denn die Meinigen
Seh' ich in dringender Gefahr. (ll. 1689–90)

[I have to follow him: for I see my own in pressing danger.]

But she has not been able to "learn" the language appropriate to her moral resolve. With the best will she cannot carry through this sacrifice of herself; not her moral intention but her innermost being makes the choice. And so she does not ask herself if she should tell the truth; the question has just answered itself. She asks:

Hat denn zur unerhörten Tat der Mann
Allein das Recht? (ll. 1892–93)

[Has only a man the prerogative of unprecedented act?]

She to whom the fate of woman seemed "lamentable" and who saw her task only in lending a pleading note to the divine inner voice in a world of amazing masculine deeds—she now only asks herself if she can hazard the feminine act, the act of speech, which will achieve what she needs and will make the divine order responsible for the consequences.

The result shows how really "amoral," how very obedient to the "project" of her being this act is. Schiller's Tell does not make his choice lightly; he is fully conscious of the gravity of his deed. But after he has decided, he is beyond all doubt; the possible consequences are morally insignificant. Should his plot be unsuccessful and bring even more tyranny upon family and fatherland, he would not have to reproach himself for it. Parricida's assertion that he too committed a Tell-act does not awaken in him the faintest doubt in himself; he turns the parricide away with horror. For the deed itself is a gamble only in the world of things; its consequences can never cast a reflection on the moral quality of the choice, since this exists and can be judged solely in the realm of values. But as Thoas appears not to hear the "voice of truth" and Iphigenia's verbal act threatens to remain unheard, that is to say, without success, she is deeply frightened, not *for* herself but *regarding* herself:

Denn nun empfind' ich, da uns keine Rettung
Mehr übrig bleibt, die grässliche Gefahr,
Worin ich die Geliebten übereilt
Vorsätzlich stürzte. Weh! . . . . .
. . . . Mit welchen Blicken
Kann ich von meinem Bruder Abschied nehmen,
Den ich ermorde? [8]   (ll. 1945–51)

[For now that no rescue is left for us, I feel the horrible danger into which I have thrust my loved ones with deliberate rashness. Woe! . . . With what mien can I take leave of my brother, whom I murder?]

This is not simply psychological realism, not just Goethe's deep understanding of the feminine soul. It is not the reaction of fright of the delicate woman when faced with the consequences of her pure act, but the inexorable judgment that these consequences themselves pass upon the act. *She* is the murderer.

The contrast to *Wilhelm Tell* is not just external. Tell has only to choose between action and non-action; still, his choice is fully moral, since in the realm of pure values the act itself is not yet act and finds therefore in non-action a sufficient counterweight. For Iphigenia there exists no true moral choice; her resolve to lie shatters on the fact that she cannot. She acts under compulsion and can be justified therefore only by the consequences of her act; the essence of such action is that it morally obligates the doer to the consequences. For Goethe the act is the point at which human resolve and material circumstance collide and mutually determine one another. The resolve may transform the circumstance or be distorted by it to a caricature of itself; the decisive element is not the pure choice but its point of incidence. So to this Goethe diverts our full attention. Schiller proceeds inversely. The act itself is a matter of chance; the choice is the essential. Like Goethe, he finds the perfect symbol. He separates the deed carefully from the doer; we hear Tell's thorough explanation of his resolve but we do not see him shoot. The arrow flies down toward Gessler from the realm of pure values and choices; the bow which removes from the point of incidence the doer, who does not really act but rather evokes a power from on high, is the ideal instrument for the Schillerian deed. Goethe's is the sword—and the word; through them the doer is joined in thrust and counter-thrust, statement and answer, most closely with act and purpose, and is thus vulnerable and responsible in all action.

Iphigenia speaks the truth "that is in her" because she cannot do otherwise. She remains even now unconditionally true to herself with the same splendid egotism with which she refused Thoas' suit. The single difference, to be sure radical, lies in the complete gamble of everything she holds dear, in the full renunciation of any refuge, any justification, except through success. She stakes everything on her word, the true word —and wins. But we saw that her truthful intention was not solely decisive; if the oracle should remain unclarified, then the sword would have to "speak" in the end. How is the dangerous error resolved? What is truth?

II

So much is clear—the divine word itself is neither true nor untrue; it is ambiguous. It is a matter of interpretation, so that our question is wrongly posed. We must ask: How does it *become* truth? Even this formulation shows how carefully we will have to proceed and how misleading any unpoetic attempt at an answer must be. If Pilate's question was calculated to shake our intellectual certainty, it is still a true rock compared with this "become." With some justification it has been claimed that western culture would be unthinkable if the original Indo-European language had not laid the little word "to be" in its cradle. To doubt the importance of this word is the deep pessimism of Heraclitus; to affirm it, the passionate intent of Plato. How comforting is the belief *that* there is truth, even if we are doubtful of ever knowing *what* it is. But to draw it into the perpetual "becoming"—the river one never enters twice—is to deprive us of any support. Goethe does this in *Iphigenie*.

Critics have not paid sufficient attention to the oracle, for otherwise they certainly would have noticed elements calling for explanation. In the first place, it does not appear in its true wording until the very end, after having been repeatedly mentioned throughout the whole play. The *ipsissima verba* are therefore, in the actions of the drama, result, not a point of departure. They do not assume full value in the world determined by the drama until they are actually uttered.

Previously the words of the oracle were always modified to suit the speaker. These paraphrases are clearly grouped: up to the recognition scene between Iphigenia and Orestes they retain the original (as we learn at the end) word "sister," which subsequently disappears and is replaced by "image."[9] This change is all the more surprising as "sister" is heard at the "breaking point" with pointed reference to Iphigenia, who is now recognized as sister. Why does neither Pylades not Orestes hear the echo?

But if we look at the paraphrases as various refractions of the original oracle, we find the following: Even the "sister" that is at first still retained must be a refraction, for otherwise it would not be subjected to a broader and deeper refraction in that moment when it is to be effective and acquire saving significance. The concrete phenomenon Iphigenia usurps the word, so to speak, so that from now on it is no longer at the disposal of the oracle. The first prose version throws clearer light upon how this happens; in it Orestes designates his "wise friend" Pylades as chiefly responsible for the false interpretation—a blame that can only bear on Pylades' belief in the obviousness of the oracle. This very belief has to generate the later, fateful refraction; after "sister" has already been *understood* as the image of the goddess, it really has to *become* the image at the appearance of an actual sister. The "simple" exegesis of the divine word leads therefore to an unrecognizable distortion.

We notice another thing: As long as the "sister" is spoken of, the related word of action is "bring away"; for "image" we have "carry off" and "rob." Here likewise the refraction and distortion; as the noun is demeaned to the purely material, so the act is coarsened to the simple physical violation, to Pylades' naive presumption:

Ich bin allein genug, der Göttin Bild
Auf wohlgeübten Schultern wegzutragen.   (ll. 1563–64)

[I am sufficient in myself to carry away the image of the goddess on my capable shoulders.]

The critic should bear in mind the fact that exegesis is no simple undertaking. In the most tragic manner words become objects of discord if they are not treated with the reticence due everything holy. Once they are demeaned to the very things of which we naively consider them a sign, they lose the divine healing power residing within them and are accursed by a sensationalism that one simply seeks to possess and twists back and forth according to desire and need. A fatality weighs upon the appropriation-to-itself of the word.

We said at the beginning that the ambiguity of the oracle had to become clear in order that everything turn out well. But now we see that the method of interpretation necessary for such language is of a very special kind. Simply to discard one interpretation in favor of another will not suffice. Pylades does this; the result is that the gods are accused of having chosen a false word: " 'Sister' you said, but really you meant her 'image'." If we explain an ambiguous word at the cost of one of its meanings, we destroy thereby the unity which it represents. But how can a word with two meanings have a single interpretation?

Really, only in the mouth of God as a word of creation: "And God said: Let there be light. And there was light." The unconditional validity of the creative word is to be found in this divine power to create what it "means." It *cannot* be untrue, but can for that reason in the human sense also not be "true." For to the human consciousness concepts which cannot be refracted are necessarily without content. If everything were green, the word "green" would have no content. The divine word therefore *must* be refracted in order that it gain content and meaning, that it become humanly "true." Yet in this refraction lies the danger of eternal discord.

The refraction, the destructive distortion of the oracle, is therefore tragic necessity for the human being; for this reason Goethe changed the sarcastic "wise friend" of the first version to "the god," who has laid error like a veil about the head of man. As long as man only interprets—and that he must—he lapses into error. But human dialectic is not purely destructive; the curse carries within it blessing; error carries truth as necessary, dialectical component. The action of *Iphigenie* is drawn with almost unbelievable exactness even here. If the second refraction had not taken place, had Orestes and Pylades heard the echo and interpreted the oracle "correctly" as early as the third act, then Thoas' condition would be fulfilled in the simplest sense; in order to keep his word he would have to let Iphigenia go. But with that his related resolve would also be strengthened, to introduce again the blood-sacrifice from which she alone had held him back. Her rescue "from life here, a second death" would be purchased with the death of all those ship-wrecked in the future. The "word" of the king (to indicate merely a further pattern which Goethe wove into the work with delicate care)—the "word," by the letter of which he can be held, would be a two-edged sword; the letter kills. It is not a free word; it obligates to nothing other than literal, tangible fulfillment. It belongs to the realm of "monstrous" things, of sword, discord, the eternally regenerative evil deed. The prematurely "correct" interpretation of the oracle would only have resulted in arguing over the word as object.

The possibility of Iphigenia's emancipating herself through speaking arises only from the tragic necessity of misunderstanding. Connected to the purely material, the idol, the oracle demands of her theft, cunning, and deceit; for in this interpretation Thoas is not bound by his word and does not need to be argued with. It is the "wrong" interpretation that subjects Iphigenia fully to the curse of being human and, as we saw, makes her capable of true humanity. In experiencing the finite limitation of the divine word she also experiences her own. Without this error the action would end in a short circuit and not just in the sense that it would be over: it would also afford no illumination. Iphigenia could simply take Thoas at his word without having to speak in her most personal language from her innermost being.

Since this error then is necessary, it is a question of reckoning with it rather than eradicating it. Otherwise, "necessary error" would be blasphemy and despair. As so often, Iphigenia says even in her last prayer more than she knows. The "if" allows the possibility that the gods lie, which they as creators really cannot do. Still, they could deny man forever the recognition of their a priori "truth"; they would do this if they did not allow the incorporation of necessary error into *human* truth. For insofar as this incorporation is necessary, it is also divinely created order and thus a part of truth, which could never be accessible to man if he did not find it through and in error. He would be forever excluded from the divine order; Iphigenia's hymns would be childish self-deception, and the Song of the Fates, terrible truth. Indeed, the gods themselves would not be "truthful," since by this they would be denying that man was their creation.[10]

In the foregoing we have had to use quotation marks repeatedly. One could perhaps say that poetry is a kind of language that makes quotation marks unnecessary. Conceptual prose gets muddled in undecipherable paradoxes which allow error to appear as truth, truth as error. However, giving substance to the intellectual and intellectualizing the material— this according to the ambivalence of him whose prose it is—it always has to say the opposite of what it intends to. Conversely, the word of the poet gives clarity by uniting these contrasts—these ambivalences—inherent in the human being, so that "no angel might divide the dual oneness of two so close." The poetic word is truly humanizing, for it creates and represents the duality which is man but which he can otherwise never express.

The divine word does not entail a separation of sign and that signified; it means nothing apart from what it is. It says "sister," and sister it is. But man in his helpless prose has to present it in reflection, as a mirroring of a truth lying beyond it. He may interpret it in a purely corporeal sense—sister as image, or in a completely spiritual sense—sister as goddess. Both are wrong, for he himself is neither the one nor the other; both are right, for he is both. As long as he just interprets, as long as he keeps language at a distance as something different, not inherent in his being, as long therefore as the word is sign and not act—he labors under a delusion. Orestes says: "Between us let there be truth," and with that Iphigenia becomes sister. But at the same time the delusion is intensified; the "sister" of the oracle now becomes "image," so that Thoas is forced to say: "Then arms would still have to decide between us." Why is Orestes' truth not redeeming? Because it is still the thing, like weapons, that is "between" men. For *one thing*, however, this truth is good and extremely necessary: for calling things, and especially ourselves, by name. "It is I myself, Iphigenia"; "I am Orestes"; "Orestes, it is I!" From the impersonal namelessness of the language of the hymns and of the Fates, this truth, which assigns a name to the indubitably existing ego, for the first time creates the possibility of human relationship and communication. But only the possibility, for it is at the same time the *principium individuationis* that makes us fully conscious of our separateness, and more than that gives power to others to treat us as object. Thoas loses little time in making use of the advantage that Iphigenia affords him by giving herself a name:

Dein heilig Amt und dein geerbtes Recht
An Jovis Tisch bringt dich den Göttern näher
Als einen erdgebornen Wilden.   (ll. 499–501)

[Your holy office and your inherited right to be at Jove's table bring you nearer the gods than an earthborn barbarian.]

He cries out in bitter scorn and asks finally also why she should expect more humanity from him than from her father. And the luring call to death with which Orestes woos his sister derives its almost rapturous power from the knowledge of who she is. The intoxicated surrender to the curse, which transforms Tartarus into an idyl, is born of the pleasurable feeling of final fulfillment of fate, according to which fratricide must be the last as well as the first act and will put an end to the accursed race.[11] The language that names and designates sets up a dangerous, because only partial, truth. If the unnameable is divine, then the merely named is thing.

The last truth, Iphigenia's confession, is thus entirely different from that of naming, which preceded it and had to precede it: it is action. Not that divine, *a priori* action which can have only itself as a measure, nor that of the descendants of Tantalus, on whose iron rule every measure shatters. It is another, whose nature we may only sketch by means of baroque-sounding pairs of antonyms. It attacks while surrendering completely. It renounces all support, all cautiousness, without however weakly delivering itself up to causality. It recognizes its involvement and yet is not that which Pylades offers:

> Schweigend herrscht
> Des ew'gen Schicksals unberatne Schwester [die Not].
> Was sie dir auferlegt, das trage: tu,
> Was sie gebeut. (ll. 1683–86)

[The sister of eternal fate (necessity), she with whom there is no consulting, reigns in silence. Bear what she gives you as burden: do what she commands.]

The fulfillment of Christian truth is named "passion" with good reason. It begins with the prayer in Gethsemane and consists not only in the fact that the Lord allows himself to be made prisoner, scorned, and crucified, but even more in the fact that he is silent. He answers the high priest and Pilate with silence or with a passive "You have said it." He does not let himself be given a "hearing," and attempts to convince no one of his innocence. So they say of him: *Ecce homo.* We think of the fact that Nietzsche too said this of himself shortly before he entered his last silence. In this "Behold!" is expressed the superhuman certainty that the last word has already been said, indeed written, and is now only to be fulfilled: "But how would the scripture be fulfilled? One must thus go ahead." The no-more-speaking, the beyond-answering, stamps truth as a final, no longer changing *fact* of action, no longer needful even of being uttered. Iphigenia says "Listen!" Through silence she would still save her unsullied purity, if not herself, and become a martyr to her steadfastness. But for her, truth is not yet fulfilled; she has still to act.

Not in servile obedience to "unheeding" necessity but freely in answer to a human "Say!" She utters the truth which is in her, and as though miraculously, without her knowledge, the words join together that previously were so threateningly separate:

Apoll schickt sie von Delphi diesem Ufer
Mit göttlichen Befehlen zu, das Bild
Dianens wegzurauben and zu ihm
Die Schwester hinzubringen . . .   (ll. 1928–31)

[Apollo sends them from Delphi to this shore with divine instructions to steal away the image of Diana and bring to him his (*literally: the*) sister . . .]

With this, identity is at last put in words, that is, created: the image of the goddess is the sister. Now the oracle is true in human terms. The divine word "sister" attains its correct meaning by having had to be subjected to the densest, most unintellectual substantiality. The refracted error is incorporated into truth, elevated to truth in the *act of language*.

That this truth is act, that it *comes into being* for the first time in speech, we are shown not only in Iphigenia's preceding monologue but also in her innocence of the significance of what she says. She still believes she is uttering a meaningless tautology while uttering what expresses everything. As human being she can not speak with purely creative intention, in words which freely produce meaning instead of being indications of meaning. She cannot intend this, but in staking everything on not letting the truth of her heart "always remain" there, but on its becoming audible and heard, she can bring it about. Her prayer, "Save me, and save your image in my soul," had already darkly implied what now becomes a truth as yet unconscious but therefore *new*. Even in prayer she implored the same thing twice; the image of the gods is not only to be found, but is set exactly in her soul. It is she herself, Iphigenia. But in order that this identity become really saving truth, it must be *said*; it is forced into the reality of truth for the first time when Iphigenia addresses the human being Thoas instead of praying to the gods.

Grasping the meaning of this truth is the task of others: Iphigenia has spoken and is now suddenly "eloquent." Not only in confrontation with Thoas, who feels his anger dissolve at her words; also with Orestes, whose gleaming sword is forced back by her word to its sheath.[12] Even Pylades speaks of the barbarians suddenly with surprising respect: "This is the king's honored head." There is left only—to understand and learn to

speak in the new tongue. For this reason Orestes' "discovery" is intro-
duced with such lack of emphasis; it represents no real reversal but only
the explanation of a state of affairs[13] already "created by words." And as
explanation it is necessarily misleading; it speaks of error and of what the
god "intended." But man is not permitted to know[14] the thoughts of
God. He has only the ambiguous word; what God thought remains for
him forever shrouded. Not until the word has been translated through
error and action into the human sphere does it become meaningful and
true; only then can it be quoted literally without causing confusion.

This word of God, transferred to human terms, is the action which
created truth, Iphigenia's truth which creates speech. It is her speech. As
such it is not either truth or "mendacious web" that we place "between"
us and another according to whether we consider him friend or foe. Still
less is it the "wily word," the continuation of war by other means. It is
not the voice of the heart, which can hide at will from the danger of the
irrevocable utterance, and yet it is not the set word either, the fixed
letter, which in its very fixedness can be gotten around so easily if the
voice of the heart contradicts it. It is none of these and yet all are part
of it. It encompasses constantly the possibility of falsehood, can always
be misused as sword; it must continually hold the balance between
enlivening but untrammeled spirit and the binding but deadening literal
word. It is always mere inheritance, that must be earned anew through
the act of language. But those establish it, and the truth in it, who hear
the voices from above and below call beckoningly and frighteningly: the
poets.

Another question to be sure confronts us here: If all this is so, if
Goethe really intended to represent language in its state of becoming
and thereby achieve truth in human terms, why did he transform the
whole into such a unified verbal form? Why do Thoas and Iphigenia
speak at the very beginning the same language as at the end? Admittedly,
there must be speech in a drama even to express non-speech; but should
not the process of development, if it is really verbal, be more clearly
delineated in a changing language-form? For answer we have to adduce
Goethe's often misused phrase about the "fragments of a great confession." Certainly Iphigenia reflects Charlotte von Stein and Orestes, the
young Goethe tormented in his Titanism; Goethe's personal experiences
are reflected in all his works. But experiences are not poems; we must
seek to understand his poetry solely from his poetic work. And then we
may say that his works are words in this confession. The task of criticism
is to interpret each of these words as accurately as Goethe defines it in
image, action, character, language-form of each work, and so hear his

great poetic confession. In the development of the poet, *Iphigenie* is one word, one act of language; image, action, character, language-form merge into one symbol. Of what? Of the moment in which Iphigenia's act seemed to him possible and realizable, and in which, renouncing his youthful Promethean claim to the immediately divine, creative, poet's word, he believed he could establish a really human, purely mediating, tangible-intangible language and through it a new kind of human community. Hankamer pertinently called the Goethean language of this time "social."[15] What Iphigenia is and accomplishes in the play, *Iphigenie* was to be and accomplish in life. She teaches Thoas at last what the work was to teach the German nation. Having travelled the path of dangerous error, she achieves and established the truth. This fact was to shine forth in full clarity through the very transparent, "very exact" language of the work. There is an incongruity here to be sure; we saw that truth can never be final possession, that it always has to be made anew. Yet even this last paradox Goethe knew how to cast into language—in the last "first" word: in Thoas' "Farewell." Goethe chose just this word of sorrowful parting in order to confirm finally the joyful resolution; one auspicious, first word is taught in this language, but it is a word that already means "end." Is it not also the word, that we designated the work as being? It carries in itself the promised wealth of everything that has gone before. But does it not also conceal the dark premonition of an end? We know that Goethe was not long able to hold fast upon this high level of belief in the social mission of the poet; the renunciation that the late work so often laments is already indicated in *Tasso*. So we must be thankful that in the moment when he indeed had to say farewell, Goethe could leave us this "Farewell" not only as goodbye but also as possession, promise, and command.

Objection may be made to the interpretation attempted here that much of what it represents is also portrayable without the concept of speech, that at times the concept indeed seems to lose substantiality. In reply to this perfectly serious objection, two things should perhaps be kept in mind. Concerning the work itself, its imagery is essentially verbal and requires being read and understood thus. I believe also that by this method of interpretation problems which have formerly remained unsolved or unrecognized are made clear and have for the first time indeed been shown necessary of clarification. (And I will confess that I must have been very clumsy if I have not succeeded in imparting a modest part of my feeling not only of the "beauty" but of the extraordinary, Shakespearean density of *Iphigenie*.[16] Still, the answer must be construed even more generally. Poetry *is* word, the poetic universe is one of language. Concerning what a word means we should never forget first of all that it is one. To be sure, on principle that need no longer be said, but in concrete cases we must on occasion recall the fact. Goethe himself takes care of this. Following the Euripidean model, *Iphigenie* is among other things also a drama that captures poetically an important cultural moment: the abolition of human sacrifice. Iphigenia, herself saved from the bloody altar, believed she recognized her mission in this. She suddenly sees her work threatened; by human calculation only a lie can save herself and her brother from destruction. She calls it a lie; but Pylades can say it differently:

> Man sieht, du bist nicht an Verlust gewohnt,
> Da du, dem grossen Übel zu entgehen,
> Ein falsches Wort nicht einmal opfern willst. (ll. 1674–76)

> [One can see that you are not used to loss, since you do not wish to sacrifice even one false word in order to avoid great disaster.]

He speaks more truly than he imagines; in saying "sacrifice" he elevates the "false word" in exactly that degree in which he intends to devalue it. When it is a matter of life or death, Iphigenia discovers that she can no more sacrifice a word than she can a real human being. Thus language, the association of words, is equated with the association of human beings. Words may not be "engaged" and "expended," like soldiers in war. For speaking is no war; it is the external and polar opposite of war. Words have a holy individuality and inviolability which may not be sacrificed to any purpose, however good it may appear; in each one of them the soul of the whole is contained and preserved. Pylades' proposal is that of the devil in Gotthelf's *Die schwarze Spinne*. He is, to be sure, not the father of lies, but all the same the unconscious speaker of the curse. His "sacrifice" should warn us never to limit the word too narrowly, and to honor it too much rather than too little—provided, of course, that it is the word of a poet.

3. The Consistency of Goethe's *Tasso*

*J*T IS no longer fashionable to dismember a work of literature for adventitious biographical reasons; our critical bias is holistic, or "organic," and we hesitate to do violence to the unity of a poem for no better reason than that we know something of the circumstances of its composition. If *Tasso* criticism seems to form an exception to this rule—if it has again and again led to attempts to separate the "Urtasso" layer of the play from the "Italian" layer—the motive is not the old positivistic delight in anatomizing, but rather a very genuine uneasiness, a real sense that there is something the matter with *Tasso* and a wish to discover what ails it.

The diagnosis has been fairly unanimous: the play is inconsistent; it suffers from undigested "Urtasso" matter. Between 1780 and 1789 Goethe—and with him his conception of the poet's function and place in the world of men—changed profoundly, so that when he tried to incorporate "Urtasso" fragments in the final version, he was bound to fail, the old conceptions and attitudes proved unassimilable. The play (so this argument runs) is therefore not comprehensible except insofar as we are able to distinguish the earlier elements and so to restore two versions, each coherent within itself and each expressing a distinct phase in Goethe's development.

Thus *Tasso* becomes something of a test case in the great critical debate: Are any data other than those given in the work itself admissible of interpretation? Can we properly understand the play if we do not know—or choose to ignore—that its inception and its completion are separated by eight epochal years of Goethe's life? The most sharply defined opposing positions in this debate have been taken by Wolfdietrich Rasch and Walter Silz.[1] Professor Rasch considers speculations about the "Urtasso" idle or even obstructive to a true apprehension of Goethe's meaning, while Professor Silz declares: "Any interpretation that would prove [*Tasso* a cogent play and unified work of art], objectively, abstracting from all genetic and personal implications, will never be satisfactory." Refusing to surrender his critical judgment to a doctrine of Goethean infallibility, Professor Silz draws up a long list of what he considers inconsistencies in the play; these, he believes, are facts which the critic is bound to mark and condemn but which the biographer can explain.

I should like to make a case for—and against—both these critics, in the conviction that at crucial points they have not fully confronted the problems which their approaches have—very properly and illuminatingly —raised. Professor Silz is right in probing sharply for inconsistencies in *Tasso*, but I find myself unable to agree with his claim that only biography can resolve them. Professor Rasch is right in insisting that we must try to understand *Tasso* as it stands, but at times he glides too easily, I think, over some of the very real difficulties the play contains. That is to say: I think that if we are to get a valid interpretation, we must try to join a keen awareness of the play's "inconsistencies" with a firm purpose to treat it as a meaningful and coherent whole.

My own position is perhaps most readily clarified by an analogy between the method of literary interpretation and that of science. Where the interpreter discovers an "inconsistency," he is in the position of the scientist who has detected an "inconsistency" in nature. To the scientist this discovery means that there is a conflict, not between two facts or sets of facts, but rather between a fact and a hitherto accepted interpretation. Since his enterprise is the formulation of principles, or "laws," which are valid for *all* the observable facts they are designed to describe—and since, therefore, the one axiom he cannot dispense with is the uniformity ("infallibility") of nature—he abandons the law or sets about revising it in such a way that it will be consistent with the new fact. If he cannot find a formula that fits all the observable facts, he may, indeed, resign himself to working with two conflicting ones, but the finding of the resolving formula remains one of his chief aims. Analogously, the interpreter's business is to find the "law," the descriptive formula which accounts for all the facts in the verbal microcosm, the poem. For all we know, there may be a Being that interrupts at will the uniform behavior of matter, but science cannot exist except as it discounts this possibility. For all we know, the poet may take liberties with the uniform behavior of the elements that constitute the poem; but interpretation cannot exist except as it discounts this possibility. To an interpreter, an "inconsistency" should mean that he has not read aright, that he must revise the categories or principles which he thought were valid.

That is why we must keep our eyes open for "inconsistencies"; they compel us to develop more and more comprehensive, valid, "true" formulas and so, we trust, to penetrate farther and farther into the heart of the matter of the poem. But it is even more important that, once we have discovered them, we do not rest satisfied with chalking up an error against the creator. Perhaps there is, in the end, no other explanation;

but the possibility always exists—and the greater the poet, the greater the possibility—that the impasse we have come to is of our own devising: that it is the result of our inflexibility, our inability to break free of deeply ingrained habits of perception and reasoning. Properly, interpretation *begins* with the discovery of an "inconsistency." If the "New Critics" seem to delight in puzzles and to find puzzling poems peculiarly suited to their method, it is not from perversity, but from a very sound instinct regarding what they are about: they are not so much critics as interpreters, and puzzles are what interpretation, like science, thrives on.

But the real problem is not to be solved *a priori;* the proof of the methodological pudding is in the eating. I must—and I think I can—show that the axiom of infallibility yields results by forcing us to try to resolve "inconsistencies." I will confine myself to a particularly flagrant one, which has troubled not only Professor Silz but virtually every critic who has not (like Rasch) preferred to pass it over in silence. The complex of facts involved is the "character" of Antonio; the scene in question is the opening one of Act V. Antonio begins by informing Alfons that Tasso stubbornly insists on leaving Ferrara, and then launches into an inventory of the poet's foibles so spiteful that, as Staiger comments, his remarks "selbst in seinem Munde fast erschreckend wirken [even in his mouth have an almost frightening effect]" (*Goethe,* I, 389). A few moments earlier Antonio had assured Tasso of his friendship and promised him his good offices, a few moments later Tasso calls him "edler Mann." In this scene, however, he employs all his considerable resources to blacken Tasso's character, to increase the ill will of Alfons (who is already "verdriesslich") and to portray his rival as an arrogant, spoiled, and ridiculous troublemaker. In fact, Antonio is so possessed with vindictiveness that he does not shrink from turning buffoon and performing a scurrilous and degrading farce to drive home his point. Or so it seems.

I think I may claim that in choosing this scene I am confronting the problem of inconsistency where it most compellingly invites us to fall back on the theory of undigested "Urtasso" matter. But again I might add: "or so it seems." For what does this theory here imply? Nothing less than that Goethe was incapable of avoiding (or eliminating) a scene so stridently out of tune that it grates on the ear of the most casual listener. Even if one were to grant (though there is not a shred of evidence for it) that the scene was already composed in 1780/81—what possessed Goethe to retain it? The play is too long as it is, and nothing in the scene is remotely necessary to the plot. By taking Goethe at his most "inconsistent," I am pointing up the inherent weakness of the "biographical" explanation: it allows of no *a fortiori;* it gets weaker where it should be getting stronger. In proportion as an inconsistency becomes more flagrant, it appears more and more "wilful"—that is, willed by the poet—so that, unless we assume that Goethe deliberately set out to write a faulty, incoherent play, we are compelled to ask: What did he mean by this? And this question does not lead us into Goethe's biography, but straight to where we, as interpreters, belong: the text. What do we find there?

The dramatic situation is this: Antonio would like to keep Tasso from leaving, not because he suddenly loves him, but because reconciliation is the task—the "Geschäft"—with which Alfons has charged him (II.v). Even Leonore's artful playing up on his jealousy (III.iv) has not succeeded in deflecting him from his goal; *he* doesn't want to bear the blame for Tasso's departure. But the poet's ultimatum leaves him no choice, if he cannot persuade Alfons to let Tasso go gracefully, Tasso, overwrought as he is, will himself demand his dismissal and not only create a disagreeable scene but, no doubt, incur the serious and lasting displeasure of the prince (IV.iv). So Antonio is in the unenviable position of having to reconcile two contradictory wishes; he has a task worthy of the highest diplomatic skill. And since he has declared himself Tasso's friend, he has not only one interest to represent in this conflict, but both; as a man of honor and a loyal subject, he must represent them equally.

Now if we assume that he is *not* a man of honor and has deceived Tasso in his declaration of friendship, his behavior is inexplicable. He might, in that case, simply have refused to be Tasso's ambassador, then Tasso would have stormed to Alfons and presumably have won a dismissal the very opposite of gracious—a banishment. And, with Tasso disgraced, Antonio would have been the final victor. But even if this course seemed still too risky to him—after all, Alfons might still have held him responsible for being the prime cause of all the unpleasantness—all such risk is at an end at the outset of our scene, because there Alfons expressly, and in retraction of his earlier judgment (II.v), absolves Antonio of all responsibility: "Ich schreib es dir auf keine Weise zu [I hold you in no way responsible]" (l. 2864). Alfons is by now so annoyed at Tasso's obstinacy that he has reassessed the guilt for the quarrel to the point of completely exculpating Antonio. All Antonio would have to do is to stand aside and let the sovereign wrath take its course.

Instead, he launches into his apparently quite superfluous attack. And what does he accomplish? The very opposite of what—if he still hates Tasso—he should wish. Alfons' first words in the scene are: "Ich bin verdriesslich [I am irritable]" (l. 2836), but his last speech begins: "Ich bin's zufrieden [That satisfies me]" (l. 2979), and he goes on to grant Tasso a leave which is not merely gracious, but actively solicitous, and which provides for the poet's eventual return to the court.

Of course we might conclude that this is an instance of Antonio's being hoist with his own petard; if we share Professor Silz' very low opinion of Antonio's diplomatic skill, this conclusion, as such, would not be unreasonable. But not only is the evidence of the play uniform in attesting Antonio's skill; more important is that this explanation would leave us still deeper in the lurch. The contradiction between a sinister intrigant and the "edle Mann" as whom we are manifestly expected to accept him a few scenes later is bad enough; it becomes wholly incomprehensible if Antonio is not left even the dignity of skill. For then the "edle Mann" is nothing more than the old farce's stock figure of utter contempt, *der geprellte Teufel*. And Goethe here is nothing more—indeed less—than a clumsy hack.

So—back to the text. The scene clearly reveals how Alfons is brought around from his initial "verdriesslich" to the final "zufrieden." His anger abates as Antonio's spite increases: "Ich hab es oft gehört und oft entschuldigt [I have often heard all this and excused it often]" (l. 2917), "Du hättest Recht, Antonio, wenn ... [You would be right, Antonio, if ...]" (l. 2935). Antonio leads Alfons to see the maligned Tasso in a more and more favorable light by forcing the prince to become the poet's advocate; he allows himself to be "set straight" and thereby provides a harmless outlet for Alfons' anger. It is hardly overstating the matter if we say that Antonio sacrifices his personal dignity to the difficult task he has assumed: to obtain for Tasso a gracious dismissal.

This reading of the scene is, I believe, at least as tenable as the traditional one, and it has the very telling advantage of making Antonio's behavior jibe with the final judgment which Goethe wants us to form of him. But does that suffice? Have I offered more than an *ad hoc* explanation which has nothing to recommend it except that it acquits Goethe of the charge of exceedingly poor judgment or outrageously poor workmanship? If it does no more than that, it only raises a new difficulty. *Tasso* criticism furnishes abundant evidence that this scene—if we assume my reading of it to be correct—is highly (indeed, it might seem: perversely) misleading. If Goethe wanted to show that Antonio turns into a loyal and effective friend, why did he write a scene which virtually everyone has felt to be completely unfitted to this end? Why should he wilfully put stumbling blocks in the path of our understanding?

To answer this objection I must be able to show that this peculiar way of exhibiting Antonio's loyalty has implications—i.e., meanings—beyond the immediate one. By a procedure apparently so strange, Goethe jars us into attending to a question quite apart from the simple one of Antonio's moral stature. The question is: Does Antonio tell the truth? Does he just "talk like that" in order to accomplish his purpose, while he "really" thinks Tasso a fine fellow? Ambassadors, by Wotton's famous punning definition, "lie abroad for their country"; does Antonio lie abroad for his friend?

No, he doesn't lie (good diplomats don't); what he says of Tasso is confirmed at every point by Alfons. But neither, surely, does he tell the truth. And precisely this, I suggest, is the intention of the scene: to show in action a mode of speech to which the categories truth and false-hood are entirely irrelevant. Antonio speaks to accomplish a certain end; and judged by his success (by which alone he *can* be judged), he speaks superlatively well. What *he* thinks, how *he* feels about Tasso, we have no means of knowing, the pure "states-man" does not speak to reveal himself and the truth that is in him, but to accomplish a purpose. What we are to discover in the scene, therefore, is not that Antonio is spiteful and treacherous, nor that he is generous and loyal, but rather that he is *not* the kind of man whose inner truth is to be got at from what he says. For him, as well as to him, actions speak louder than words; he is to be known only by what he *does*.

This leads us farther, because Tasso is Antonio's antithesis. Tasso, we may infer, judges language solely under the categories truth and false-hood. Because he does so, he considers all speaking that is *absichtlich* as lying. It is worth noting that in the whole play he is the only one who utters real lies, as when he answers Leonore's proposal to come to Florence:

Gar reizend ist, was du mir sagst, so ganz
Dem Wunsch gemäss, den ich im stillen nähre. (ll. 2426–27)

[What you say to me is quite attractive, so entirely in agreement with the wish that I secretly foster.]

In fact, he raises deception to the level of a principle of conduct:

Wer spät im Leben sich verstellen lernt,
Der hat den Schein der Ehrlichkeit voraus.
Es wird schon gehn, nur übe dich mit ihnen. (ll. 3107–9)

[If one learns to dissemble late in life, he has the advantage of the appear-ance of honesty. You will manage, just practice the art with them.]

He does so, not, of course, because he is by nature dishonest, but on the contrary, because he is so fanatically honest—has so absolute an idea of the truth function of speech—that he feels surrounded by "liars": people who talk to gain ends.

It is for this reason that, in one sense, Antonio and Tasso exchange roles midway in the play. Until the end of Act II Antonio is the divisive force, while Tasso strives for union; in the last two acts Tasso is the divisive force, while Antonio strives for union. Why the turnabout? In the beginning, Tasso's mode of speech is the appropriate one: the speech of friends who pursue no hidden designs, who want only to reveal themselves and their truth to each other. In the half real, half unreal world of the idyllic park Tasso feels at home; but for Antonio it is "fremdes Land," so that he says:

Vergebt, wenn ich . . .
. . . weder Zeit noch Ort,
Noch, was ich sage, wohl bedenken kann.   (ll. 736–38)

[Forgive me, if I . . . can properly consider neither time nor place, nor what I say.]

What *he* needs in order to speak properly is a purpose; so that when he is given a beneficent one (at the end of Act II), he speaks admirably—to the purpose. (When his passions give him a malignant one—in the quarrel scene—he speaks equally admirably—to *that* purpose.) But a purpose in speaking is precisely what Tasso despises and fears; and so, as soon as he feels compelled to speak in this fashion, he lies and with every word widens the gap between himself and the others.

It has often been observed that Goethe took the greatest pains to keep the two antagonists *morally* equivalent. I hope the preceding paragraphs have further buttressed that observation. The moral balance is so exact because we are not supposed to sit in judgment over the two men; we are supposed to apprehend two modes of being—which in Goethe's poetry always means two modes of speaking. When Antonio "etwas Menschlichs in dem Busen fühlt [feels human frailty]" (l. 2004), he becomes dangerous; to speak properly, he must have a proper purpose assigned to him by the state, since he is the "states-man," the functionary": "Was gelten soll, muss wirken und muss dienen [If something is to count, it has to function and be of use]" (l. 671). But when Tasso speaks in this manner, denying his true "Gefühl," *he* becomes dangerous, to speak properly, he must give voice to what is within him:

Doch schöner ist's, wenn uns die Seele sagt,
Wo wir der feinen Vorsicht nicht bedürfen   (ll. 1211–12)

[But it is finer if our soul tells us when we do not need subtle caution.]

And so it is that in the final scene Antonio is almost silent (of 167 lines
he has a mere 24) but *does* the deed that puts his humanity beyond
doubt: wordlessly, without protestations of friendship, he steps up to
the desperate poet and takes his hand. He is *ein Mann der Tat*. Tasso,
conversely, accepts the impossibility of fulfilling himself in action: "Ich
gebe mich, und so ist es getan [I surrender, and thus all is over]"
(l. 3381). He *speaks*, and in speaking discovers his true function, his
mode of self-fulfilment:

Und wenn der Mensch in seiner Qual verstummt,
Gab mir ein Gott, zu sagen, wie ich leide.   (ll. 3432–33)

[And when in their torment men remain mute, a god gave me the power
to tell how I suffer.]

He is *ein Mann des Wortes*.

A full development of this theme would finally involve, I am convinced, a full interpretation of the play—that is to say, the formulation
of the "law" which would reveal *Tasso* as a wholly consistent verbal universe, or "consequente Composition" (to quote Goethe's own judgment
of his play). This is not the occasion to attempt such an interpretation;
but I trust that what I have suggested of it is enough to prove my point:
that Goethe had a compelling reason for writing V.i precisely as he did.
Not a compulsive reason, as though he had to get some old hatreds off
his chest, and let the devil take the play. But a compelling one: a certain
meaning had to be put across, and he saw no other—at least no better—
way to do it.

Here, of course, the critic may step in and say: "I still don't like it.
This is not the best of all possible worlds; the thing could have been
done more simply, more neatly, without creating so much puzzlement."
Saying this devolves upon the critic the task of showing how it *should*
have been done; but that, surely, is not an unfair demand to make of
those who reject the doctrine of the poet's infallibility. And there is still
another position the critic can take: even though he admit the play to
be perfect, he needn't like it. We may justifiably feel that the best of all
possible worlds is nevertheless pretty miserable, or pretty dull. I don't
believe that *King Lear* could be shown to be as perfect as *Tasso*; but I

should think him a very poor critic who therefore decided that *Tasso* was the greater play. The critic works with a set of values different from those of the interpreter, since he is not concerned solely with meaning but with that elusive quality—beauty—and since, where he finds it, he tries to be contagious about it. The interpreter tries to demonstrate; it is not his business to persuade us that the poem is beautiful, any more than it is the scientist's business to persuade us that the world is glorious. He tries to show how it works; having done so, he leaves the critic to decide whether his demonstration has sharpened our sense of the poem's beauty. (I believe that in some way and in some measure it inevitably will, though I am not prepared to say how. In any case, the problem is in good part academic, since no interpreter in his right mind would bother to waste the very considerable effort of an interpretation on a poem that he did not, as critic, think highly of.)

I should say, then, that we cannot dispense with the "toughminded-ness" which frankly recognizes and probes the apparent errors and inconsistencies of even the most venerable poets. But neither can we dispense with the working hypothesis that the poet is infallible. For if we do, we are, in the face of an "inconsistency," committed to judging before we have made every effort to understand. That is why biographical information so often is more of a hindrance than a help: it offers us far too easy an escape from the possibly laborious task of pushing through to the poet's last intention. There are two kinds of response to the reading of poetry: the too ready acquiescence and the too ready judgment. What poetry of the first rank demands of us is a precarious balance between acquiescence and judgment. If we can maintain it, poets like Goethe will reward us with unsuspected meanings and, beyond them, with the severe pleasure we derive from seeing a grand and yet minutely articulated structure.

4. *Die natürliche Tochter*: Goethe's *Iphigenie in Aulis*?

Was bedeutend schmückt,
Es ist durchaus gefährlich.

[That which ornaments with meaning, is fraught with danger.]

DIE NATÜRLICHE TOCHTER [*The Natural Daughter*], according to Goethe's own statement, is a torso; thus the temptation to understand it from the outside—from the plans for continuation or from Goethe's pronouncements about the French Revolution—is obvious. Nevertheless, current criticism, in keeping with its fundamental position, has been at pains to interpret the work in and of itself, alone; and I at least—particularly since the quite illuminating interpretations of Emil Staiger and Verena Bänninger—have no doubts that the newer method proves itself the truer and more reliable even for this fragment.[1] Nevertheless, a third path may be pursued here, proceeding from the assumption that *Die natürliche Tochter* must surely be a part, but part of an actually executed whole: Goethe's dramatic trilogy in blank verse.

Whether and how far this assumption is justified can only be shown by its fruitfulness. But one thing may be said at the outset: it is consonant with the guiding critical principle valid above all for Goethe, that form is always a bearer of meaning in a work of art, perhaps indeed the most important bearer of meaning. *Iphigenie auf Taurus, Torquato Tasso*, and *Die natürliche Tochter* are not less closely bound together by the form of blank verse than *Agamemnon, The Choëphori* and *The Eumenides* by the curse of the Atridae. For form is body, shape, and hence in the work as a whole, metaphor. So when Staiger writes: "The lines of *Die natürliche Tochter* . . . should be read for long stretches in different fashion from those of *Iphigenie* and of *Tasso*,"[2] he seems to me to miss somehow their true nature. For, as Goethean blank verse, they should also be read like those that come in the plays before. As shape and metaphor they should be and mean the same in this play as in the others; if they do not, then something decisive has been stated about them by virtue of pointing out the very non-realization of their nature. If one capacity above all characterized Goethe, it was that of considering absolutely everything that happened to him as symbolic. He hated the fortuitous; he overcame it by forming it, with his own impressive

66

devoutness, into a symbol. How much more he must have understood and preserved with reverence what he had created with effort! Would not blank verse have to embody for all times in his mind the moment that granted him the completion of *Iphigenie?* "You were, you are"—this certainty which comforts the Duke is valid, in the full weight of the little word "to be," also for blank verse.

The epigraph above is to be understood then as the axiom of the following attempt at interpretation. Form is "ornament with meaning" and therefore "fraught with danger." For by giving meaning it is in danger of doing violence to that of the subject matter through its own meaning, or of being itself violated by the subject matter. If form as well as subject matter is a statement, then they must either coincide or the work must break to pieces under the pressure of their contradiction. I hope to show with what severity Goethe submitted his work (and thereby in a certain sense himself) to the judgment of this alternative.

I

Mysteriously banished by the King, threatened by the conspirators with death, Eugenie seeks in vain a way out of the choice between exile in the "islands" and marriage with the Magistrate, a commoner. Despairing, she turns finally to the Monk from whom, to be sure, she no longer hopes for rescue, but perhaps for divine instruction. The Monk refuses this last, but he gives her human counsel:

So ziehe denn hinüber! Trete frisch
In jenen Kreis der Traurigen. Erheitre
Durch dein Erscheinen jene trübe Welt.
Durch mächt'ges Wort, durch kräft'ge Tat errege
Der tief gebeugten Herzen eigne Kraft;
Vereine die Zerstreuten um dich her,
Verbinde sie einander, alle dir;
Erschaffe, was du hier verlieren sollst,
Dir Stamm und Vaterland und Fürstentum.   (ll. 2756–64)

[Go forth then! Enter the circle of the sad with fresh spirit. Bring cheer to that gloomy world by your appearance. By a powerful word, by a forceful act, arouse the inborn strength of deeply bowed hearts; unite the scattered about you, bind them to one another, and all to you; create for yourself what you are to lose here: family and fatherland and princedom.]

What is offered to Eugenie (and the poet) here is the image of Iphigenia—in Aulis. The innocent victim of a curse is to allow herself to be removed "in pious compliance" to the "islands" and thereby begin again the cycle, which had its blessed beginning with the advent of Iphigenia in Tauris. From her word, her act, a true community of human beings is to arise; a new "fatherland and princedom" is to replace the older order, which is visibly disintegrating and no longer to be saved. The development (and writing) of a second *Iphigenie* is what appears to Eugenie and her poet as temptation. But only those most worthy could feel this to be temptation.

Still, the counsel of the Monk *is* temptation. The natural daughter rejects it not from arbitrary principle but because she recognizes that such a "turning-back" would in truth mean a betrayal of the Iphigenian heritage. The Iphigenia of Aulis made no choice; a divine will controlled her destiny. Her own longing was concerned entirely with her fatherland and her accursed race. She did not wish to flee and save herself; on the contrary, she became a blessing for her people and for the barbarians in that she was loyal to her family without reservation. Her happy fate was to be able to become a complete human being because she remained completely the daughter of the Atridae and a Greek.

Her successor conversely is asked to leave her fatherland by her own accord and decision and to regard the curse driving her away as an "alien error." Just because she is a genuine offshoot, Iphigenia's question —"Can an alien world become our fatherland?"—forces itself again upon her almost word for word:

> Doch wär' es fremd, was deinem Vaterland
> Begegnen soll?
>
> [But would what must befall your fatherland be alien?]

In order to be able to answer the question in Iphigenia's spirit, Eugenie has to withstand the temptation to become a second Iphigenia. No god carries her off in a rescuing cloud, from which she will come forth gradually into the clarity of conscious decision; she already bears the burden of consciousness and has to choose. But her choice forces her to became a counter-Iphigenia. Instead of refusing marriage, she goes to the marriage-altar; instead of revealing her identity, she conceals it as an inexplicable "talisman"; instead of departing, she remains; instead of lifting a race to the community of human beings, she binds herself to a kingdom doomed to a "rapid fall."

She is also the true descendant of Iphigenia in that she possesses an incorruptible sensitivity to words. Cast forth and orphaned, she seeks a new father, referring the word in the "transferred," purely spiritual sense to a "cleric":

Mein Vater! lass den ach! mir nun versagten,
Verkümmerten, verbotnen Vaternamen
Auf dich, den edlen Fremden, übertragen.   (ll. 2682–84)

[My father! let me transfer to you, the noble stranger, the name of father,
now alas denied me, spoiled for me and forbidden me.]

From the father thus "created" she then hears the counsel: "Win . . .
for yourself family and fatherland." But this contradiction by which the
fatherland becomes an alien world, an alien world the fatherland, causes
her to pay great attention and finally reject this spiritual advice. "*Ubi
bene, ibi patria*": this tenet, however ennobled, would be a betrayal of
the Iphigenian inheritance, which consisted in the very incarnation of
the divine word "sister." [3] Blood is a very special fluid, as even the devil
knows. Fatherhood is in the final analysis not a purely intellectual
"relationship," to be interpreted according to desire or necessity, but
also a physical, corporeal bond. Even the apparently rejecting father is
still a father; even the word apparently becomes meaningless, cannot be
attached arbitrarily to a more fitting meaning. In the very incompre-
hensibility of word and bond still fraught with literal obligation, Eugenie
discovers what is holy. If body and spirit can no longer be united in the
form of pure humanity, as in *Iphigenie*, then nothing remains other than
to "cling fast" to the completely inanimate and corporeal, the "soil,"
and wait for a future "miracle" with a "steadfast heart."

Eugenie thus becomes Iphigenia's true heiress by taking upon herself
the opposite destiny. The "harbor city" could have become Aulis; but
then Eugenie would have been cheated of her own truth. The altar—the
last word of the play—could not simply be Agamemnon's sacrificial altar
without being demeaned to a stage prop; in order to be able to hope for
a renewed life, Eugenie could not be permitted to wish to die once again
the "death" of her forebear. She earns her own death:

Sobald ich mich die Deine nenne, lass,
Von irgendeinem alten zuverläss'gen Knecht
Begleitet, mich, in Hoffnung einer künft'gen
Beglückten Auferstehung, mich begraben.   (ll. 2911–14)

[As soon as I call myself yours, let me, accompanied by some old trusted
servant, bury myself, hoping for a future happy resurrection.]

And as always with Goethe, here too *language* accomplishes the real
action. Language—the once transparent veil that reveals truth—becomes
in this sentence a densely entangled hymeneal and burial veil which is

scarcely transparent any longer. Language loses all vitality and will not rise again in its present form.

The conversion of her father—we may perhaps term the end of his interview with the Abbé thus—stands in remarkable contradiction to Eugenie's resolve. Here the Duke, robbed of the body of his daughter forever (as he believes), is thrown back upon the spirit:

> Getrenntes Leben, wer vereinigt's wieder?
> Vernichtetes, wer stellt es her?
>   Der Geist!
> Des Menschen Geist, dem nichts verlorengeht,
> Was er von Wert mit Sicherheit besessen.   (ll. 1698–1701)

[Who will unite sundered life again? Who will restore what is destroyed? —The spirit! Man's spirit, that loses naught of value that it has possessed with certainty.]

And this consolation is effective. From a despair compared with which the outcast Tasso offers a mild complaint, which in destructive frenzy surpasses Faust's curse and has its counterpart only in the curses of the storm-lashed Lear, the belief in the protecting strength of the spirit helps the Duke gain inner peace.

But the riddle of the contradiction is thereby in no way as yet exhausted. A true spiritual guide attempts to convince Eugenie, who is only too conscious of her true situation, by means of a truthful analysis; but he has no success. A false spiritual guide undertakes to comfort the cruelly deceived Duke by means of "lies," and he is successful. His eloquence is unnatural, as indeed the whole scene probably belongs to the most monstrous that dramatic literature can show. For what we hear happen is the legitimation of falsehood.[4] If we forget for a moment—and does not Goethe almost force us to forget it?—that Eugenie is not really dead and buried, the scene is characterized by a power of conviction which is only due the truth. If we look about for the most terrible example of the power of falsehood, we think of Iago and Othello. But what is it compared with that of the Abbé? In Shakespeare we never forget the truth for a moment; and more important—the lie is destructive. It is a bitter solace but still a solace, that its triumphs are bloody. But in *Die natürliche Tochter* it speaks with an authority it should never have. No "aside," no "look," no false tone of voice betrays the Abbé. Who of us can deny him consent, when with a commanding and "true" word—"the spirit"—he puts an end to the despairing questions of the Duke?

Even as dramaturgy the third act is an impropriety. The action of *Iphigenie* develops in harmonious regularity; two only apparently independent destinies are revealed in the third act as sprouts of one root. *Die natürliche Tochter* on the other hand separates into two actions, which after initial unity lead to conclusions without relation to one another. And Goethe takes great pains to lend to this third act ending in a blind alley the full pathos and the poetic rounding fitting for a true end; in the closing words of the Duke, as we feel and we must feel, final words are spoken. The "action"—the dramatic happening around the heroine as a physical person—ends with the last act; but her fate as a being with a name, as Eugenie, comes with the composed mourning of the Duke to an end that has lost all character of what is false, miscarried, or provisional. From this moment on "Eugenie" is indeed no longer among the living; she is called here for the last time by her name, the further action concerns only the nameless one:

Von hohem Haus entspross die Bittende;
Doch leider ohne Namen tritt sie auf. (ll. 2426–27)

[The petitioner is descended from a noble house; but she appears, alas! without a name.]

In view of this peculiar structure, which mocks all dramatic rules, the interpretation of *Die natürliche Tochter* as a purely classic or classicistic fragment seems to me not very convincing. Much has been said about the stylization and treatment of the figures as types, as an attempt to approach the essential quality of classicism.[5] But where, we may well ask, do the Greek tragic poets deny their characters proper names? And if we want to explain the structural "defects" by the fact that the play is only a fragment, that does not satisfy either: the *Oresteia* is a trilogy too, but for all its continuity of action each of its parts is self-contained. Goethe, having had his drama produced and printed, must therefore have been convinced that it would be effective even as a part. It is thus more than probable that with the dramaturgical caprices stressed above he pursued intentions that we may not approve critically, but which as interpreters we must try to fathom.

Considered from the point of view of speaking, at all times important for Goethe, drama is the poetic form that does not allow the poet to say his own word. He may not address us directly, as in a lyric poem, nor is he permitted, as in the epic, to play an active role as narrator in presenting, describing, and interpreting at any point. In straight drama the poet is allowed no voice and granted no platform permitting him to take up a position, while he offers explanations and "revelations," between the half-truths (or even falsehoods) of his characters and his listeners. In this sense drama is the touchstone by which the possibility of a "natural religion" is determined in poetry. This means that, if a perfect drama were possible, the poet as creator could reveal himself fully in his creation without special revelation. In such a self-contained and self-creating work, he would be wholly expressed and wholly understandable. Without arbitrariness, without miracles or any kind of stage magic, such a world would revolve with inspired regularity, directly accessible to our senses and our human reason. And it is not too much to say that *Iphigenie* realizes this ideal situation. What in the beginning is still false, distorted, dark and misunderstood in it, is revealed *from within itself,* without additional divine explanation, as pure harmony and truth. Through the continuous speaking in the play the truth which is the play is created. Everything in it is necessary, even error, in order to bring forth this truth; and if Goethe had written only this work, we could be critical deists and say: here we have him as a whole; we need nothing more in order to understand him, his true nature and his creative will. And thus, I believe, Goethe himself looked back upon *Iphigenie* when in *Die natürliche Tochter* he wrote his last drama in lofty style. The final recognition of Orestes:

Wir legten's als Apollos Schwester aus,
Und er gedachte Dich . . .

[We explained it as Apollo's sister, and he [the god] meant you.]

is echoed once again in the closing words of the Duke:

Die Gottheit hatte dich
Vollendet einst gedacht and dargestellt.   (ll. 1722–23)

[The Godhead once conceived and represented you as perfect.]

Iphigenie is the perfect revelation of the creator in his work; the interpretation of it is "natural theology," the veneration of it is "natural religion."

If *Die natürliche Tochter* has two conclusions and Eugenie two destinies, this indicates that the one revelation no longer suffices. The dead Eugenie lives in the mind of her father as indestructible spiritual possession; the living, anonymous woman buries herself as a mysterious talisman. Which of these is semblance, which true being? Eugenie believes she has the answer:

Der Schein, was ist er, dem das Wesen fehlt?
Das Wesen, wär' es, wenn es nicht erschiene?   (ll. 1066–67)

[What is the semblance that lacks true being? Would there be true being if it had no semblance?]

But paradoxes are not solved by being expressed in antithetical aphorisms—on the contrary. With this question that only she deems rhetorical, Eugenie disregards the paternal ban, puts on the treacherous adornments and so seals her antithetical fate. "Dear friend, my good fortune cannot be revoked," she cries; and who would want to deny it? In the "semblance" of eternal youth, beauty, and vitality she will remain preserved in the mind of her father. But the hollow echo of the Governess replies: "The lot that befalls you cannot be revoked"; and this proves just as true. It is thus advisable to understand Eugenie not in the singular but in the plural, if we want to do justice to her and to the work.

II

It is not alone the dramatic structure that forces us to this interpretation. Eugenie in fact speaks of herself in the plural in her first words after her prefiguring fall: "What has happened to us?" and again: "Who brought us under these trees?" Only after hiding her face in the "white kerchief" does she say: "Here I am again." In this prelude, this first "rapid fall" that she suffers, she already has a premonition of what the later fall will mean: a splitting of her very self.

But if we are inclined to disregard the "us" as a sign of momentary confusion, the weightier circumstance remains that Eugenie appears on the title page and in the *dramatis personae* with two different designations. Even she, the only one with a name in the play, is deprived of her name as titular protagonist. Iphigenia had one name, Torquato Tasso a double name; Eugenie has one and again none. As illegitimate child, she is without name and function; but just for this reason she needs a name more than all others and is provided with one: she exists in this impersonal world of functions only as a private individual, as natural man, in the love of those who are devoted to her.

Basically, the very title justifies calling the play a "tragedy." If we keep our ears open for the resonance the words "nature" and "natural" had for the eighteenth century and especially for Goethe, we hear the tragic disharmony that vibrates in the phrase "natural daughter." Here too *King Lear* comes to mind: perhaps the monologue of Edmund the bastard ("Thou, Nature, art my goddess") or Lear's reason-shattering discovery of the "unnaturalness" that hides behind the legitimacy of his daughters. That human society can develop in such a way that "natural" and "illegitimate" become synonymous, is reason enough for sadness.

And yet society has developed in this way. In *Iphigenie* the word "nature" is not yet known, for in that drama everything *is* nature. The stage setting is a "grove," covered with growth and still not overgrown—neither the virgin forest which we are to imagine as the first scene of *Die natürliche Tochter*, nor Tasso's "garden." What in a real sense *is*, does not demand conceptual definition; a concept always makes itself questionable, "nature" necessarily conjures up "non-nature." It has not yet come to this in *Tasso*; Tasso in the end realizes that Antonio too is natural:

> die mächtige Natur,
> Die diesen Felsen gründete, hat auch
> Der Welle die Beweglichkeit gegeben.

[... mighty nature, that established this rock, also gave mobility to the wave.]

The fair world of morality, in which instinct and law stood in free cooperation—the world of cultivated gardens and polite human society—proved itself too fragile to be assured; from this unique union nature turned back into its elements, the enmity of which is natural law and the momentary harmony of which nothing guarantees other than the handclasp of two men. Only in the world of *Die natürliche Tochter*, which has as it were become monolithic, do nature and the human order oppose one another in unbridgeable division, so that both have become "unnatural" in the Iphigenian sense:

> Wie du auf einmal völlig abgeschieden
> Hier unter diesem Bollwerk der Natur,
> Mein König, dich empfindest, fühl' ich mit.
> Hier dränget sich der Unzufriednen Stimme,
> Der Unverschämten offne Hand nicht nach. (ll. 21–25)

[I understand, my king, how completely isolated you suddenly feel here behind this bulwark of nature. Here the voice of the discontented does not force its way, nor the open palm of the brazen-faced.]

The human element penetrates this virgin forest as a jarring note, and the "natural" rite here performed is not a religious service nor the crowning of statues of poets, but the hunt (as indeed it was also the hunt that in Aulis led to the sacrifice of Iphigenia). Everything, even this "return to nature," is purposive and for that very reason leads astray:

Das flüch'ge Ziel, . . .
Der edle Hirsch, hat über Berg and Tal
So weit uns irr' geführt . . .   (ll. 1–4)

[The fleeing object, the noble stag, has led us across mountain and valley so far astray.]

As nature and human order thus become antithetical, both lose: nature degenerates to wilderness, order to rigidity. In their conflict Eugenie is torn to pieces. She,

                    das Vollkommne,
Das ernst und langsam die Natur geknüpft,
Des Menschenbilds erhabne Würde . . .   (ll. 1542–44)

[. . . the perfected whole that Nature joined with slow and earnest case, the noble dignity of a human being]

would still be the only one who could hinder the final rift; in her banishment the state delivers judgment on itself as well as on Iphigenian nature. The wilderness the Duke intended to set in order will become a "wasteland," and the structures of human settlement are accursed. At the end of the play the stage set is one of symmetry in stone: church to the right, palace to the left, with a view upon that elemental force, the sea. And beyond the sea a nature that is everywhere the opposite of Tasso's paradisiac vision—a nature pregnant with malice and poison:

Ein feuchtes, kaum der Flut entrissnes Land.
Um Niederungen schwebet, gift'gen Brodens,
Blaudunst'ger Streifen angeschwollne Pest . . .
. . . wo sich in Sümpfen Schlang' und Tiger
Durch Rohr und Dorngeflechte tückisch drängen.   (ll. 1984–96)

[. . . a damp land, hardly snatched from the waters. The swollen plague of blue-vapored clouds hovers in hollows with poisonous exhalation . . . — where in swamps snake and tiger make their way with malice through reed and thorny web.]

All this is included in "natural." And the word itself—and the figure of Eugenie—holds all this together in an undivided whole no longer credible. Not only was she joined by nature; she *is* also joined to it and threatens in her ruin to relapse into the chaos of elemental forces:

> O! Wehe! dass die Elemente nun,
> Von keinem Geist der Ordnung mehr beherrscht,
> Im leisen Kampf das Götterbild zerstören. (ll. 1533–35)

[O woe! that now the elements, ruled no more by any spirit of order, in muted struggle destroy the god-like image.]

But it will not do to consider Eugenie simply a victim. Behind the change and rift in meaning of the word "nature," there is active not only arbitrariness but at the same time a fatal logic. The distrust of society has a certain justification, even though self-produced.

This is also evident from the *dramatis personae*: the mere given name, Eugenie, represents a kind of throw-back, an over-emphasis. Because law has hardened against nature, nature itself has become Rousseauistic. This is felt particularly in the description of the "fairy kingdom" into which the Duke wishes to transform the virgin forest:

> Den wilden Wald, das struppige Gebüsch
> Soll sanfter Gänge Labyrinth verknüpfen.
> Der steile Fels wird gangbar, dieser Bach,
> In reinen Spiegeln fällt er hier und dort . . .
> . . . Hier soll kein Schuss,
> Solang' ich lebe, fallen, hier kein Vogel
> Von seinem Zweig, kein Wild in seinem Busch
> Geschreckt, verwundet, hingeschmettert werden. (ll. 619–27)

[A labyrinth of gentle paths is to unite the wild forest and the unkempt brush. The precipitous rock will become passable, this brook will fall there and here in clear mirrorings. Here no shot shall fall as long as I live, here no bird from its branch and no game in its bush shall be frightened, wounded, struck down.]

This is rococo "nature": the temple that is dedicated to no god; the labyrinth that leads to no minotaur; the game park in which one can only imagine tamed or peaceable animals. The attempt to construct again the scene of *Iphigenie* conjures forth a "féerie."

Even the language is disquieting. Coming from *Pandora* or the Helen episode of *Faust*, we may still feel this style to be natural; but whoever has the lines of *Iphigenie* or of *Tasso* ringing in his ear, notices something forced. Let us consider *Tasso*:

Ja, es umgibt uns eine neue Welt!
Der Schatten dieser immer grünen Bäume
Wird schon erfreulich. Schon erquickt uns wieder
Das Rauschen dieser Brunnen. Schwankend wiegen
Im Morgenwinde sich die jungen Zweige.

[Indeed, a new world surrounds us. The shade of these trees forever green already affords pleasure. The murmuring of these fountains already refreshes us again. Waving to and fro, the new branches rock in the morning breeze.]

If indeed such an observation of nature itself—one looks for it in vain in *Iphigenie*—is no good omen, at least it is unforced; the language, in order to produce the feeling of harmonious animation, can safely entrust its own rhythm to the meter of blank verse. When, towards the end of the play, Tasso wishes to remain at any price in the vicinity of the princess, he offers himself to her as solicitous custodian; and as the mania for integration and subordination increases in him, his individual note yields more and more to the meter:

Es soll das Estrich blank und reinlich glänzen,
Es soll kein Stein, kein Ziegel sich verrücken,
Es soll kein Gras aus einer Ritze keimen!

[The stone floor shall shine in gleaming purity, no stone or brick be out of place, nor any grass sprout from a crack!]

Here, to be sure, grass grows no more; here not only the poet but the free-born human being abdicates. We would do the Duke an injustice if we said that such a cadence would be more appropriate for him; but somehow his language longs for an ordering not granted it. It is neither completely composed nor even trusting; it hesitates in mid-course, and loses the courage for a simple statement by timidly adding an adjective, by repeating a noun unnecessarily in a pronoun, and by employing an almost baroque series of verbs (in order that full justice be done the preceding subjects). These are, to be sure, traits of Goethe's late style; here they are not yet a style but compulsive verbal gestures that express themselves without or even against the will of the speaker. And when we observe this rather jittery animation even in the pedantically jouncing chancery-language of the Secretary:

Und was Erfreuliches
An Waldung, Busch, an Wiesen, Bach und Seen
Sich Phantasie zusammendrängen mag,

Geniessen wir, zum Teil als unser eignes,
Zum Teil als allgemeines Gut. Wobei
Noch manche Rente gar bequem vergönnt ... (ll. 677–82)

[Let us enjoy, in part as our own, in part as a shared possession, whatever
pleasure the imagination can win from woodland and bush, from meadows,
brook and lakes. At the same time, too, many a revenue will comfortably
allow ...]

we may indeed long to have back Tasso's honest "It shall ... it shall ...
it shall. ...

The quality of aloofness, indirectness, and stiffness in *Die natürliche
Tochter* has been remarked upon often and explained variously. But the
characteristic note that the blank verse in this work often assumes can
hardly be described more aptly than in Staiger's words: "Blank verse by
nature approaches more the tempo of ordinary discourse. The artificial
distension [of this meter in *Die natürliche Tochter*] is the audible sign
of disturbance of equilibrium of the physical-spiritual existence."[6] Still,
this tone, with its palpable overburdening of the meter, does not govern
the whole play. Often within the space of a few lines we are tossed from
passages which could without break be inserted in *Iphigenie* over to
others which can hardly be distinguished from the trimeters of *Pandora*:

Du wirst es anders finden! Ja, du bist
In eine Zeit gekommen, wo dein König
Dich nicht zum heitren, frohen Feste ruft,
Wenn er den Tag, der ihm das Leben gab,
In kurzem feiern wird; doch soll der Tag
Um deinetwillen mir willkommen sein. (ll. 328–33)

[You will find things different! For you have come at a time when your
king will not summon you to a gay and happy celebration, when he will
presently commemorate the day that gave him life; yet for your sake the
day shall be welcome to me.]

But immediately thereupon:

Der freud'gen Überraschung lauter Schrei
Bedeutender Gebärde dringend Streben,
Vermöchten sie die Wonne zu bezeugen,
Die du dem Herzen schaffend aufgeregt? (ll. 339–42)

[The loud cry of joyful surprise, and the urgent striving of significant gesture, would these be able to attest the rapture that you, creating, have
roused in my heart?]

Here—and not only here—there is a stylistic shift which resists any description aiming to show homogeneity.[7]

For the full understanding of the meaning to be attached to style and structure, we have to allow such inconsistencies their full value. We must not even be afraid of the figure of Eugenie, as insensitive as that may seem. Certainly she is "enchanting" in her naiveté (Staiger); certainly she is "the symbol of individual existence in a world which threatens demonically in the form of history" (von Wiese); but Goethe himself found the epithet "childlike" insufficient and with his "even childish" made it questionable.[8] It is evidence neither of true cultivation nor of genuine naiveté when a young girl distributes gratuities with the words:

Verweilt!
    (Sie reicht ihnen einen Beutel hin.)
      Zum Vorgeschmack eures Botenlohns
Nehmt diese Kleinigkeit, das Bessre folgt.   (ll. 1004–5)

[Tarry! (*She hands them a purse.*) Take this pittance as a foretaste of your messenger's reward—something better follows.]

On the contrary, these are grand, "princely" manners, which we may indulge in one suddenly elevated but which we must not overlook. It is not a sign of natural or cultivated taste when a sweet little versifier speaks of an undistinguished sonnet of homage as though it were a unique inspiration of the divine muse which will press "a stamp for all time" on the emotions. These are rather the "arty" phrases of a dilettante.

In any case: if Goethe intended to create here a "chaste drama of style without subject matter" (Gundolf), why do we see in it the heroine running back and forth on the stage in order to find a hiding place for her poem, but hear this still quite material behavior accompanied by the words:

Du, den mir kindisch allausspähende,
Von Neugier und von Müssiggang erzeugte,
Rastlose Tätigkeit entdecken half,
Du, jedem ein Geheimnis, öffne dich!   (ll. 990–93)

[You whom tireless activity helped me discover—activity childishly spying out everything and spawned of curiosity and idleness—you, a mystery to everyone, open up!]

This apostrophe is directed to a cupboard! Goethe's dramatic art is here anything but chaste; rather it plays consciously with the danger of falling into the ridiculousness of incongruity.

Accordingly, I am, unlike May, completely unable to regard the dramatic action and language as "controlled movement that is regulatively encased by permanent being and, as it were, flows along beneath it." Almost the opposite seems correct to me: as Eugenie shows herself to be unequal to the hope proffered her, so the language is not equal to the events which it should cope with; both betray a certain incapability. As play as well as figure "the natural daughter" is no longer an Iphigenia; she has the misfortune of having to be natural in a world in which the word—and indeed with a certain justice—also means "illegitimate."

With this we have touched upon the difficult question of the moral principle of the play. It will not do to regard Eugenie simply as the victim of a ruthless conspiracy;[9] for the piece of writing that banishes her is signed by the King himself. We do not know how he was persuaded to sign. But we do know one thing: Eugenie presumed to construe an unambiguous command of the King as well as of her father according to her own construction of it. It may seem an insignificant offense that she confides her happy secret to the Governess who knows it anyway; it is also not clear how strict obedience would have been able to alter her destiny. But so much can be said: in this arbitrariness of interpretation she who is illegitimate and nameless according to the law renounces the only protection that she has—reverent respect for true being as such (be it word or man). Her justification:

Mit Sinn befahl er, zum bestimmten Zweck;
Der ist vereitelt: alles weisst du schon.   (ll. 1028–29)

[He gave his order with a definite purpose in mind; the purpose has been frustrated: you know everything already.]

we must read as commentary on the conversation between the Secretary and the Governess, on the principle:

Und was uns nützt, ist unser höchstes Recht.   (l. 861)

[What serves our needs is highest law.]

According to positive law, Eugenie has no rights:

Und gönnt ihr dieser köstlichen Natur
Aus Fürstenblute nicht das Glück des Rechts?   (ll. 754–55)

[And do you not grant this precious being of princely blood the happy benefit of law?]

For this very reason she is thrown entirely upon unwritten natural law, upon the feeling

Dass über Schuld und Unschuld lichtverbreitend
Ein rettend, rächend Wesen göttlich schwebt.   (ll. 851–52)

[... that, spreading light, a saving and avenging being hovers divine over guilt and innocence.]

But as *Iphigenie* had already taught, the sacrifice of a word equals that of a human being. Eugenie makes this sacrifice. To be sure she does not lie, but on the other hand neither is she slain; she disenfranchises the word at her discretion and thus she herself is disenfranchised at the discretion of state interest. For her above all others reverence is fitting, a feeling for the absolutely binding quality of the word merely sopken, of the commandment not established in law and not confirmed by sense and purpose. But in the intoxication of her joy she loses this feeling, until she ultimately rediscovers it under tragic coercion.

The pitiless royal decree speaks, then, instead of pardon. Whatever reasons may have moved the King to banish her, it cannot be denied that there is a certain "poetic" justice in the decree. For if society sins against the natural law of human beings in regard to Eugenie, *she* has transgressed the natural law of language; she, the last token of nature in a world rigidified and hence already chaotic, betrays what is sacred in her sphere—that of language—for an expedient functionalism.

III

A great deal thus lies here behind the word "natural"—the faith of an age and the faith also of a Goethean period of creation. Here it is weighed and found too light, not only considering the age, but also in its peculiar character as conditioned by this age. The net in which "the natural daughter" is caught is woven of a joining together of historical compulsion and personal impotence deliberately concealed by Goethe and perhaps hardly to be untangled completely; and the net is called arbitrariness. Eugenie is conceived in arbitrariness and pursued by arbitrariness; arbitrarily she disregards the injunction of silence and arbitrarily she is banished. And with amazing and yet necessary arbitrariness of speech and dramatic means, the poet produces the picture of her fate.

Since Lessing, there has been much ridicule of the "classical" rules of the unities; and certainly if they lead us to value Addison's *Cato* highly and, instead, to condemn Shakespeare, they are indeed ridiculous. As soon as one feels a rule as an inhibiting constraint and makes unwilling sacrifices to it, it may easily come about that the sacrifice has not been worth it. But who is willing to assert that *Oedipus Rex* is not only not inhibited by the "keeping" of the rules but gains infinitely? The confining of an action widely dispersed in time and space into a compact process of self-discovery—the realization that an episodic destiny, which seemingly evolves without design, had nevertheless to be brought together beneath the surface as an unknown and terrible unity—this is just what lends the drama its power and makes it in the true sense classical. Unity in some sort of sense *is* law, actually capturing the essence of this very law in a poetic work so that it becomes a metaphor of the whole is the masterstroke of Sophocles; this is classicism.

And who is willing to assert that *Iphigenie* would have become the masterwork of German classicism if Goethe had not obeyed the "unities"? His obedience was anything but aesthetic pedantry; it was the realization that the redeeming sense of the whole could only be embodied in the harmony of inner necessity and outer constraint. That in one place and at one point in time seemingly unreconcilable demands clash with one another and then unite anyhow—that in the transcendent order of space and time human needs can be fulfilled—this lends the play its singular harmony, its truth and classic "naturalness."

About *Tasso* Staiger nicely observed that the unity of time is already felt to be a constraint.[10] With the exception of the princess (who also once betrays impatience, however), all the characters repeatedly enjoin themselves to haste. That this is only an "artifice" with which Goethe "carelessly gives the theater what the theater demands" (Staiger) seems to me, however, doubtful; for this very haste is calamitous. Gently urged by the princess, Tasso pushes himself "prematurely" upon Antonio; Leonore is in a hurry with her destructive work; and in the end Tasso's insistence upon his immediate dismissal contributes decisively to his misfortune. Even the unity of place is not completely observed, again because the characters cannot be calm. "Uncertainly my steps follow you," Tasso says after leaving the happy garden, "and thoughts without moderation and order are stirring in my soul." This uncertain following about then brings him to the confinement to quarters, in which he can hear from the princess only through the mediation of Leonore. Whereas Iphigenia remained "steadfast," at all times available and approachable, there is noticeable now an urgency, a striving after goals, a slightly irritating purposiveness.

In *Die natürliche Tochter* the striving has now become an irreverent, almost brazen and yet again compulsive, arbitrariness. Led astray "by the fleeing object," it races destructively through the order of nature. Eugenie disregards both impassable acclivities and mild warnings; her brother "contradicts the demand of nature, the voice of law, and reason." In the interest of their purpose the Secretary and the Abbé commit crimes with open eyes. An uncanny precipitance holds sway over the whole play:

> O diese Zeit hat fürchterliche Zeichen:
> Das Niedre schwillt, das Hohe senkt sich nieder,
> Als könnte jeder nur am Platz des andern
> Befriedigung verworrner Wünsche finden,
> Nur dann sich glücklich fühlen, wenn nichts mehr
> Zu unterscheiden wäre, wenn wir alle,
> Von *einem* Strom vermischt dahingerissen,
> Im Ozean uns unbemerkt verlören. (ll. 361–68)

[Oh! this is an age of terrible signs: what is low rises, and what is high subsides, as though each could find only in the other's place satisfaction of confused desires, only feel happy if there were no more distinctions and all of us, carried away commingled by one stream, were to be lost unnoticed in the ocean.]

If the drama thus finally bursts through the frame of the classical unities—if, as we saw, not only unity of place and time but even that of action and of style are violated—this testifies to a failure of a special, "meaningful" kind. Here a form fails the world that it should comprehend—or a world the form which alone could bring it about. Faced with such a reality, form is disconcerted; in such a form, reality is unintelligible. As Eugenie puts on the decoration at the completion of her hasty self-adornment, she says boldly: "That which ornaments with meaning is fraught with danger":

> Was reizt das Auge mehr als jenes Kleid,
> Das kriegerische lange Reihen zeichnet?
> Und dieses Kleid und seine Farben, sind
> Sie nicht ein Sinnbild ewiger Gefahr? (ll. 1137–40)

[What charms the eye more than the garb that designates long rows of warriors? And this garb and its colors, are they not an emblem of eternal danger?]

The sash stands for the military uni-form, for the rows of iambic five-footers which—arranged in larger units—stride along in even measure. But Eugenie herself knows that the uni-form is ornament with meaning. Of course it means for her here only soldiering and fighting for the fatherland, but it signifies more: the unifying order of the world which it represents and protects—and the punishment which is meted out for the unjustified wearing of the uniform. As "the natural daughter" puts on the uniform that the King has as yet failed to grant her and that a world rushing toward chaos has already denied her, she too fails.

The equation of blank verse with uniform may seem forced. In the final analysis, it is also the form of *Iphigenie*. And what could more miss the mark than to characterize it there as "uniform"? But here, as with "natural," we encounter the same unfortunate consistency of intention —the same distortion of a possession no longer tenable because of the mania for possessing it:

Er ist entschwunden! Was uns übrig bleibt,
Ist ein Gespenst, das mit vergebnem Streben
Verlorenen Besitz zu greifen wähnt.   (ll. 2836–38)

[It has disappeared! What remains for us is a spectre, that thinks to seize a lost possession with vain striving.]

In *Iphigenie* we remain unconscious of costume. The veil—the light woven fabric more revealing than enshrouding—plays a thematic role, which however only the perspective from other works of Goethe makes us notice. In *Tasso* the motif gains considerably in meaning: the "rare, festive garment of the beautiful" in the beginning; nature, which "covers her inmost fruitful breast with a green bright garment"; Leonore's domestic concern with Tasso's linen—these are only some examples. Garment is here the symbol of what is "seemly," of what surrounds the civilized human being with hardly noticeable constraint. But in *Die natürliche Tochter* clothing becomes the predominant symbol; almost the whole *physical* action of the play is concentrated in the dressing-scene. While Goethe does not show us the signing of the decree and Eugenie's abduction and so does not allow the causally important elements of the action to assume shape, he squanders a considerable amount of "material" and words on this causally unimportant scene. We are spared no single detail of the inventory:

Komm! Reiche mir die Teile, nach und nach.
Das Unterkleid; wie reich und süss durchflimmert
Sich rein des Silbers und der Farben Blitz . . .
Das Oberkleid, das goldne, schlage drüber,
Die Schleppe ziehe, weit verbreitet, nach.
Auch diesem Gold ist, mit Geschmack und Wahl,
Der Blumen Schmelz metallisch aufgebrämt.   (ll. 1046–56)

[Come! hand me the pieces, one after the other. The undergarment—with what sweet richness the sparkle of silver and of colors shimmers clear . . . ! Throw over it the golden outer garment, pull the train back and spread it wide. On its gold the gloss of flowers makes a metallic border too, done with taste and judgment.]

And so on to the pearls, jewels and ribbons until this uniform of princeliness is fully donned. From pliable veil the attire stiffens to metallic brocade, and natural beauty is no more.

IV

If I have up to now examined chiefly the first two acts, there is a reason: it is in them that the will to unify shows itself. And they are the really disquieting acts: the language changes suddenly without obvious necessity; the action moves perkily and with an excess of motivation that is, however, unnecessary. We might say, everything is under the simultaneous prohibition of "Not yet!" and "No longer!" However incomprehensible from the point of view of motivation Eugenie's banishment may appear, as *figure* she is thoroughly meaningful, for in this world of premature and belated action she confirms the unattainability of the purely present.[11] Even a clear, regularly motivated course would be unsuited to this world, and so Goethe does not let it come about. Even a symbolism entirely of the present and self-contained would contradict the meaning of the work, and thus Goethe pushes the symbolism further into a parabolism that forces us to see through it and speculate about it. The riddles—that of the cupboard that is so palpably a "mystery," or even that of the jewel casket—may be solvable, but their immediate effect is that they do not allow any graspable present to take shape on which our senses and thoughts might rest. We are neither invited to a direct perceiving, as in *Iphigenie*, nor forced to a complete and unified point of remove, as in *Pandora*; we never know where we are and what position we are commanded to take.

The third act now follows this unrest and uncertainty as a release. We are returned again to the world with which this form can cope and with which it stands in full accord. Nor is it simply a return; for here is wrested from the blank verse a new tone, even fuller than in *Iphigenie* and *Tasso*:

Doch jede Hand soll feiern! Halb vollbracht
Soll dieser Plan, wie mein Geschick, erstarren!
Das Denkmal nur, ein Denkmal will ich stiften,
Von rauhen Steinen ordnungslos getürmt,

Dorthin zu wallen, stille zu verweilen,
Bis ich vom Leben endlich selbst genese.
O lasst mich dort, versteint, am Steine ruhn ...
Ich fühle keine Zeit; denn sie ist hin,
An deren Wachstum ich die Jahre mass.   (ll. 1578–93)

[But every hand shall be idle! This plan, half completed, shall come to a
halt, like my destiny! I shall set up a memorial, the monument only of
rough stones piled high in disorder, to make pilgrimage there and to
linger there quietly until I myself recover at last from life. O let me rest
there by the stone, myself a stone ...! I have no sense of time, for she is
gone by whose growth I measured the years.]

By the removal of everything distracting and precipitous, and of all
impious desire and intentionality, in these scenes a human being finally
utters his despair, his lament, his grief, and his solace.

And yet both despair and solace are based on illusion. Everything is
true and everything false, inasmuch as we know that the natural daughter is alive. We need an almost abnormal bridging of a sense of reality
and immediate receptivity in order to preserve the proper equilibrium
demanded by the poet. One almost hesitates even to speak of dramatic
irony; for this too would mean a depreciation of the truth of the dialogue at the expense of the reality underlying it.

Here then begins the dissolution of an unstable substance into its
component parts. If in *Iphigenie* two divided and in their division dangerous elements united in a saving union, this proved to be impermanent
in the course of time—of Goethean as of historical development, and
finally became explosive:

Sie, als des Haders Apfel, warf ein Gott
Erzürnt ins Mittel zwischen zwei Parteien,
Die sich, auf ewig nun getrennt, bekämpfen.   (ll. 1776–78)

[An angry god cast her, like the apple of discord, into the very middle of
two parties that, now divided forever, fight against each other.]

Repose is only to be found in dissolution and peace only in the hope
for a future, "higher" reunion. By the twofold sacrifice of a lovely but
already deeply ambiguous creature, the confusion of the first two acts
clarifies itself to become the various consonances of the third and of the
two that follow.

The variousness can probably best be understood in the concept of
the power of language. The dialogue between the Duke and the Abbé is

a triumph of effective speaking. And not in the elementary sense that the Duke falls victim to the "story" of the Abbé; speech also reacts upon the latter. His proposal had been complete annihilation:

> Sie ist dahin für alle, sie verschwindet
> Ins Nichts der Asche. Jeder kehret schnell
> Den Blick zum Leben und vergisst, im Taumel
> Der treibenden Begierden, dass auch sie
> Im Reihen der Lebendigen geschwebt.   (ll. 1183–87)

[She will be gone for all, she will disappear into the nothingness of ashes. Everyone will quickly turn his gaze back to life and forget, in the flush of driving passions that she too moved in the dance of the living.]

But he ends differently:

> So lebt Eugenie vor dir, sie lebt
> In deinem Sinne ...
> So fühle dich durch ihre Kraft beseelt,
> Und gib ihr so ein unzerstörlich Leben,
> Das keine Macht entreissen kann, zurück.   (ll. 1702–12)

[Thus Eugenie will live in your presence, she will live in your mind. So feel yourself renewed by her strength, and in this way give her back an indestructible life that no power can take away.]

It is as though speech, however severed from reality it may be (or perhaps just because of this severance), had life-bestowing power. In order to persuade one with a death wish, the preacher of destruction becomes the advocate of life. Thus, as it were, this scene, like the great dialogues in *Iphigenie* and *Tasso*, sustains and creates itself on its own, or at least far beyond its factual elements. Once more utterance becomes an act creating truth—but only by surrendering to an "untruth." It derives its power from the certainty that Eugenie is not to be recalled to corporeal life; without this certainty there would be no solace, no life, but only muted grief and sombre doubt. From the paradox become destructive—for Eugenie *is* one buried alive—a partial truth is detached, which no longer redeems—such truths cannot accomplish this—but which may give strength for living.

The last two acts are also in accord, though under the sign of linguistic impotence. All utterance is of no avail against the physical, concrete prop—the royal decree.[12] The dramatic action is the erratic racing of one ensnared toward "outlets," at the end of which the inexorable watcher is always standing. And the only way open is discovered not as it could have been at the end but shown to us and to Eugenie right at the beginning, in order that the hopelessness of what follows may become that much plainer.

The speech of the "initiated" characters—the Governess and the Magistrate—accordingly betrays a reserve which might often be called dissimulation. The proposal-scene (IV,2)—counterpiece to Thoas' offer of marriage—makes this especially clear. While the barbarian, who did not know the art of "directing" a conversation "slowly and delicately towards his goal," stated what he wanted without beating around the bush, the Magistrate sees himself forced to an indirect, almost cunning way of speaking. Since he is determined from the beginning to offer Eugenie his hand, his repeated "Let me go!" and his "Nothing!" to her imploring of counsel and support, can only be a cruel game of hide-and-seek, such as a Kleist might have liked, but hardly Goethe. Yet the world is now so fashioned that even the language of love must awaken distrust. Words no longer suffice. "Action alone proves the strength of love."

To Iphigenia as well as to Eugenie the question of marriage comes in the form of an ultimatum. That is, the most intimate union of two human beings is to be brought about by means of physical coercion. As we know from diplomacy, an ultimatum means the end of speech; at bottom it is immaterial whether one answers yes or not. But the difference between the ultimatum of Thoas and that which the royal decree entails is this: the former is not yet language and the latter is no longer language. The barbarian has not yet learned speech, the King has had to unlearn it. The forces of language which establish community are potentially present at Tauris and await birth; in the nameless realm of *Die natürliche Tochter* language no longer possesses freely disposable energies. The law of linguistic entropy has run its full course, so that ossified human order can only look forward to a new chaos, as is prophesied by the King and the Monk.

Thus if the "truth" created in lively dialogue in the third act is detached from reality, that of the end is chained to static reality. The bond that still joins Tasso and Antonio in friendship and handclasp at the end is riven, and with it the form that had become the metaphor of this bond in and through *Iphigenie*. But Goethe, whose forms are never garments interchangeable at will but are meaningful, dangerous and endangered, draws his own conclusion: *Die natürliche Tochter* means the end of his mission in the theatre.

V

Goethe took pains to keep secret the origin of his play; what can be concluded about its genesis has been carefully put together by Gustav Kettner.[13] So much seems clear: the original plan was probably first expanded to that of a trilogy, to be limited to a double drama later; in this expansion the original first act was stretched to the two first of the play as finally executed, the second to the two last. The peculiar third act seems to have been added as new material. We know from statements in letters to Christiane that Goethe busied himself intensively with this act in May, 1802. It is further probable that the change of name from "Stefanie" to "Eugenie"—and probably that from Parliament Councillor to Magistrate—was made around this time; in any case "Eugenie" appears in a diary entry for the first time on August 6.

Is it then pure chance that the origin of the third act coincides with Schiller's preparation of the first performance of the blank-verse *Iphigenie*? Regardless of how plainly Goethe refused any part in the directing—he did not respond to Schiller's half-questioning suggestions of alteration and in the end attended the performance not as author but "like any other citizen of Jena"—this attempt at revival of his "child of sorrow" must still have touched him more deeply than he professed. Schiller's somewhat drastic criticism directed at stage effectiveness—read his letter of January 22, 1802—can hardly have left Goethe untouched either. I must limit myself here to the assertion that a basic misunderstanding of *Iphigenie* comes to light in this criticism. Was not the revival at the same time a kind of tearing apart?

It is not to be wondered at that Goethe let his friend "have his way in everything." It would have contradicted his lofty and stringent concept of the poet's word if he had sought to "explain" its meaning. If it could not make itself understood, no verbal intercession could help, for the very nature of *Iphigenie* consisted in complete self-revelation. It was not Goethe's way either to complain about the stupid public; when speaking of his works, he preferred to assume a joking nonchalance. But if one considers what effort he expended on *Iphigenie* and *Tasso* and how they then remained almost without success—and further, what a high opinion he had of the social function of the stage—there remains hardly a doubt that the failure of the best that he was able to accomplish in the dramatic genre affected him more deeply than he let be noticed. Not from hurt artist's vanity, but because it became clear to him what a severe and incomprehensible judgment his time had thereby passed both on him and on itself. He never forgot what we forget so easily: that a *threefold* consonance is necessary for complete truth—the consonance of subject, statement, and *understanding*. An unheard or not understood "truth" is not true in the fully human sense. It is a measure of Goethe's poetic integrity that, faced with such a lack of understanding, he condemned neither the time nor his work alone, but understood the misunderstanding as tragic and gave it shape in this remarkable tragedy.

All this is of course surmise, not proof; but let it be allowed me as a hypothesis arising from the facts, so that these may be in turn illuminated. The facts are that Goethe wrote the third act of *Die natürliche Tochter*, which is difficult to explain, while *Iphigenie* and her fate on the stage appeared once again tangibly before his eyes; that about this time he chose the name "Eugenie"—and surely without question by aural association with the name of the earlier heroine; and that he let the act become a grand obituary, a lament over unavoidable physical disintegration of the "image of the gods," of "form." In the earlier drama the ambiguous word of the oracle ("sister") achieved saving clarity in taking on human form and the human name "Iphigenie"; material and spirit found one another, the word became flesh, and, in the all-decisive scene, speaker, hearer and reality met in a new creating truth. Everything pushed toward Revelation, toward interpretation of word and intention still mysterious at the beginning. Now there is a reversal: the human name "Eugenie" is separated from the ambiguous designation ("natural daughter"), body and spirit are divided from one another, speaker and hearer meet in unreality, and fair form is concealed in a mystery hardly to be unriddled.

In *Die natürliche Tochter* everything presses toward mystification, and for a good reason. Right at the start the Count speaks with scorn of the "open secret":

> was für Hof und Stadt
> Ein offenbar Geheimnis lange war. (ll. 188–89)

[. . . what was long an open secret to court and town.]

The adept courtier and man of the world thus depreciates a term [14] belonging originally to the religious sphere, an expression paraphrasing with reverent paradox the essence of the Logos, to an empty phrase of a modern world. It is a world which arrogantly believes that it has unveiled all mysteries and solves the sacred contradiction by hearing only the "open" still. In view of this effrontery, this desecration of the word, the word must dissolve into mystery and renounce form.

A peculiar law is at work, here to be only suggested, the law that governs the Goethean group of concepts "middle," "means," "mediator," "mediating." Though, significantly, never so named, Iphigenia *is* in the purest sense a mediator; and the word that stands almost exactly at the middle of the play is "truth." But Iphigenia's role of mediator is only permanently secured at the moment when her sanctity is recognized by all. Though from the noblest motives, both Pylades and Arkas attempt to make use of her as a means for the benefit of others; should she accede to these temptations, she would be incapable of the role of mediator destined for her. And again, exactly at the midde of *Tasso*, the "sly little mediator" Leonore speaks her disastrously decisive monologue (III, 3), in which she decides to use for her own purposes the function of mediation she has been commissioned with; by her gentle, though to the poet palpable, distortion of the truth necessitated by her "purpose," the already distrustful Tasso is driven completely into a persecution mania. Language has now become a means and can for this very reason no longer mediate truthfully. Eugenie finally, is completely debased to a means; in the beginning the King uses her, also in noblest fashion, as a political means of exchange, and for this reason he also has to sacrifice her cruelly to the interest of the state later. Instead of becoming a mediator, as she hoped, Eugenie becomes the apple of discord which "an angry god" cast "into the very middle of two parties." As a living figure she has now been pushed entirely from the middle of the play; in the third act she appears only as one dead.

The surprisingly concrete and poetic definition of the concept of the "middle" seems to me also to explain the formal mediacy of language often observed in Goethe's late work and already noticeable in *Die natürliche Tochter*. When in *Die Wahlverwandtschaften* (*Elective Affinities*) a mediator appears as a figure once again, he produces only disaster; given Eugenie, one might say that the presentation of the figure of a "mediator" is made impossible. With the secularization of the "open secret," natural language—the language of *Iphigenie* which *Die natürliche Tochter* also attempts to speak once more—has proven itself too helpless and unprotected and has been entirely debased to a means. In order to be able to fulfill her own function of human mediation, she needs a defense that now to be sure forces her into an alien, unnatural, mediating *form*. This "form" is marriage:

Gewiss! dir gibt die Kenntnis jener Formen,
Für Hohe wie für Niedre gleich verbindlich,
Ein Mittel an. Du lächelst. Ist es möglich!
Das Mittel ist gefunden! Sprich es aus!   (ll. 2068–71)

[Surely, your knowledge of those forms which are equally binding for the high-born and for those of lesser rank will suggest a means! You smile. It *is* possible! The means is found! Say it!]

Why does the Magistrate smile? Quite possibly because Eugenie herself names the means she seeks so desperately: *form.* Of course, he smiles too soon; he still has to learn that even this form may only be entered *pro forma*, so that untouchability may be concealed beneath the semblance of taking possession.

An examination of Goethe's concept of marriage would lead us here too far astray; for the dramas in blank verse, in any case, marriage must have the value of a tragic solution. To the tragic irony that can be heard in the "natural" of the title there corresponds another, that this tragedy (*Trauer-spiel*) ends at a marriage-altar (*Trau-altar*)—and I am tempted to consider Goethe himself capable of this pun. Marriage is a substitute for language, a union of two human beings in or beyond that community which language establishes. The taking possession of woman, expressed in the sacrifice of her name, is the danger to be warded off, is the fatal wish—clearest in Tasso's embrace of the princess, but plain too in Thoas' desire and in the timid circumspection with which the Magistrate leads Eugenie to a recognition of this evil necessity. Distance, over which a mediating word casts a bridge: this is the image of the happy ending of *Iphigenie*; distance and immediacy are the hallmarks of the Iphigenian art of language. In it form can give shape to matter; form itself is a field of forces, as such hardly perceivable and only appearing phenomenally as shape. Conversely, the "natural daughter's" semblance of marriage represents a heightening of the form that alone permits the once clear and immediate figure of Eugenie to take refuge from the impudent assault of a world afflicted by an obsessive concern with the means of achieving its ends.

Thus the end of the play gives us the key to Goethe's late style. How bitter the sacrifice of shape was for him we hear not only from the laments of the Duke; also in *Pandora*, five years later, the sound of grief is still unsubdued:

Mühend versenkt ängstlich der Sinn
Sich in der Nacht, suchet umsonst
Nach der Gestalt. Ach! wie so klar
Stand sie am Tag sonst vor dem Blick.

[Toiling and fearful, the mind subsides in the night, and seeks in vain the shape. Alas! how clearly once it stood before the eye in light of day.]

But life, whose servant the poet will remain until the last, is stronger and raises loftier demands than even perfection once achieved. Indeed, life revokes this perfection, simultaneously destroying and, by force of the human spirit, sustaining. Iphigenia survives because she was truthful; "you were, you are." But while *she* could go from semblance of death—"from life here, a second death"—into a valid human life that is given unambiguous shape, her descendant returns to a two-fold, ambiguous semblance of death, where she must await an other resurrection than did her happier, more natural, and—as Goethe well knew—more perfectly realized forebear in Aulis.

5. *Egmont* and *Prinz Friedrich von Homburg:*
Expostulation and Reply

HERE IS no need to labor the point that Goethe's *Egmont* must have been very present to Kleist's mind when he wrote his last testamentary play. The parallels, both in general conception and in details, are many and manifest. My purpose is, rather, to understand *Homburg* as Kleist's specific and conscious answer to Goethe, his way of saying: This is *my* Egmont, or even perhaps: This is the real Egmont. Duelist that he was at heart, Kleist here chose the proper weapons and the only meaningful arena for a decisive trial by combat with his great rival; he joined the issue on the stage and in dramatic action and language. As in his story "Der Zweikampf," the true verdict was slow in coming, but I think that there can be no doubt any longer who the victor is.

How minutely conscious Kleist was of his opponent is evident from his formulation of the death sentence. In *Egmont* the sentence is read in full—except for one seemingly inconsequential point, to which Goethe calls our attention by an odd stage direction: "Datum und Jahreszahl werden undeutlich gelesen, so, dass sie der Zuhörer nicht versteht [Day and year are read indistinctly, so that the listener does not understand them]." When Homburg writes his reply to the Elector—which is to say, *his* death sentence, since the Elector has just made him supreme judge of his own cause—Kleist withholds from us what Goethe supplies—the text of the sentence—but gives us what Goethe withholds—the date: "Homburg; gegeben, Fehrbellin, *am zwölften* [Homburg; signed at Fehrbellin, *on this twelfth day*]." It would seem that Kleist saw this event—and with it the whole play which pivots on it—as an inversion of Goethe's point. The accused is judge rather than mere victim; the sentence is implicit rather than explicit; the time, instead of being left indeterminate, is specified.

At issue in both plays is the role of the exceptional man—the man who believes he can and must follow the promptings of his genius—within the social order. And there can be little doubt that Schiller—and Kleist also, as I shall try to show—were right in judging that Goethe's solution, or rather dissolution, of the issue was operatic. Klärchen, appearing through dissolving prison walls as the goddess of liberty, is

literally a *dea ex machina*; her comfort and promises do not spring from
the inner necessities of the plot, but are a divine dispensation by the
omnipotent playwright. Goethe turns the tragedy into a kind of "Mär-
tyrerspiel," removes the hero from a wicked world into a higher, supramundane jurisdiction, a realm of the spirit in which the positive judgments of the existing order can be morally rescinded.

Throughout the play, Egmont does not act; he *is*, and suffers for
being as he is. He refuses to plan, to calculate, to take steps which, to
secure him a measure of freedom, would compromise that absolute
liberty to be himself which he considers his essential being. In other
words, he is a radically un-dramatic figure—not necessarily in the sense
that he makes a poor hero for a drama, but rather that he is lacking in
precisely those qualities which a dramatist must possess. A dramatist
must be a statesman, must manoeuvre, make binding choices; he must
deny himself direct self-expression in order to achieve it more truly
through the grand design. He must acknowledge that he progressively
binds himself with each word he writes; his sole chance of creative freedom lies in the conscious acceptance of this fact. By refusing this knowledge, Egmont ends in prison walls so massive that only "Bühnenzauber"
can penetrate them.

For it is in good part his doing that the world about him turns monolithic; he is one of Alba's summoners. Because he prefers love idyls with
Klärchen to the austere demands Margaret of Parma would make on
him, the state's authority stiffens. The possibility of a saving interchange
between the individual and the order, between feeling and form, recedes
to the point where the dialogue between the two is merely a trap and an
illusion. The meaning of the great scene between Egmont and Alba lies
not in what they say, but in the fact that what they say is to no purpose;
the scene is dramatically sterile. We know from the start what Egmont
discovers too late: "Umsonst hab ich so viel gesprochen, die Luft hab
ich erschüttert, weiter nichts gewonnen. [I have spoken so much to no
purpose, I have disturbed the air, achieved nothing else]." Effective
action—that is, drama—now takes place in extraverbal silence.

It is fitting, therefore, that in the end we hear Egmont as an ineffec-
tive voice beating vainly against impenetrable masonry and its verbal
equivalent: the sentence of death. With this wholly impersonal order,
discourse is impossible; when it speaks, it has spoken—*dixit*—and whatever is said to it or against it is futile expostulation rather than reply.
Goethe supplies Ferdinand and the vision of Klärchen to soften the
rigor of the final impasse; but Klärchen is dead and Ferdinand illegitimate and helpless. No solution is possible, only dissolution, as Egmont

himself knows: "Süsser Schlaf! ... Du lösest die Knoten der strengen Gedanken, vermischest alle Bilder der Freude und des Schmerzes; ... eingehüllt in gefälligen Wahnsinn, versinken wir und hören auf, zu sein. [Sweet sleep! ... You unravel the knots of tense thoughts, and mingle all images of joy and pain; ... wrapped in pleasant delusion, we submerge and cease to be]."

I suggest that this is, very roughly, the interpretation of Goethe's play implicit in *Homburg*. Kleist reverses the play as he does the sentence; he makes the action move from the deadlock of counterposed absolutes to their dramatic interaction. What with Goethe is a sentence of death, both for the hero and ultimately for the petrified order, Kleist turns into a true sentence, genuine speech. In contrast to Egmont, who learns nothing (not even that Klärchen is dead; he dies deluded), the Prince learns how to become a dramatic poet.

To this end Kleist grants him Egmont's final vision at the very outset, as though to say: this is not a consolation prize but a task, the dream of a play that still demands to be written. The very structure of *Homburg* is Kleist's programmatic announcement that he intends to give reality, dramatic validity to Egmont's illusory triumph. To this end he makes a significant change in the vision itself: the state, embodied in the Elector, plays a significant role in it. When Schiller prepared *Egmont* for the Weimar stage in 1796, he eliminated the dream vision and instead brought Alba into the prison, concealed in a cloak which Egmont finally tears off. Though the change violates the essentially undramatic logic of the play, it shows Schiller's keen sense of what true drama demands. Goethe's ending is operatic because an essential partner to the transaction—the state—is lacking, has been dissolved into an illusory nonexistence. Egmont's triumph—quite unlike that of, say, Maria Stuart—remains essentially private, essentially lyrical. Kleist, like Schiller, brings the state back into the action—not as a villain to be exposed, however, but as a genuine, fully implicated partner.

Through this re-entry, the plot develops the complex urgency which genuine drama shares with political reality. There is no purely private sphere for Kleist, nor a purely public one, though the Elector mistakenly thinks so. Even love, the most private of feelings, has public consequences. Unlike the blissfully and later pathetically inconsequential love of Egmont and Klärchen, that of Homburg and Natalie propels the action at crucial points, creates confusions and dilemmas, forces vitally necessary confrontations. Goethe's play moves toward a simplicity which is as undramatic as it is unpolitical. As Oranien and Margaret disappear, meaningful choice and interaction become impossible. And as the possibility of action recedes, rhetoric inevitably takes over; language which cannot act *within the play* has no one to address except the feelings of the chairbound audience. In *Homburg* the movement is opposite: from a relative and illusory simplicity toward increasing complexity and involvement. What the characters say and write becomes ever more decisive, until at the climactic moment the fate not only of the hero but of the state hangs on one utterance, one sentence.

That sentence, of course, is the one Homburg composes in reply to the Elector. I use the word "compose" advisedly. The entire and still inconclusive debate over the meaning of Kleist's play centers ultimately on *one* question: What does the Prince say in his answer? If, instead of speculating about the "what," critics had paid closer attention to the "how," the dispute might be nearer a solution, because here, as in all true poetry, it is through the "how" that we discover the "what," through the form that we discover the meaning. Again, a glance at *Egmont* proves helpful. Egmont cannot be bothered with the drudgery of writing, will not bend his spontaneous genius to the chore of careful and definitive formulation. He makes his feelings known and leaves the rest to his secretary, so that—by a justice truly poetic—in the end his writing is done *for* him, by Alba. A comparable impatience with writing down the battle plan is in part responsible for the as yet unsigned death sentence that hangs over Homburg's head; but now, given the opportunity to write a sentence of his own, he buckles down to the hard labor of composition.

The opportunity, we must note, is one he is invited from every side to ignore. The phrasing of the Elector's note, Natalie, his own feelings urge him simply to seize upon ready-made formulas—whether of defiance or contrition—and to let the form shift for itself, as something purely external. In Natalie's words:

Doch nun tu auch das deine du, und schreib
Wie er's begehrt; du siehst, es ist der Vorwand,
Die äussre Form nur, deren es bedarf.   (ll. 1346–48)

[But now, you do your part too, and write as he desires; you see, it is the excuse, simply the outer form, that is needed.]

But instead, and in the face of powerful temptations, the Prince composes with almost comical care: he begins to write, tears up what he has written, rereads the Elector's note, starts to write anew, gets up to reconsider, tells Natalie that he is on the point of finding the satisfactory phrasing—"die Fassung eines Prinzen"—and finally does write. In short, we see him bodily as a "Verfasser," an author, with the author's pain-staking concern over the "how": "Gleich werd ich wissen, *wie* ich schreiben soll [I'll know in a moment *how* I am to write]." Expostulation would have won him his life, though it would have ruined the state. But with a suicidal insistence on the perfect and perfectly expressive form, he would rather die than use "die Fassung eines Schuftes."

Thus, in the effort of composition enacted before our eyes, Homburg "composes himself." The play on the words "Fassung" and "sich fassen" is Kleist's, not mine. The Prince, who, confronted by the deadly writ of the law, had become completely "fassungslos," completely unresponsive to the Electress' "Fasse dich!," now assumes the fearful responsibility of composing his own, sovereign sentence; having been thrust into nothing-ness—"Ins Nichts mit dir zurück, Herr Pinz von Homburg, / Ins Nichts, ins Nichts! [Back to nothingness with you, Prince of Homburg, to nothingness, to nothingness!]"—he now composes himself out of that nothingness in a free creative act. His letter is not "self-expression" in the normal sense—expression of his feelings, thoughts, judgment or what not; it becomes himself and he it, so that he and it are, in the act of writing, self-composed.

Even in his final words, Egmont speaks disdainfully of "das hohle Wort des Herrschers" and rests his faith on "Gemüt." Homburg learns that the state's word has the deadly solidity of chains and bullets. That is why at first he abjectly begs rather than nobly expostulates; death reduces rhetoric to irrelevancy. And that is why, when he sees a possibility of replying, he accepts it as an absolute responsibility to find words equally solid. Again in sharp contrast to Egmont, who in his dealings with debtors, heretics and soldiers refuses to make his word the law, determines each case, by feeling, as an exception to the general principle which—except for this one case, of course,—is to govern such cases. Homburg replies in the awareness that he is sovereign, that *his word is law*. For this reason he concludes his letter with the sovereign word "gegeben," which in Goethe's play concludes Alba's sentence. For this reason he can issue it, not "im Namen des Königs," but in his own. For this reason his letter almost literally invests the half-dressed, half-divested Elector with the authority to deal with the manifold challenges to himself and the state. Homburg acts truly—i.e., sovereignly—not when he leads his cavalry into battle but when he puts pen to paper, because he comprehends writing as a fully political act, defined by and in turn defining the legal order in which it takes place.

My criticism of Goethe's play has been severe—as severe, I believe, as Kleist's implicitly is. But I have left out of consideration one crucial fact, which I rather suspect Kleist ignored. *Homburg* is Kleist's last drama, not merely in the sense that he wrote no more plays after it, but that it was final *for that moment*. There is nothing final about *Egmont*; when Goethe finished it in 1787, he had already completed what we must call a later play: *Iphigenie*. This is not the occasion to show how the problems which are evaded, the questions which are begged in *Egmont* are confronted—and solved—in *Iphigenie*; I must confine myself to asserting that *Egmont* was not, even at the moment of its writing, Goethe's last dramatic word. Rather it was a funeral elegy, a final tribute to the beauty and grace of a past and imperfect incarnation. Ultimately it was Goethe himself who condemned the play, as surely as Alba condemns its hero; the play is an instance of the axiom: *Nemo contra Deum nisi Deus ipse*. Goethe, with his incomparable piety toward himself, his deep reverence for all organic development, however incomplete it might seem in retrospect, could not help seeing, and sorrowing over, the lyrical splendor he had to bury, because it was inadequate to the demands of true drama, which is to say, of a truly social poetry. His sorrow was gentle rather than bitter, because in *Iphigenie* he already had assurance of a metamorphic resurrection. Later, in *Die natürliche Tochter*, his grief was to be vastly more bitter and unrelieved, for then he knew that he was compelled to bury the dramatic form altogether. Moving rhetoric no longer provided adequate consolation against so final a loss; Goethe took refuge in enigmatic irony. But in 1787, something better, something hardier and purer was already waiting in the wings to take over the stage left vacant by *Egmont*.

This, I believe, is the secret of the withheld date. Because Goethe was so supremely scrupulous a poet, he had to betray, at least to the attentive reader, the fact that this play was not, as it were, contemporary to itself, not a present enactment of present problems. Egmont's sentence is not what the later sentence of arrest is for Tasso or the sentence of exile for Eugenie, or the death sentence for Homburg: an incomprehensible catastrophe which leaves the poet's world in fragments and demands a reconstruction from chaos. Egmont never loses composure; the words "Fasse dich" are not addressed *to* him, but *by* him to the disconsolate Ferdinand. The dramatic present is, in truth, no present; nothing of absolute consequence, nothing that cannot be managed by the rhetoric of splendid defiance and unshaken self-assurance, is transacted.

True drama is a life-and-death trial. In it a mode of speech, a conception of language in action, is tested; and a conception of language means, for the poet, a conception of himself and his social function.

This is what happens in *Iphigenie*, which is genuinely political, because it asks the question which Egmont never really asks: How must men speak in order to make true communion, and hence true communities, possible? When Iphigenia says:

> Ich werde grossem Vorwurf nicht entgehn
> Noch schwerem Übel, wenn es mir misslingt;
> Allein Euch leg ich's auf die Kniee! Wenn
> Ihr wahrhaft seid, wie Ihr gepriesen werdet,
> So zeigt's durch Euren Beistand und verherrlicht
> Durch mich die Wahrheit.   (ll. 1914–19)

[I shall not escape great reproach nor serious harm, if I do not succeed; however, I lay it on *your* knees! If you truly are as you are extolled for being, demonstrate it by your support and exalt truth through me.]

in that moment she transforms language into action. This is *dramatic* speech, very different from Homburg's, but forged by the same pressure of unsecured risk, unqualified reply. Goethe said of himself that he could never have written a real tragedy; it would have killed him. He called *Egmont* a "Trauerspiel," but I think we can take him at his word and conclude that he himself did not think of it as a real tragedy. The decisive risk had already been taken, and won, elsewhere; so that *Egmont* is an expression rather than an enactment.

While Egmont expresses his being, Homburg defines himself in action. His reply to the state, as expression implicit, is fully explicit as act, fully enmeshed in circumstance and tied to the moment. And when he is finally crowned victor by Natalie von Oranien, who, "gedrängt von Spaniens Tyrannenheeren," had to seek refuge and protection in Brandenburg, the victory is not only over the Swedes, over himself, or even the more complicated one over the Elector, but also the victory over the appealing and eloquent Netherlander, who only dreamed of laurels and should have started where he left off. Homburg, like Yeats, discovers that responsibilities do not end in the pleasing madness of dreams but rather begin there; and that they are discharged, not in expostulation but by reply.

6. Heinrich von Kleist: The Poet as Prussian

MY SUBTITLE may sound incongruous, even paradoxical. Prussia, it would seem, is dead: a name in history books, a slogan in old newspapers, surviving only as an adjective to denote goosestepping regimentation, monocled arrogance, and bureaucratic aridity of heart. What could the poet *as* Prussian have written but heavy-footed marching songs and odes to duty? If he sprang from that infertile soil, it must be *in spite* of his having been a Prussian; it must be because, in a stiffly uniformed society, he refused to let the subtle rhythms of the heart be drowned out by the brutal cadence of command.

But even if this is too stereotyped an image of Prussia—and of course it is—there is still good reason to feel that something radically unpoetic, even anti-poetic, clings to its name. Consider the potency of names of countries: of sweet France and Mother Russia, to say nothing of Greece and Rome. Even to the stranger, names like these call up a rich penumbra of meanings, feelings, and memories: of landscapes and climates, art and architecture, song and legend and history; the names are distillates of abundant and colorful national being. Prussia, by contrast, has about it an abstractness, a univocal poverty of connotation, which forbids us to speak of it as the *Song of Roland* speaks of France or as Shakespeare's John of Gaunt speaks of England: "This royal throne of kings, this sceptred isle ... this precious stone, this blessed plot, this earth, this realm." Prussia means not earth nor realm, even less a precious stone; it means a *state*.

It is for this reason that Prussia poses, far more nakedly than other such names, the question of *order*: political, moral, even universal. For John of Gaunt, England by herself exists in all her inalienable splendor; of herself she is sceptred, a throne and a diadem, endowed with all the attributes of royalty; that in Richard II she has a king unworthy of her is her temporary misfortune. But if it were meant for Prussia, Gaunt's plaint would make no sense; for Prussia *is* its government. It exists only in and as the order by which a group of territories were welded into a state.

To use an analogy: the state should stand to the nation in a relation like that of a prose abstract to a poem; the poem is there in its rich and

101

incommensurable primacy, and the abstract expresses it more or less adequately. On this analogy, the poem of which the Prussian state should have been the abstract never existed. There are, of course, historical reasons for this, which it is not my purpose to go into. But it is worth noting how programmatically the true founder of Prussia— Frederick William I, the father of Frederick the Great—went about making this state what it was to be. Admittedly Frederick William was penurious, anti-intellectual, and brutally despotic; but he did have a perfect sense of the fitting political style. Instead of following an irrelevant tradition, he ruthlessly stripped himself, his court, and his administration of all the symbolism and ritual in which other states still garbed the nakedness of power. He saw Prussia in the image of an army—which is to say, of that pure, abstract order which scorns disguise and makes its austere appeal through the rigorous logic of its own structuring. Frederick William's fame rests not so much on his having been the effective founder of a major European state as on having discovered a new political style. He reduced to Newtonian simplicity and explicitness a traditional model of political order that was still Ptolemaic in its profusion of colorful mythical constructs.

The style was sheer prose, sheer function. The state articulated Prussia, not as a statement articulates feeling or experience, but as syntax articulates a sentence. No richly fraught words were admitted, no rhetoric of pomp and circumstance, nothing that would make the harsh voice of authority fall more melodiously, more insinuatingly and majestically on the subjects' ear. In Prussia, order did not express a higher harmony beyond it: It was—and, by being—it lifted incoherence into meaning.

There is, I think, a far from superficial relation between Prussia and the United States, though in part it is a relation by contraries. The United States also was somewhat abstractly conceived, a traditionless, functional, and—some thought—essentially prosaic order. Many of her artists have felt her to be anti-poetic. But Walt Whitman, the American poet *par excellence*, felt very differently; "the United States themselves," he said, "are essentially the greatest poem." The difference, amounting almost to an inversion, between America and Prussia was that America was conceived as somehow exempt from the Fall, Adamic, a virginal commonwealth. It was no syntax but rather an unabridged dictionary, an inexhaustible reservoir of natural and moral resources begging to be tapped and shaped. Her basic charter was not the state's definitive utterance so much as it was a self-denying ordinance, as open as the Western frontier. We can almost hear Whitman shaping for himself and his countrymen the first elements of ordered speech. He is as a child, enraptured by the verbal riches about him, speaking words as though he were the first to say them, sure that of themselves they glow with the meaning and beauty of discovery and creation. America, for Whitman, is the very opposite of prose; if she, like Prussia, does without all the traditional ceremony of "poetic" splendor, the reason is not that she is prosaic, but on the contrary: because she is, of herself and naturally, a poem—still in that blessed state of innocence in which natural speech *is* poetry.

There was nothing virginal or Adamic about Prussia. By a singularly expressive accident of history, its colors were black and white, the abstract poles where color in its rich multiplicity ceases. Prussia's sense of order was Hobbesian, a desperately functional shoring against chaos. The prose of its political habitus was no self-denying ordinance; it claimed to be the last word, the definitive proposition. Like its army, it was so fully and tautly articulated that it seemed to leave no room for spontaneous communion and free creativity.

II

Into this Prussia Kleist was born, not as an ordinary subject but as the son of an old family of officers. As a matter of course he was brought up to be an officer himself and duly entered the king's service. So that, when the inevitable moment of rebellion came, his rebellion was bound to be absolute. He could not rebel in the name of a higher patriotism— to restore his fatherland to its true self. Prussia *was* itself, the state *an sich* as it were, the very thing he was rebelling against. Thus the question of a higher legitimacy—in the name of what do I rebel?—assumed for him from the start an extraordinary bareness and urgency.

What makes this question so acutely modern is the progressive weakening of Western man's belief in a higher jurisdiction: a divine or natural law to which the positive laws of the state are morally accountable and by which they can be pronounced just or unjust. The problem is by no means merely, or even primarily, a philosophical one. For unless the idea of a supra-political order receives some palpable symbolic embodiment—as it used to in the religious ceremonial that enveloped even the secular power—it is unlikely to maintain its hold on men's minds with sufficient authority to withstand the very palpable images of order and power the state surrounds us with. In *Darkness at Noon* Koestler has furnished a frightening demonstration of how weak the naked human consciousness is against this massively concrete order, how it will betray its own certainties, in fact its very existence, in the attempt to escape from its fearful seclusion, to become once more a meaningful part of a greater, ordered whole. The advocates of natural law, whatever the strength of their case in logic, are defeated by the brute fact that their ideas have increasingly lost those symbolic embodiments by which vital ideas of order demonstrate and maintain their vitality.

Of course, the ideas and ideals of his time stood ready to furnish Kleist with an answer to his question; the great legitimator of rebellion was Nature. For a brief space he thought the answer would do. He had only to believe that Nature was innocent and existing society unjust, that simple men were noble and benevolent—in short, that the Fall was reversible. In one of his earliest stories—"The Earthquake in Chile"—he shows how the destruction of a merciless, petrified order releases men, now stripped of law and rank and prejudice, to join in natural fellowship and harmony. But even in this story the end is tragic; it turns out that the shattering of the order releases not only benevolence but likewise fear and brutal unreason. However cruel the law, it is less cruel than man's unchained emotions can become.

This insight also—at a time which had just witnessed the Reign of Terror in France—is commonplace enough, though the intensity with which Kleist pits the cruelty of order against the savagery of chaos and between them embeds a poignantly brief moment of paradisal harmony is far from commonplace. But what is unusual even here is that Kleist measures the order, not so much by a higher order, whether natural or divine, but by its capacity, or incapacity, for *inclusion*. Morally, the element before which the order breaks is a pitiful and disreputable datum: an illegitimate child. With this story, illegitimacy becomes one of Kleist's major motifs. But unlike many of his contemporaries, he does not celebrate it as an assertion of nature over artificiality and convention; he uses it, in what I will call a characteristically Prussian manner, to test the orders men live by.

What is order? There are those—Goethe was perhaps their last great spokesman—for whom it is the outer expression of an inner harmony, something that is generated rather than imposed. But there are others— more numerous and, I fear, more modern—for whom order is a construct, moral, legal, or conceptual, which divides the world of phenomena into an inside and an outside, which purchases intelligibility at the cost of inclusiveness, coherence at the cost of relevance. This kind of order is wholly explicit and tends to justify itself by the tautological perfection of its interior workings. Franz Kafka invented the ultimate metaphor of it in the execution machine of his Penal Colony, that cruelly perfect and self-defining mechanism which in one precise opera-tion communicates to its victims their crime, their punishment, and the release of full comprehension.

To seek refuge in such an order, to condemn in oneself and others what the order defines as irrational and illegitimate, is a great temptation. No man can live for long in chaos, a rebel without a cause; and where he has no higher order to appeal to, he must, it seems, succumb to the positive and explicit one, which rewards his submission by assigning him a place and a role. There are many who make this submission with a mental reservation, who cling to the sentimental belief that there is a public sphere and a private one, who learn to split their individuality and their moral responsibility, until finally as men they can grow roses while as functionaries they run concentration camps. But there are others, though few, who will not recant, with or without mental reservation, but will keep faith with the inchoate and incomprehensible stirrings within them. Of these Kleist was one.

It was, he found, his art that was illegitimate; the words, images, and tales he felt himself unaccountably pregnant with were offensive and disorderly in an order that was, within its own terms, definitive and complete. And so he shaped a style and a series of great fables which are unmistakably his own and have, nevertheless, an authoritative impersonality. The motif of illegitimacy takes various forms. It is translated into religious mystery in the high comedy of *Amphitryon*, where, after first following Molière, Kleist suddenly breaks into the easy ménage of classical French comedy, a god in disguise, to extort from Alcmene a glory of knowledge and purity she never knew she possessed. But next to this play he puts the prose narrative of the "Marquise of O.," who likewise finds herself mysteriously pregnant, but who must solve the mystery with pain and reproach before her purity is vindicated. No divine epiphany announces the impending birth as virginal; the Marquise is compelled to discover her child's very natural father by the sordidly secular means of advertising for him in the public prints. This descent from the sphere of classical and religious myth to the level of prose and ordinary reality is Kleist's decisive step, for it forces his characters to find *within themselves* the strength to defend their inner truth against the legitimate claims of the establishment. The Marquise's pregnancy seems to defy reason as well as morality; it is an inexplicable *novum*, which everyone tries his utmost to deny and ignore, until at last it can be ignored no longer. At that point the pressure to recant and repent becomes almost irresistible; the order puts all its vast authority into the effort to sustain itself, to compel submission. But at the decisive moment the Marquise does not break; she stands by the reality within her and submits only, to quote Kleist, "to the great, holy and inexplicable scheme of things." Because she does so and at the same time honors the claims of legitimacy enough to wish to find her child's father and to marry him, she succeeds in solving the mystery and in establishing a truer, *i.e.* more encompassing order.

As with other great poets, so with Kleist, a problem once worked through becomes implicit, enters wholly into the body of his language. Every sentence almost of Kleist's mature prose style is a verbal re-enactment of the illegitimacy motif, a little victory of inclusion. His syntax is notorious, even in German, for its tense complexity, which strains at the limits of rational order. What Kleist does is to call into question the easy rationality of the classical sentence, which gains its victories by keeping out unfitting detail—the streaks of the tulip that Samuel Johnson forbade the artist to paint. What the rational order—which claims to be "natural" but in fact is as positive as Prussia—proscribes as illegitimate, accidental, and irrelevant, Kleist forges into a larger, tenser structuring. He does so, not with the naturalist's comfortable faith that out of accumulation order will somehow arise, but from the positivist's knowledge that there can be no truth without order, yet that every order stands under the judgment of what it can*not* admit.

III

But self-vindication, however impersonal and unsentimental, was not enough for Kleist. As a poet he was bound to aspire to being a founder of unions in his own right, to perform what Shakespeare calls "the marriage of true minds," independent of, even in opposition to the social order. Like Shakespeare, Kleist wanted and needed to be a matchmaker in the most profound sense—*i.e.*, to be a writer of comedies. But, again like Shakespeare, the intensity of this need drove him to test all hidden assumptions, all built-in safeguards, which would beg the question of unmediated human fellowship. And so he took the classical test case— the Romeo-and-Juliet situation—and divested it of its consoling elements. Shakespeare had shown the way when he made his lovers re-enact their story in the guise of Troilus and Cressida and watched with bitter cynicism how a love that is buttressed by nothing but private faith and feeling turns into betrayal. Kleist chose as his lovers Achilles and Penthesilea, Queen of the Amazons. Their only possible meeting place is the battlefield, and combat their mode of union. By the contradictory laws of their sexes and nations, to possess each other they must vanquish each other; the whole play moves at the driven and driving pace of attack and counter-attack, flight and pursuit. There is a central interlude of illusory peace: the warrior-lovers sit together, divested of their armor, in what appears to be intimate and unguarded understanding. But the deception is revealed and the battle resumes; only now it has turned bestial. In the end Penthesilea kills Achilles, not in human combat but in a hunt; maddened by what she sees as a betrayal, she tears her lover's flesh.

It is easy to interpret this play, and much else in Kleist, as evidence of a deep psychic disturbance, an obsessive sado-masochism. But such an interpretation misses the essential point: that the play is a test, arranged with a scientist's cunning guard against specious solutions. Unsupported by any common order—of thought or custom or law—what promised to be the sweetest fulfilment turns into the most savage tragedy. What we are being shown is not merely the battle of the sexes, but rather the truth that outside some sustaining order union is not to be had. The poet's highest ambition—to show and celebrate the possibility of men joining beyond the preestablished orders into which they normally must fit themselves before they can hope to reach understanding—this ambition had proved unattainable. Union, it seemed, must remain the question-begging achievement it is, possibly only where the community is already there to found and guarantee it. There is no realm which is the poet's own, no marriage which he alone can perform, unless he has the prior sanction of the state. As Achilles lies mutilated and Penthesilea is killed by the comprehension of what she has done, the *tertius ridens* appears to be the authority Kleist had desperately tried to prove superfluous—Prussia.

But before I pass beyond this tragic failure, let me stress once more that its being a failure is its greatness. Kleist did not pride himself on his "tragic sense of life," did not try to provide us the inhuman satisfaction of being able to look unflinching into the face of horror. The modern tendency to proclaim tragedy as the highest and truest attainment of art should leave us suspicious and dismayed. Shakespeare wrote, as his last play and testament, *The Tempest*; Bach ended the *St. Matthew's Passion* with something very much like a cradle song; Goethe said of himself that he could never have written a real tragedy, because it would have killed him. Kleist, who did write one under the bitter compulsion of his need, did not think that he had thereby shown humanity raised to its highest form and potential. Precisely because he was capable of creating Penthesilea, he was able to have her say, at the moment of seeming fulfilment, lines which show that a genuine tragedy is a comedy that failed:

Das Unglück, sagt man, läutert die Gemüter,
Ich . . . empfand es nicht. . . .
Wie seltsam war, auf jedem Antlitz, mir,
Wo ich sie traf, der Freude Spur verhasst;
Das Kind, das in der Mutter Schosse spielte,
Schien mir verschworen wider meinen Schmerz.
Wie möcht ich alles jetzt, was mich umringt,
Zufrieden gern und glücklich sehn! . . .
Der Mensch kann gross, ein Held, im Leiden sein,
Doch göttlich ist er, wenn er selig ist!   (ll. 1686–97)

[Misfortune purifies the soul, they say; but I . . . did not have this feeling.
. . . How strange that I should find hateful the trace of joy on every face in
which I encountered it; the child playing on its mother's lap seemed to me
to conspire against my pain. How gladly would I now see everyone about
me contented and happy! . . . In suffering man can be great, a hero, but in
joy he is divine!]

IV

Thus Kleist painfully discovered that as a poet he could not escape
from the state, any more than man could; that man is a political animal,
and if the political is subtracted only the animal is left. At this point
Kleist must have felt tempted to foreswear a faith in creative autonomy
which had proved so disastrous, to return contritely to the bosom of the
state, and to find purpose and reward through submission and service.

The temptations were manifold and subtle. Prussia, proud and self-
reliant when he had defied it, now was a humiliated and occupied country, struggling feebly to regain its self-respect. The political cause drew
dignity and passion from the patriot's just hatred of Napoleon; Kleist
himself had become a fanatical anti-French publicist. More importantly
and insidiously, the rising Romantic school of political philosophy—led
by his friend and collaborator Adam Müller—furnished him with a per-
suasive rationale for surrender. It offered him the mystique of the
organic state, in which man, self-exiled from the City of God, could
escape from his cold isolation and find a new matrix. (What a consol-
ingly maternal metaphor we have found for a coordinate system!) In the
state, relation and relatedness were still possible; and if this kind of
relatedness seemed to be lacking in warmth, one could always endow it
with an oversoul. To poetize Prussia—to dissolve its explicit, denotative
outlines in the soft focus of patriotic feeling, to give the harsh rectangu-
larity of its matrix the gentler curvature of a womb—this must have
seemed to Kleist a very seductive way out of his dilemma.

The state itself beckoned him. King Frederick William III, to arouse his people's spirit, had called for patriotic art, and Kleist now set himself to writing what he called a patriotic drama, which he intended as his last word and testament as a poet and a Prussian. The play, *The Prince of Homburg*, celebrates the victory won by the Great Elector over the invading Swedes in the battle of Fehrbellin. The Prince of Homburg, in command of the Elector's cavalry, attacks in violation of explicit orders; it is not clear whether, in doing so, he wins the battle or prevents a more complete victory. The Elector, in any case, is wholly committed to the view that the state rests on the law; he appoints a court-martial, which duly condemns the Prince to death. Faced with this verdict, the Prince collapses and miserably begs for his naked life; he surrenders all claims to rank, honor, even love, if only he is pardoned. Up to this point the Elector has rejected all pleas on the Prince's behalf on the grounds that he cannot arbitrarily intervene in the workings of the law without becoming a despot; but when he learns of the Prince's collapse, he completely reverses his position. He notifies Homburg that he need only declare himself unjustly condemned to win full reinstatement. Thus made judge in his own cause and thereby in effect sovereign, the Prince responds with a letter of which we are not given the text, but which must contain, or imply, an acceptance of the verdict. He recalls his comrades, who are close to mutiny for his sake, to their duty and calmly, in fact triumphantly, prepares for his execution. At this point the Elector feels empowered to do what before he could not do: he vacates the judgment, and instead of being executed the Prince is proclaimed the true victor of the battle and crowned with laurel.

The subsequent fate of this play is in the highest degree ironic; it is hardly too much to say that by its gradual acceptance on the German stage we can measure the progress of a creeping political malaise. At first it was condemned and neglected, because it presented the hero in a state of demoralization unthinkable for an officer and nobleman. But from the 1860's on it steadily gained in popularity. It was interpreted to show that the individual, acting in arrogant reliance on his private judgment, is bound to fall, but that the state, personified in the Elector can reclaim him by wise pedagogic management. By judicious dosages of power and manipulation, the erring individual can be made to acknowledge the state's overriding claims; by a genuine inner acceptance of his fault and the state's justice, he can regain grace and reinstatement. There was, in fact, greater rejoicing over one reclaimed sinner than over a hundred of the just.

The religious analogy underlying this interpretation is obvious; and it means that the divine and the political orders have become one. Where formerly the political order was understood to be, at best, a metaphor of the divine one, it now *is* that order; the vehicle has become the tenor. And where the ruler used to rule by the grace of God, he now *is* God— the dispenser of ultimate justice and, upon the proper conditions, of mercy.

There can be no question that Kleist himself saw the Prince's fate under the aspect of the archetypal drama of man's fall and redemption— nor that he saw the state as an ultimate order, with no possibility of appeal to a higher jurisdiction. But what this meant to him was not that the state had to be deified so as to provide man with an *ersatz* heaven, but that the divine order had become secularized. In Adam's fall we fell all—God included; it was irreversible and continuous. There was neither a paradise to which contrite man could be readmitted nor a utopia which proud man could construct. There were, instead, the positive, unanswerable order of the law and man's inchoate intuitions of freedom and harmony; these, improbably, had to come to terms with each other, with no third, supramundane term provided in which, by definition, they were blissfully fused.

The remarkable thing about Kleist's play is that it does not in any way soften the rigor of this polar opposition but on the contrary increases it. More and more, ruler and subject withdraw from each other until at the climax the subject is *mere* man, stripped of all the dignity and dignities society has to give, while the ruler has retreated into the order, a wholly impersonal embodiment of the law. The spheres no longer touch each other.

The moment has come, it would seem, for either tragedy or compromise. But Kleist gives us neither. When the Elector is made aware of the total irrelevance of the absolute order to the absolute individual, he abdicates. He does not try to preach to the Prince, to insinuate himself into the defenseless soul of his victim and lead him to contrition and amendment. He respects the Prince's moral inviolability at the moment of his deepest degradation and takes the unsecured risk of entrusting him with the sovereign power. By making the Prince judge in his own cause, he throws himself and the state upon the mercy of the individual, as unreservedly as the individual had thrown himself upon the mercy of the state.

This transfer of sovereignty creates a strange and paradoxical situation, which I will try to make clearer by comparing it to an analogous one. When Socrates is asked to speak in his own defense, and later, after his conviction, to propose his own punishment, he faces a choice not unlike the Prince's. He could employ the formulas of contrition and beg for lenience; by speaking as his judges expect him to speak, by making himself an echo of the public voice, he could save his life. But instead he speaks freely, by the sovereignty of the divine voice within him; doing so, he provokes a sentence of death, as surely and as knowingly as though he had pronounced it himself. Confronted with the ultimate authority of the state, he acknowledges it more fully than it wants to be acknowledged. What *it* wants is submission; but Socrates honors it by fulfilling his inalienable duty: the duty to speak truly. He sees himself so wholly pledged to the state that he cannot submit his inner truth to it; for if he did, the state would have no truth but turn into an empty tautology irrecoverably sunk into the error of its own devising. Hence Socrates is perfectly consistent when later he refuses to flee; for the laws, whose child he considers himself, have as just a claim to his life as to his truth.

The difference between Socrates and Kleist's Prince is that Socrates has a divine warranty; he knows he is not guilty as charged. The state has the right to translate its sentence into act, but it cannot thereby make it true. Truth resides elsewhere. Homburg, on the other hand, has no divine warranty; his inner voice was not infallible but has led him into an act which, by the only possible criterion—the law—must be defined as a crime. With Truth no longer resident among the absolute ideas, there is nothing for him to plead except guilty and to accept the verdict as just, not merely in the limited and contingent sense in which Socrates accepted it, but absolutely. His private sense of what he is and has done, unlike Socrates' daimon, is irrelevant to the matter, has no guarantor outside himself, makes no sense; there is nothing he has to offer the state, not even a meaningful death. Hence his demoralization.

But when he gets the Elector's note, his situation becomes still more confusing: he is put into the strange position of being whatever he *says* he is. By the terms of the note, he need only say: "I am innocent," and he *is* innocent. The Elector had the law to fall back on; in calling the Prince guilty he spoke meaningfully, for the law had pronounced him guilty. But the Prince now has nothing to tell him whether or not he speaks the truth if he pronounces himself innocent. Since whatever he says becomes true by his saying it, to say that he is innocent is nothing more than if he said: "I am that I am"—an empty tautology.

Thus, at this moment two tautologies face each other, self-referential, without meaning each for the other: the absolute law and the sovereign individual. The Prince could save his life by pronouncing himself innocent, by accepting the proffered role of being a creative speaker; but if he did so, he would deprive himself permanently of any possibility of vindication. He would encapsule himself in an unchallengeable emptiness, without reference or relation. He would, to put it differently, be a Poet, with a capital P, the kind whose utterances do not mean but are. This, then, would be one way out of Kleist's dilemma: to become a "pure" Poet.

If, on the other hand, Homburg pronounces himself guilty, his judgment merely endorses that of the law; his voice and the state's will be one, and he signs his death warrant, not merely in the sense that he is killed, but that he confirms the law in *its* self-defining perfection. When Socrates provoked his condemnation, he achieved something by it; he was able to tell the truth, to provide a point of reference by which the state's sentence could be judged. The Prince, by condemning himself, would accomplish the opposite; he would surrender whatever truth he has in him and thereby deprive the order of *its* chance of meaning and reference. The other way out of the dilemma would be to become the state's mere echo.

But in this seemingly hopeless dilemma the Prince does keep hold of one saving fact: that, like Socrates, he has been addressed and asked to reply. Moreover, he has been made sovereign, which means that he is not bound by the self-defeating alternatives of saying either yea or nay, the only possible discourse the absolute individual can hold with the absolute order. He recognizes that, oddly, in order to use his sovereignty for his own justification, he would be bound by the formula prescribed in the Elector's note; he might be speaking creatively but the very opposite of freely. But most importantly, he accepts the challenge, implicit in the note, to *speak*. He has no God to speak for; he can speak only in his own name. But he speaks *to* some one, and though he does not surrender to the state, he does deliver himself over, as every true speaker does, to the man he answers.

We do not know what he says in his reply; the only part we are told of it is the concluding formula. But this formula makes it clear that the Prince considers his letter at the same time his sovereign utterance and his death sentence. It could hardly be otherwise. It must be his death sentence because he has refused to accept the formula and definition of sovereignty which were the condition of his self-acquittal. It is his sovereign utterance because he has chosen to speak, freely and truly, rather than let himself be enslaved by the deadly alternative of absolutes.

As the sequel shows, he has also spoken to some purpose. True speech is between men, and by his answer he has freed the Elector, who, in fear of destroying the state, had retreated behind the gates of the law. As soon as the Elector receives the Prince's answer, he turns from an administrator of the law into a ruler, a man who takes the risk of action. The law is by no means set aside, but it becomes responsive to the needs and intuitions of those whom in the last resort it is meant to serve. Autonomy has replaced automatism; the communion of men in genuine speech lifts function into service, coordination into consonance, obedience into loyalty.

The first risk and action the Elector takes is the tearing up of the death sentence. He can take the risk now, not because the Prince has contritely acknowledged the necessity of absolute obedience—learned his Prussian lesson, in other words—but because has has demonstrated that where there is no divine law to fall back on, the burden of order need not be carried entirely by the state's positive law. Autonomous man can bear his share and yet not diminish the order's authority but rather increase it. While God can be merciful because He is omnipotent, the secular power can grant mercy because the risk rests not on it alone. Nor need law assume the certainty of self-definition, because where there is meaning, ambiguity can be chanced.

V

This, then, was Kleist's response to the King's demand for patriotic art. It probably was not what the King expected, any more than Homburg's reply was what the Elector expected. It is, in fact, unlikely that the King ever read it or, if he had, that he would have understood it. The future, and not only in Prussia, listened to different and mostly worse replies; and when it finally gave Kleist a hearing, fifty years of drill-field barks and sentimentally patriotic warblings had dulled its ears. But all this did not matter to Kleist; two years after the completion of the play, disavowed by his family, largely ignored as a writer, in difficulties with the Prussian Government, and in despair over Prussia's servile foreign policy, he committed suicide.

It may seem that what happens to Kleist's work is of little relevance to Walt Whitman's country, that his was a special and desperate case. But there is not only the threat of losing the spirit of Whitman's America; there is also the threat implicit in that spirit itself. If the extreme metaphor for the Prussian kind of order is Kafka's execution machine, the one I would propose for us is Univac. A democratic order develops its own kinds of automatism. The daring democratic faith in free trade—of goods and, much more importantly, of ideas—this faith has a dangerous affinity to reliance on poll-taking, statistics, and market research. To flee from risk is a tendency from which no political arrangement exempts us;

the difference will be merely in the kind of security we seek. There is not much to choose between a cog and an IBM card; and a crystal may seem a more appealing arrangement than a colloid.

At times there is something distinctly colloidal even about Walt Whitman:

> I speak the password primeval, I give the sign of democracy,
> By God! I will accept nothing which all cannot have their counterpart of
>   on the same terms.
> Through me many long dumb voices,
> Voices of the interminable generations of prisoners and slaves,
> Voices of the diseased and despairing, and of thieves and dwarfs,
> Voices of cycles of preparation and accretion,
> And of the threads that connect the stars, and of wombs, and of the
>   father-stuff,
> And of the rights of them the others are down upon,
> Of the deformed, trivial, flat, foolish, despised,
> Fog in the air, beetles rolling balls of dung. . . .

Here is plenitude, but is there sufficient reason? One cannot quite escape the feeling that Whitman, having given the sign of democracy—and what with the United States already being the greatest poem—hoped that things were given a voice simply by being present and voting. "By God! I will accept nothing which all cannot have their counterpart of on the same terms." It has a certain nobility, but it is the nobility of an unrealized sentiment. It is what a speaking super-Univac might say in rejecting an unrepresentative sample.

But there is another American writer, whose vision was shaped, not by the democratic vistas of a continent opening limitlessly toward the West, but by the gunwalls of a man-of-war: Melville. Human society as a ship's company—a floating island of precarious and hence rigorous order on the chaotic waters: this is an image very close to Kleist's of the embattled state. Billy Budd, suddenly transferred from the *Rights of Man* to the martial law of the *Indomitable:* this has a very close counterpart in Kleist's development and that of his Prince. The automatic definition of crime by mere act, regardless of motive and provocation; the imperious need for punishment, regardless of personal feelings; the direct confrontation, outside the law, of judge and victim and the absolution of the judge by the victim: these parallels suffice to show how close Melville's final vision came to that of Kleist's last play. They argue that Prussia is not a local accident of history but a form or order with which modern man needs to come to terms. Kleist did: laboriously, unlyrically, with a rather obsessive and constrained energy, because

lyricism is like to find itself helpless before such an order; a tougher
poetry, a harsher speech is needed for man's necessary discourse with it.
The sheer poetry comes only at the end, after the confrontation: in the
description of Billy Budd's hanging, or in what Homburg thinks are his
last words before his execution:

> Nun, o Unsterblichkeit, bist du ganz mein!
> Du strahlst mir, durch die Binde meiner Augen,
> Mit Glanz der tausendfachen Sonne zu!
> Es wachsen Flügel mir an beiden Schultern,
> Durch stille Ätherräume schwingt mein Geist;
> Und wie ein Schiff, vom Hauch des Winds entführt,
> Die muntre Hafenstadt versinken sieht,
> So geht mir dämmernd alles Leben unter:
> Jetzt unterscheid ich Farben noch und Formen,
> Und jetzt liegt Nebel alles unter mir.   (ll. 1830–39)

[Now, immortality, you are entirely mine! Through my blindfold, you
radiate for me the splendor of a thousand suns! Wings are growing on both
my shoulders, my spirit soars through calm, ethereal regions; and as a ship,
driven by the gentle wind, sees the lively seaport sink away, so everything
living is submerged in twilight: now I still discern colors and forms, and
now everything lying beneath me is mist.]

7. Kleist's *Hermannsschlacht*: The Lock and the Key

ISTORY sometimes seems to do the work of interpreting for us. Since World War II we can hardly help accepting Hitler and Goebbels as authoritative interpreters of Kleist's *Hermannsschlacht* and the events of 1933 to 1945 as its gruesomely faithful translation into fact. The play has become the "unbewältigte Vergangenheit" of Kleist criticism, something we would avoid rather than contemplate. How, we wonder, could it ever have been talked about as Gundolf talked about it some forty years ago?

> Comparatively speaking, the least convulsed. . . . of his plays to date. . . . Controlled, firm, with a goal kept tenaciously in sight. . . . the unrestrained ecstasies of sheer impulse and somnambulistic escapes from self are almost completely lacking in it. . . . The language is more alert, purer, sturdier, pithier [than up to now]. . . . He had finally found an area outside of himself which he did not have to compress into himself first, but in which he could extend himself with some freedom—an answering element that he found responsive even before he shouted at it.[1]

Gundolf writes without embarrassment, almost innocently, as though he were dealing with a work of literature. We "Nachgeborenen" cannot be so untroubled; for us it is not a play so much as an issue.

In this feeling we are, I think, partly right—which is to say, we react as Kleist meant us, *initially*, to react. Whatever its precise meaning may turn out to be, the play is first of all an act of calculated violence, an assault on our moral convictions. But if we think it worth knowing what Kleist had in mind with this piece of "Schrecklichkeit," we must do more than react; we must look. For Gundolf also is partly right: Kleist here *is* "controlled, firm, with a goal kept tentatively in sight . . ."— exactly like his protagonist Hermann. We are wrong in describing the play as an "eruption" or "fit," a "running berserk" of irrational hatred; it is no such thing. It is what it represents: a coldly planned and executed ambush. Like all drama worth talking about, *Die Hermannsschlacht* constitutes a careful *design* both moral and metaphoric, though a design of a strange and shocking sort. I shall try to read it accordingly.

I

The reading must begin with the distich—often quoted and almost as often misunderstood—which serves as the play's motto:

Wehe, mein Vaterland, dir! Die Leier, zum Ruhm dir, zu schlagen
Ist, getreu dir im Schoss, mir, deinem Dichter, verwehrt.

[Woe unto thee, my Fatherland! Faithful to thee in my heart, I as thy poet am debarred from striking my lyre in thy praise.][2]

To read the critics, one would think that Kleist had written "Wehe, mein Vaterland, *mir!* [Woe unto *me*, my Fatherland!]"; the distich is commonly taken to be the poet's bitter plaint that his work has been spurned by the very nation it was meant to glorify. But it says nothing of the sort—almost the contrary. It employs the formula of the scourging prophet's curse; Woe unto *thee!* In what follows, the fatherland will be sung; but we are not to expect that the song will redound to its glory. We will not leave the performance as though we had listened to one of Klopstock's "Bardiete" or Ayrenhoff's *Hermann und Thusnelda*: with a heightened sense of our worth as bearers of so proud a "Volkstum." We will not be invited to see ourselves as the heirs of a race of nature's noblemen, whose purity of soul and greatness of spirit puts to flight and shame a corrupt and decadent enemy. We will not find ourselves consoled for our manifest inferiorities by a flattering contrast between "echtes Deutschtum" and "falsches Weltentum." Rather, the song will issue "aus tiefster Erniedrigung"—from abject degradation. We will be whipped into a redoubt of self-assertion so final as to be worse almost than none—the den of the wild beast. The noble speeches, generous acts and grand exits will be given to the "villains," while the "heroes," more often than not, will be without manliness or dignity, as fulsome in their remorse as they are cruel in their enmity. By the time Kleist concludes his demonstration of what it means to be "getreu im Schoss" of *such* a fatherland, every patriotic stereotype will have been called into question.

Kleist knew that he was working within a well-established literary tradition; the meaning of *Die Hermannsschlacht* lies in good part in the jarring contrast between that tradition and what he does to it. There are the studiedly irregular, often grating lines, the frequent passage of prosiness, the sheer ugliness of the sounds:

Pfiffikon! Iphikon!—Was das, beim Jupiter!
Für eine Sprache ist! Als schlüg ein Stecken
An einen alten, rostzerfressnen Helm!
Ein Greulsystem von Worten, nicht geschickt,

Zwei solche Ding wie Tag and Nacht
Durch einen eignen Laut zu unterscheiden.
Ich glaub, ein Tauber wars, der das Geheul erfunden.
Und an den Mäulern sehen sie sichs ab.   (ll. 1897–1904)

[Pfiffikon! Iphikon!—What language that is, by Jove! As though a stick were beating an old, corroded helmet! An abominable system of words, ill-suited to tell apart by sounds of their own two such things as day and night. I think the man who invented their caterwauling was deaf. And they read it on each other's coarse lips.]

True, the speaker is a Roman; but throughout the play, Kleist insists on reminding us that these Germans are savages in every sense:

Wie wollt ihr doch, ihr Herrn, mit diesem Heer des Varus
Euch messen—an eines Haufens Spitze,
Zusammen aus den Waldungen gelaufen,
Mit der Kohorte, der gegliederten,
Die, wo sie geht and steht, des Geistes sich erfreut?   (ll. 286–90)

[My, lords, just how do you propose to rival this army of Varus'—at the head of a swarm that has come together from the woodlands, to rival the well-ranked cohort that rejoices in morale wherever it may be?]

Kleist himself drives the point home, in his stage directions: "Im Hintergrund sieht man die Wohnungen der Horde [In the background are seen the dwellings of the horde]." Surely a patriot might have it on the word "Stamm" rather than "Horde."

But to cite a more more telling and significant instance: the death of the unfortunate Hally, who, violated by Roman soldiers, is killed by her own father and then cut up into fifteen pieces, to be sent into all parts of Germany (IV, vi). The motif, of course, is a grandly tragic one; it traces its descent from Appius and Virginia and the Rape of Lucrece; a recent forebear was Lessing's *Emilia Galotti*. The tradition called for the victim nobly to kill herself or to demand her own death. To underscore Roman villainy, the motif had already been employed by Lohenstein, whose lecherous Varus drives a German princess to suicide. Wieland, in his fragmentary Arminius epic, took it over; and though there is no external evidence that Kleist knew the fragment,[3] it is instructive to see how the episode was handled in the pre-Kleistian tradition. Hulda, Wieland's violated princess, speaks—in hexameters, of course:

Grausamer Varus!
Welch eine Unschuld, o was vor Hoffnungen hast du zernichtet!
Götter! ihr sehet mein Unglück, und rüstet den strafenden Donner,

Ja, dis hoff' ich, und seelig! wenn mein unbeweinbarer Jammer
Dich, gleich leidendes Vaterland, heilt! Wie gern will ich sterben
Wenn aus meinem zu frühen Grab and der kläglichen Asche
Deine Freyheit, o mütterlich Land, schnell sprossend emporsteigt.
. . .   O weinet nicht, Liebste,
Lasst mich dahingehn im süssen Bewusstseyn der göttlichen Tugend,
Die zwar leiden kann, aber im Leiden nur herrlicher glänzet.

[Cruel Varus, what innocence, O what hopes you have destroyed! O Gods,
ye see my misfortune and are preparing the avenging thunder!—verily,
this is my hope, and bliss it will be if my unlamentable despair heals thee,
O equally suffering Fatherland! How gladly will I die, if thy freedom,
O land maternal, shall rise quickly blooming from my premature grave and
pitiful remains. . . . O do not weep, dearest ones, let me depart in the
sweet consciousness of heavenly virtue, that can suffer to be sure, but in
suffering shines only the more gloriously.]

She speaks—for another 33 lines—and dies:

Bleich, wie sterbende Lilien, sank sie, mit welkenden Gliedern
In die Arme der winselnden Mutter; die schönen Augen
Schlossen sich dämmernd, den Lippen entwich der reizende Purpur,
Noch im Sterben voll Anmuth, entschlief der erkaltende Körper,
Und die Seele verliess, mit stillen Seufzern, ihr Wohnhaus.
Würdiges Kind!

[Pale, like dying lilies, she sank with wilting limbs into the arms of her
wailing mother; her lovely eyes faded and closed, the charming crimson
vanished from her lips; still full of grace in death, her body growing cold
breathed its last, and the soul departed its abode with quiet sighs. Noble
child!]

But what used to be matter for pathos and tragedy, Kleist makes into
the stuff of butchery: a passive, helpless, wordless female is brutally
grabbed and stabbled, without the speech or even the posture that might
redeem the savagery of the act. Into the very stage direction Kleist pursues himself and us, hunting down the last furtive trace of tragic
response:

(*Sie fällt, mit einem kurzen Laut, übern Haufen.*)

[(*With a short cry, she falls headlong.*)]

The poor creature is not even granted a "sinkt nieder" or "bricht
zusammen"; in the vile "übern Haufen" she suffers the unkindest cut
of all.

This is a hunting play; there is open season not only on bisons and

Romans but on all kinds of sentimentality, more particularly on patriotic sentimentality. Are we to suppose that Kleist was insensitive to the pawing intimacy of Hermann's "Kosenamen" for Thusnelda—Thuschen? If we are tempted to honor the renegade Fust for his (very belated) desertion of the Romans and contrite return to the German cause, the manner of it promptly reawakens our disgust:

> Das hab ich heut, das musst du wissen,
> Gestreckt am Boden heulend, mir,
> Als mir dein Brief kam, Göttlicher, gelobt.   (ll. 2498–2500)

[This you must know: when your letter reached me, excellent one, I took this vow, howling outstretched on the ground.]

Spoken like—Caliban. Varus and Septimius are noblemen next to these German princes, the "best" of whom, in his resolute reserve, is the unregenerate and unforgiven Aristan. (Of the Greek meaning of Arist-an Kleist was assuredly not unaware.) It would be only further sentimentality to think that the manner does not matter—that Teutonic feeling, however revolting, is better than Roman posturing, however noble. A dramatic poet above others knows that manner *is* matter; Hermann responds to the slavering of Fust and his kind exactly as we do (cf. ll. 2527–38). The Germans are far from being of Tacitean cast—outwardly or inwardly.

II

To the play's insistent aesthetic inversions there corresponds the upside-down morality. The point needs no spelling out; Hermann himself is quite explicit:

> Die Guten mit den Schlechten!—Was! Die Guten!
> Das sind die Schlechtesten! Der Rache Keil
> Soll sie zuerst vor allen andern, treffen!   (ll. 1697–99)

[The good with the bad—How so, the good! They are the worst! The spearhead of revenge must strike them first, before all others!]

Most critics have assumed that there is, for Kleist, a value so absolute and ultimate that it can transform all other values. It does not much matter whether we identify this value as nationality, national independence or the inviolability of the "Volksseele"; the meaning is pretty much the same and reasonably clear. And the implication is equally clear: *if* we accept Kleist's absolute as our own, we will also accept the inverted morality as being a true one.

H. A. Korff's judgment is representative of this mode of reading the play—and of its consequences for the normal reader:

> Hier ist der Punkt, wo der Dichter Kleist *überall versagt.* . . . Hier ist der Punkt, wo jeder gesund fühlende Mensch dem Dichter entgegenrufen muss: "Verwirre das Gefühl uns nicht!" Versuche nicht, *uns* etwas als absolut verehrungswürdig und gross einzureden, was in Wahrheit als etwas höchst Fragwürdiges und bestenfalls als eine tragische Notwendigkeit, ein düsteres Mahnmal an die Unvollkommenheit der Welt zu batrachten ist. . . . Weil [*Die Hermannsschlacht*] uns vorbehaltlos begeistern will für die vernunftlose Verabsolutierung eines Gefühls und sei es des höchsten . . . darum ist [sie]als Dichtung ein tief fragwürdiges Gebilde.

> [This is the point at which the poet Kleist fails everywhere. . . . This is the point at which every human being with normal instincts must confront the poet with: "Do not confuse our feelings!" Do not attempt to convince *us* that something is absolutely venerable and great, that is really to be regarded as something most questionable and at best as a tragic necessity, a sad reminder of the imperfection of the world. . . . Just because [*Die Hermannsschlacht*] is intended to fill us with unconditional enthusiasm for the irrational autonomization of a single emotion and be it the highest . . . it is, as poetry, a deeply questionable creation.][4]

But surely something is wrong here. Korff's vocabulary—"verehrungswürdig und gross," "Verherrlichung," and "und sei es des höchsten"— sorts oddly with "fällt übern Haufen" and "Horde," and even more oddly with the title of the distich that serves as the play's motto: "Die tiefste *Erniedrigung.*" The argument proceeds a priori: since Kleist justifies lying and cruelty by their service to the national cause, therefore he "must have" felt—and meant us to feel—that the national cause is a value higher and more venerable than truth, kindness, justice and all the other virtues. But while this might pass for sound reasoning, it is poor reading. Kleist refuses to embody the national cause in figures, actions and words which will persuade us of its moral supremacy. What he makes us see is pelt-clad savages rejoicing in the kill; what he makes us hear is the disheveled fury of Thusnelda shouting fiendish witticisms at the man she is tearing to pieces. Again and again we witness mean stratagems and hideous vindictiveness; the mere invocation of the word "Vaterland" is quite inadequate to restore the moral balance.

To put it differently: the common view of the play implies a putative "ideal" audience—one that, having learned fully to accept Kleist's absolute, would no longer feel horrified and violated by what it sees on the stage. But this is clearly not the audience Kleist wanted, for he does nothing to persuade us of the overriding grandeur and splendor of the national cause. On the contrary, the play relies for its effects precisely on the brutal shocks it administers to our normal moral responses (including those of normal patriotism). Only an audience of totally brainwashed SS functionaries could watch *Die Hermannsschlacht* with simple assent.

In fact, not even they. The grisly rhetoric of heroic self-abnegation which Himmler employed to buck up the morale of his exterminators is the exact opposite of Kleist's technique. Even an SS man—unless he is a psychopathic sadist and needs only to be let loose—must be *persuaded* that acts which humanity has agreed to call evil are in fact good; and for that the rhetoric of high moral purpose, the constant glorification of the "Cause" are absolutely essential. But this is just what Kleist denies his Germans, himself and us. Even in his soliloquy Hermann does not seize the opportunity to tell us how hard he finds it to have to act as he does, how he has had to conquer his naturally "good" self for the greater good of German freedom. Nor, for that matter, does he break out into a hymn of hatred and *furor Teutonicus*. He speaks with the detachment of a commercial traveler:

> Nun wär ich fertig, wie ein Reisender.
> Cheruska, wie es steht und liegt,
> Kommt mir, wie eingepackt in eine Kiste, vor:
> Um einen Wechsel könnt ich es verkaufen. (ll. 1656–59)

> [I am ready now, like a traveler. Cheruska, just as it stands, looks to me like something packed in a chest: I could sell it for a bill of exchange.]

And elsewhere his attitude toward his scheme comes close to being one of relish; he is a man who enjoys his work.

Hermann, it is true, does try to whip *his* audience, the Germans, into a fury so savage that they reject all distinctions but one: Roman or German? But we are not Hermann's audience, we are Kleist's. Kleist takes pains to make us see; he manipulates our feelings not to deceive us but on the contrary to make us discover certain truths about ourselves as moral and political beings. These truths are not arrived at by logical deduction; they are defined by the play itself. Clearly we are asked to accept Hermann's conduct as justified and necessary; but it is justified only within the framework of circumstances—factual *and* formal, moral *and* metaphoric—which the play establishes. In the face of the play's paradoxical inversions, the question remains: what are these circumstances?

III

The place to look for an answer, then, is still the text—more particularly the Thusnelda plot. For Thusnelda is the "problem" character, the only one who significantly develops, who moves from error to truth. But merely to say this of her is to underscore once again how radically and pointedly Kleist inverts all traditional patterns. Flaw or error, insight and subsequent atonement and purification—that is the tragic mold. But Thusnelda's flaw is that she shows self-respect and generosity; her insight consists in the realization that by showing these she has become "unworthy" of her husband: "Arminius' muss ich wieder würdig werden [I must again become worthy of Arminius]." And her purification is her turning into a beast. Her development is rigorously anti-tragic.

Nor is this all. Into the bear's den Thusnelda carries a burden which we can be sure was precious to her author: *Penthesilea* and "Die Verlobung in St. Domingo." She is not merely an anti-tragic heroine, in impersonal contrast to an impersonal aesthetic type; she is an anti-Penthesilea and anti-Toni. To become worthy of Arminius, she tears not just a false Roman but two of the noblest creatures of Kleist's imagination.

The use of the Penthesilea motif need not be labored. What Penthesilea did in a trance and a delusion, Thusnelda does knowingly and by design. What in *Penthesilea* we experienced through the merciful and even ennobling medium of tragic poetry, we are now made to witness with brutal directness and to the accompaniment of vile sarcasms. The horror which in the earlier play had to be, and was, atoned for is now itself the "atonement." If *Penthesilea* contained "den ganzen Schmutz zugleich und Glanz" of Kleist's soul, here the motif appears stripped of all its splendor; nothing remains but the filth. Perhaps no poet has pushed so close to the precipice where terror falls into shock and awe into revulsion as Kleist did at the high point of his tragedy:

So war es ein Versehen. Küsse, Bisse,
Das reimt sich, und wer recht von Herzen liebt,
Kann schon das eine für das andre greifen. . . .
Du Aermster aller Menschen, du vergibst mir!
Ich hab mich, bei Diana, nur versprochen,
Doch jetzt sag ich dir deutlich, wie ichs meinte:
Weil ich der raschen Lippe Herr nicht bin;
Dies, du Geliebter, wars, und weiter nichts. (*Sie küsst ihn.*) (ll. 2981–88)

[It was a mistake then. Kissing delights, bites, these rhyme, and if one loves most fondly, he can easily take the one for the other. . . . Poorest of all humankind, you will forgive me! By Diana, it was only a slip of the tongue, for I am not in command of my hasty lip; but now I'll tell you clearly, how I meant it: it was this, belovèd, and nothing more. (*She kisses him.*)]

Incredibly, he managed to stop short and thereby gained for tragedy a realm of experience and a dimension of feeling it had not included before him. But now he shoves us over the edge with ghastly glee:

Ach, wie die Borsten, Liebster, schwarz und starr,
Der Livia, deiner Kaiserin, werden stehn,
Wenn sie um ihren Nacken niederfallen!
Statthalter von Cheruska, grüss ich dich!
Das ist der mindste Lohn, du treuer Knecht,
Der dich für die Gefälligkeit erwartet! (ll. 2406–11)

[Ah, dearest one, how becoming the black, stiff bristles will be to Livia, your empress, when they fall about her shoulders! "I hail you Governor of Cheruska!"—that is the least reward that will await you for your obligingness, O faithful servant!]

Psychologically, of course, this change—this transmogrification, rather—of the motif may be accounted for by Ventidius' perfidy; but *symbolically* it is much harder to explain. What we need to see, and feel, is not the difference in motivation so much as the sameness of the event itself; how could Kleist have sacrificed *this* of all his metaphors to such a purpose? It is as though Shakespeare, in *Troilus and Cressida*, had made Thersites smother the faithless heroine in a parodistic re-enactment of the scene in which Othello kills Desdemona. If we have no sense of what it must have cost Kleist to use the Penthesilea motif in this manner, we lack the first prerequisite for understanding him.

The reappearance of the "Verlobung" motif[5]—that of the love tryst as a device to ensnare and destroy the lover—adds greatly to the cost. Gustav von der Ried, the hero of "Die Verlobung," made the fatal error of interpreting Toni's actions in the light of a prefigurative story he himself had told: that of the negress who lures her former master to her bed and infects him with the plague:

Der Unglückliche ... kam und schloss sie ... in seine Arme; doch kaum hatte er eine halbe Stunde unter Liebkosungen und Zärtlichkeiten in ihrem Bett zugebracht, als sie sich sie plötzlich, mit dem Ausdruck wilder und kalter Wut, darin erhob und sprach: "Eine Pestkranke, die den Tod in der Brust trägt, hast du geküsst: geh and gib das gelbe Fieber allen denen, die dir gleichen!"

[The luckless man ... came and took her ... in his arms; but hardly had he passed half an hour in her bed amid caresses and sweet words, when she suddenly rose up with an expression of wild and cold rage and said: "You have kissed one stricken with the plague, who bears death in her bosom: go and give the yellow fever to all those like you!"]

On which Gustav's judgment had been:

dass nach dem Gefühl seiner Seele keine Tyrannei, die die Weissen je verübt, einen Verrat, so niederträchtig und abscheulich, rechtfertigen könne. Die Rache des Himmels ... würde dadurch entwaffnet: die Engel selbst, dadurch empört, stellten sich auf Seiten derer, die Unrecht hätten, und nähmen, zur Aufrechterhaltung menschlicher und göttlicher Ordnung, ihre Sache.

[that according to the feeling of his soul, no tyranny that the whites had ever perpetrated could justify a betrayal so base and horrible. The vengeance of heaven ... was disarmed by it: the angels themselves, outraged by it, would place themselves on the side of those who were in the wrong and would espouse their cause for the sake of supporting human and divine order.]

This judgment applies with full force to Thusnelda.

The parallel between "Die Verlobung" and *Die Hermannsschlacht* is still more pervasive and telling. For as the negress is the prototype of Thusnelda, so Congo Hoango is Hermann's: the merciless leader of an enslaved people, who, to avenge his race and destroy the enslavers, avails himself of any means, even that of using the women of his family as love-bait. The parallel needs insisting on because it shows not only how the play's moral configuration appears once it is divested of its German garb, but also that it had already so appeared in Kleist's own imagination and work. The moral accents—so perverse and intolerable to our feelings—have been placed by Kleist himself with the most deliberate care, in a manner which shows that he found them as intolerable as we do. More so, in fact, because for him it was not just a matter of presenting the morally repugnant as somehow justified and even admirable, but of sacrificing Toni, and Penthesilea, in the process.

IV

If, aware of these antecedents, we ask what they have in common, the answer is evident. *Penthesilea* and "Die Verlobung" are tragic commentaries on the faith that lovers can join across all the barriers which society has erected. Achilles and Penthesilea, Gustav and Toni are "meant for each other"; they seem destined to prove that men can form a natural community—or could, if external, artificial divisions did not separate them in enmity and distrust; that, in Schiller's hyperbole, it should be possible to unite "was die Mode streng geteilt," to embrace and kiss all of humanity.

But, unlike Schiller, Kleist permits himself no hymnic exaltation; he does not brush off the things that keep men apart as "Mode." Stubbornly matter-of-fact, he observes how these differences penetrate into the very tissue of our bodies: Toni is yellow-skinned and Penthesilea is one-breasted. The happy union, if it is to be achieved, must have withstood the severest tests of reality; Kleist is one of those poets whose works are acid tests rather than "expressions" of cherished feelings and beliefs. Again and again it turns out that the bond of pure humanity cannot withstand the strain of opposed social claims. At first—in "Das Erdbeben in Chile" and *Die Familie Schroffenstein*–the failure is due not to a weakness in the bond but to the malign force of outward circumstance. But as Kleist confronts the fact that "natural" and "social" man is an inseparable amalgam—as he becomes aware how deeply the social invades man's very being—he inevitably discovers that it is the bond of trust itself which is flawed. Ottokar and Agnes, once they have bound themselves each to the other, hold firm; they are destroyed from without, as are Jeronimo and Josephe. But Penthesilea and Achilles, Toni and Gustav are, in the last resort, destroyed by themselves—not because they trust less but because a much greater trust is demanded of them. Their natural being is so inextricably intertwined with their social being that it is far too ambiguous for simple trust. True, Toni's dying words are: "Du hättest mir nicht misstrauen sollen! [You should not have mistrusted me!]"; but Kleist has seen to it that the demand is well-nigh unfulfillable. And in *Penthesilea* tragic guilt is so ineluctable that we cannot assess blame at all.

The vision of union beyond all social orders and barriers remains the informing principle of both these works; they end tragically because the vision is not realized. But especially *Penthesilea* does not just end tragically; the failure issues in a fearful backlash. Once man breaks free of the confines of social order, he is in danger of becoming a beast. Society "restrains"—in the ambiguous sense which Kleist feels repeatedly compelled to probe: it restrains man both from the sweet fulfillment of utterly free, direct, personal union—and from the animal within. So that the vision, benign in Kleist's earliest work, is later seen to harbor threats and even horrors. Man outside society is still a noble savage, perhaps, but the accent has shifted from the adjective to the noun.

In *Die Hermannsschlacht* the beast is loose. All Kleist's works abound with animal images and metaphors; but no other is as intensely bestial as this play. The Cheruscans are not in the state of nature, to be sure, but they are very close to it. They are, we noted, a "Horde." Their social structure is primitive; it rests, as Kleist takes pains to make clear, on feeling and force rather than on law. When Varus condemns a disobedient Roman soldier, he can speak with the austere dignity of *Homburg's* Great Elector:

> Den einen nur behalt ich mir bevor,
> Der, dem ausdrücklichen Ermahnungswort zuwider,
> Den ersten Schlag der Eiche zugefügt. . . .
> Und das Gesetz verurteilt ihn des Kriegs,
> Das kein Gesuch entwaffnen kann, nicht ich. (ll. 1156–62)

[I will reserve for myself only him who, contrary to my expressed word of admonition, gave the first blow to the oak. . . . And the articles of war that no petition can disarm condemn him, not I.]

When Hermann, on the other hand, is told that his men refuse to fight against the Suevians and with pretended wrath sets upon their spokesman, there is no law he can invoke, only force:

> HERMANN (*indem er sich den Helm in die Augen drückt*):
> Nun denn, bei Wotans erznem Donnerwagen,
> So soll ein grimmig Beispiel doch
> Solch eine schlechte Regung in dir strafen! (ll. 2149–51)

[HERMANN (*while pressing his helmet down over his eyes*): Well then, by Wotan's brazen thunder-chariot, a grim example shall yet punish so base an impulse in you!]

In this setting Thusnelda embodies what we may fairly call the cosmopolitan vision. She is realistic enough to accept intrigue and war as facts of life; but she believes that there is a personal sphere transcending the sordid arena of politics—a republic of the human spirit in which every gentle soul holds immediate citizenship. And this sphere she wants to keep out of Hermann's schemes—"aus dem Spiel," as she says, with what we shall presently recognize as a significant play on the double meaning of "Spiel":

> THUSNELDA: Lass mich mit diesem Römer aus dem Spiele.
> HERMANN: Dich aus dem Spiel? Wie? Was? Bist du von Sinnen?
> Warum? Weshalb?
> THUSNELDA: Er tut mir leid, der Jüngling.
> (ll. 511–13)

[THUSNELDA: Leave me and this Roman out of it.
HERMANN: You out of it? What do you mean? Are you crazy?
Why? For what reason?
THUSNELDA: I am sorry for the youth.]

If she does not passionately lash out at the artificial divisions the political game creates, she does protest against Hermann's refusal to make any distinction between the individual and the social group to which he happens to belong:

Dich macht, ich seh, der Römerhass ganz blind.
Weil als dämonenartig dir
Das Ganz' erscheint, so kannst du dir
Als sittlich nicht den Einzelnen gedenken.   (ll. 685–88)

[I see that hatred of the Romans completely blinds you. Because the whole race seems to you demon-like, you cannot imagine a decent individual.]

Her protests against her husband's "Unmenschlichkeit," her pleading for the lives of the *good* Romans are of a piece with Toni's defense of Gustav:

Zeigt nicht vielmehr alles, dass er der edelste und vortrefflichste Mensch ist und gewiss das Unrecht, das die Schwarzen seiner Gattung vorwerfen mögen, auf keine Weise teilt?

[Rather, does not everything show that he is the most noble and superior person and certainly has no share in the injustice with which the blacks may reproach his race?]

Thusnelda's trust is bitterly betrayed by Ventidius. And betrayal of trust, real or imagined, drives Kleistian characters into frenzies of vengeance, as old Piachi of "Der Findling" and Penthesilea show. It seems clear that, in part, Kleist scourges himself, through Thusnelda, for his earlier, mistaken faith in a transcendent community of men. Yet this explanation is inadequate; it does not account for the moral placing of Thusnelda's vengeance. A trust, however misplaced, does not cease to be noble—least of all in Kleist, that fanatic of "Vertrauen"; yet Thusnelda feels polluted by hers. She lacerates her moral self—and ours— almost as much as she does Ventidius; it is not just the Roman whom she punishes for having betrayed what used to be Kleist's highest value, but herself for having held it.

She subjects herself, we saw, to a purifying rite which is to make her "worthy again" of Arminius. These words imply an ascent from a lower to a higher moral plane; but how can this be? Unless we are prepared (as I am not) to attribute the abnormality to Kleist himself—to think of him as morally so unstable and untrustworthy that he is coldly capable of condemning the good, the true and the beautiful and, in the name of nationalism, of enthroning evil, falsehood and ugliness—we must believe that he saw, and meant us to see, this purification as a *descent*, unredeemed and unrevoked, into bestiality.

V

Having traced the thematic antecedents of the Thusnelda plot and their implications, we must now look at that plot itself and its function within the play. It may seem that I attach undue importance to what is, after all, only a secondary element; but I think it is demonstrable that the subplot is in fact the key element. Not merely because in it the moral question is more harshly put than in the main plot, nor because it furnishes the play's emotional climax, nor because in it Kleist undertakes some strange reckoning with his earlier work—though all these are substantial reasons. My best warrant for taking the subplot to be the *key* element is that Kleist himself literally points to it as such, by the almost obsessive verbal iteration he often employs in similar cases:

CHILDERICH: Wo ist der Schlüssel, Gertrud?
GERTRUD: Der Schlüssel, Gott des Himmels, steckt er nicht?
CHILDERICH: Der Schlüssel, nein!
GERTRUD: Er wird am Boden liegen.
—Das Ungeheur! Sie hält ihn in der Hand. . . .
Reiss ihr das Werkzeug weg! . . .
CHILDERICH: (*da Thusnelda den Schlüssel verbirgt*):
Wie, meine Königin?
GERTRUD: Reiss ihr das Werkzeug, Childerich, hinweg!
(*Sie bemühen sich, ihr den Schlüssel zu entwinden*)
VENTIDIUS: Ach! O des Jammers! Weh mir! O Thusnelda!
THUSNELDA: Sag ihr, dass du sie liebst, Ventidius,
So hält sie still und schenkt die Locken dir!
(*Sie wirft den Schlüssel weg, und fällt in Ohnmacht*)
(ll. 2414-23)

[CHILDERICH: Where is the key, Gertrud?
GERTRUD: Heavens, is it not in the lock?
CHILDERICH: The key, no!
GERTRUD: It is probably on the ground. —That monster! she has it in her hand. . . . Snatch the tool away from her! . . .
CHILDERICH (*as Thusnelda hides the key*): How now, my queen?

GERTRUD: Childerich, snatch the tool away from her!
              (*They endeavor to wrest the key from her.*)
VENTIDIUS: Alas! O the misery! Woe unto me! O Thusnelda!
THUSNELDA: Tell her you love her, Ventidius, and she will hold still and
              give you her locks as a present!
              (*She throws away the key and falls in a faint.*)]

Clearly here, if anywhere, the key must be looked for.[6]

But as soon as we do, we are baffled by the realization that the
Thusnelda plot has no causal connection with the main action. What
Thusnelda says and does has no effect on Hermann's schemes; it neither
furthers nor impedes them. Her dealings with Ventidius, which so
cruelly lash our feelings, remain entirely without issue; for all the bearing
they have on the title action, they might as well have been omitted.

This is odd—especially since Thusnelda begs at the outset "aus dem
Spiele gelassen zu werden." We are told, it is true, that *in the past*
Thusnelda's complaisance toward Ventidius has been part of Hermann's
strategy. But Kleist has placed his scenes with meticulous care to show
us that by the time Thusnelda asks to be left out of the play, she has
fully served her political purpose. Nothing would have been simpler
than to place II.v–vii—by virtue of the "rape of the lock" the beginning of the subplot proper—*before* rather than after II.i, where Hermann
agrees to let Varus march into Cheruska. Had Kleist done so, the subplot would have had a clear though still slender connection with the
main action, since its crucial complication would then have occurred in
the course, and as a result, of Hermann's deceptive stalling. But with the
"Einmarscherlaubnis" all these maneuvres have served their purpose; in
II.iii there is no further reason why Hermann should not grant his wife's
wish.

In fact, Kleist goes to perverse length to keep Thusnelda *out* of the
main action, even as he keeps her *in* the play. In II.vi, to shield herself
from Ventidius' importunities, she calls for her children; here is the
scene in full:

(*Gertrud und Bertha treten auf. Die Vorigen.*)
THUSNELDA: Gertrud, wo bleibst du? Ich rief nach meinen Kindern.
GERTRUD: Sie sind im Vorgemach.
                                    (*Sie wollen beide gehen.*)
THUSNELDA: Wart! Einen Augenblick!
              Gertrud, du bleibst!—Du, Bertha, kannst sie holen!
                                    (*Bertha ab.*)

[(*Enter Gertrud and Bertha. Thusnelda and Ventidius.*)
THUSNELDA: Gertrud, where have you been? I called for my children.

131

GERTRUD: They are in the anteroom.
             (*Both start to leave.*)
THUSNELDA: Wait a moment! Gertrud, you stay! —You, Bertha, can
             fetch them!
             (*Exit Bertha.*)]

But, for reasons never explained, the children fail to appear; nor does
Thusnelda, throughout the rest of the play, so much as mention the fact
that she *has* children. Yet these are the very children—Rinold and Adel-
hart—whom four scenes later Hermann orders to be delivered into
Marbod's hands as hostages of his, Hermann's good faith—the very
children, that is, whose lives are risked as stakes in a dangerous political
gamble. Of Hermann such a measure does not surprise us; but what of
their mother? Surely here was the occasion to involve her in the main
action; surely the woman who is so moved by a Roman centurion's
generous courage—

Der junge Held, der, mit Gefahr des Lebens,
Das Kind, auf seiner Mutter Ruf,
Dem Tod der Flammen mutig jüngst entrissen—   (ll. 1715-17)

[The young hero who, risking his life, not long ago at the mother's cry
courageously snatched her child from a flaming death—]

would have something to say about her own children being staked on
the cast of the political die. (Implausibly, she does not even notice their
being gone.) If she did, her protest—quite unlike her politically inconsequential affair with Ventidius—would have the most direct bearing on
Hermann's plans, to which the children are essential. Moreover, Kleist
was practical dramatist enough to know a good scene when he saw one:
Thusnelda passionately disputing her husband's right to gamble with
their boys' lives would have been not only much better dramaturgy but
effective theatre. And if, after such a scene, she had learned to understand the greatness of her husband's cause and hence of the sacrifices he
must make and demand, how different, how much more comprehensible
and noble would she sound saying: "Arminius' muss ich wieder würdig
werden! [I must again become worthy of Armenius!]"

It is treacherous, and often presumptuous, for the interpreter to use
the subjunctive mode, to speculate what the poet "could" or even
"should" have done. But here, I submit, Kleist himself demands of us
just this kind of speculation. I do not see how the abortive scene I have
quoted can be explained except as a pointer intentionally placed to
direct our expectations along a road which then is *not* taken. Kleist

sacrifices legitimate dramatic effects, creates implausibilities, writes a puzzling and pointless scene—to what end? To make sure that his sub-plot will be effectually cut off from his main plot? Clearly we are asked to speculate.

She-bears are proverbial, not for their black bristles but for the ferocity with which they defend their young. Let us imagine another subplot:

> At the beginning of Act II, we see Ventidius passionately declaring his love to Thusnelda; she rebukes him and has her children brought in, for whom she shows tender concern.—Ventidius and Hermann negotiate; Ventidius demands the children as hostages of Hermann's good faith; Hermann sees no choice but to agree. [This would be in keeping with the Arminius tradition, in which just this cruel dilemma was a major motif.] —Thusnelda complains bitterly to Hermann about the demeaning role he makes her play; Hermann pleads necessity and tells her that they must sur-render their boys as hostages; she, distracted, accuses him of unfatherliness and inhumanity; he remains firm.—Thusnelda seeks out Ventidius to beg her children of him; he pretends sympathy and, amid renewed professions of love, promises that instead of sending the boys to Rome as he is ordered, he will restore them to her at the earliest possible moment (per-haps as soon as Varus and the Roman army have left Teutoburg).— Thusnelda confronts Hermann with the rumor that the Romans are to be massacred; she violently denounces him, contrasting his treacherous cruelty with Roman (Ventidius') humanity; when he refuses to yield, she begs that at least Ventidius be spared and the children, if possible, saved; Hermann agrees—and only then calls in the children, whom Ventidius, contrary to his promise, had sent off to Rome but who have been recap-tured by Hermann's men; Thusnelda is shattered by the discovery not only of Ventidius' perfidy but more of her own blindness and inner betrayal of Hermann; saying: "Arminius' muss ich wieder würdig werden," she resolves on a fearful revenge.—The she-bear scene.

I do not claim any sort of textual actuality—in some putative "Ur-Hermann"—for this speculative construct. It rests entirely on one prin-ciple: the substitution—or *re*stitution—of the children for the lock of hair. And it has only one object: to make more concrete the possibilities Kleist rejected when he chose the subplot as we have it. But I do claim this: (a) *some* such plot was considered and rejected by Kleist; (b) he thought the very rejection so essential a part of the play's meaning that he left clear traces of it in the play.

The substitute, then (and thus the metaphoric equivalent) for the children is—a lock of hair! This noble German heroine, this bearer of the heritage of Penthesilea and Toni, this mother robbed of her children turns into a beast over losing a snippet of her abundant tresses! I know that I exaggerate; of course, the loss of hair stands for something that

Wildroot cannot cure. But with metaphors, especially with Kleistian metaphors, it is never safe to leap too quickly to what they "stand for"; witness Kohlhaas' horses, who indeed "stand for" justice but who bring justice only after they have been suffered in their absolute, non-interchangeable and disreputable particularity and "an-sich"-ness. The lock of hair is as insistent and as crucial to the Thusnelda plot as the blacks are to *Michael Kohlhaas*; it introduces the complication, causes the peripety, and furnishes the controlling image for the catastrophe. I exaggerate to drive home the point that if we want to plumb Kleist's full meaning, we must be alive to the enormous disparity between physical cause and moral effect—and more still between what Kleist does and what he could, indeed "should," have done but deliberately chose not to do.

VI

What does it matter, we ask, whether the poet chooses this symbol or that, a trivial or a less trivial one, as long as we know and care about what it stands for. As Kleist writes of Kohlhaas:

> Kohlhaas, dem es nicht um die Pferde zu tun war—er hätte gleichen Schmerz empfunden, wenn es ein paar Hunde gegolten hätte—Kohlhaas schäumte vor Wut. . . .

> [Kohlhaas, who was not concerned with the horses—he would have felt as hurt if a pair of dogs had been at stake—Kohlhaas foamed with rage. . . .]

Justice is justice, trust is trust, betrayal is betrayal, whether the object at issue is a child or a strand of hair.

But of course it isn't so; the object does make a difference. A pact can be signed in ink as validly as in blood, but the devil knows that "Blut ist ein ganz besondrer Saft [blood is a very special juice]." People for whom "it's not the thing, it's the principle involved" surrender (as Kohlhaas does for a time) one half of their humanity. Humanity means, among other things, the knowledge that things must never be treated as mere signs. The metaphor which man himself is and which the world becomes in the very act of his knowing it—the embodiment of the spirit in the flesh, of the abstract in the concrete—is intricate and inextricable; the sign defines its meaning as much as the meaning defines its sign.

These are truisms; but they have implications which we easily ignore or forget. From the chaotic multiplicity of particulars we must rise to the ordering purity of universals by laborious steps; if we leap, we are in danger of plunging universals, ourselves, and the world back into chaos. The ordering of experience which we call abstraction is safe, and true, only if we carry upwards with us as great a burden of concreteness as we can manage—which is to say, if we *earn* our abstractions. If there is one thing that characterizes Kleist—makes him unmistakably "Kleistian," as it were—it is his obsessive need and will to create orders which leave the particularity of things intact. His typical prose sentence is the syntactic analogue of his mature stories: a bitterly fought, hard-won battle between the multifarious, "incidental" elements of experience that demand recognition and the periodic syntax that must shape them into an intelligible, ordered whole. I know of no writer who felt the opposed pulls of concreteness and abstraction—i.e., of individuality and order, of reality and truth—as keenly as Kleist did.

We are all intuitively agreed that certain things are exempt from the process of ordering by abstraction: the things we love. Of these, our children are the most signal, the archetypal instances. What distinguishes God from a chief magistrate of the world is that He in His omniscience is able, and in His paternal goodness willing, to see each one of us in full, unique individuality—as His child—and does not need to classify us in order not to lose sight of us altogether. But in the human, the social sphere this—our intuitive agreement—creates an unhappy split between the public and the private sectors of our lives. Love (ideally at least) rules the private sector, while order—the law—rules the public one; private means personal, particular, concrete, while public means impersonal, generic, abstract.

From the unease that necessarily attends this split there springs the ideal image of the "family of man," the all-embracing community in which men live together in spontaneous harmony, under the "law of love" (which is not a law, of course, but an oxymoron). And though this ideal is far from realization in political fact, we can realize it in spirit and sing "Odes to Joy" by employing its great metaphor:

> *Brüder*, unterm Sternenzelt
> Muss ein guter *Vater* wohnen!

[There must be a good *Father, brothers,* beneath the canopy of stars!]

In this way—as always when we dream paradisal dreams—we set up, in the very effort to escape the curse and cost of abstraction, the most impersonal, featureless abstraction of all: MAN. Nor only that: we drive the actually existing social orders—the state and all that Schiller calls "Mode"—even farther into impersonality, because we withdraw from them all particularizing love so as to invest it in a shapeless ideal. The "family of man" is too often a ready device by which we give our retreat into privacy the appearance of social principle; it is a blind leap from the most particular to the most universal—a leap for which the metaphor, with all its vague but intense feeling, serves as a spring board.

I have been leading up to *Wilhelm Tell*, a play which I feel sure was very much in Kleist's mind when for his part he decided to write about the founding of a free state. What damns Schiller's tyrant beyond all mercy, what draws the apolitical Tell into the main action, what prompts Bertha and Rudenz to side openly with the oppressed—what, in short, stands at the play's dramatic, spatial and emotional center—is Gessler's inhuman demand that a father stake his son's life on a desperate gamble. There, on a pole, hangs the hat—symbol of an order that is utterly disembodied, divested of all human content and particularity, the pure, empty, arbitrary sign of authority as such. Here stands Walter, the beloved son, on his head an apple—

Aus diesem Haupte, wo der Apfel lag,
Wird euch die neue, bessre Freiheit grünen

[A new, better freedom will blossom for you from this head on which the apple lay]—

embodiment of all that is organic, concrete, harmoniously held together by the bond of love. The dichotomy is as complete as Schiller's genius knows how to make it; so that we "know," by intuitive assent, that true order, though perhaps not identical with nature, must spring from it and is justified only to the degree that it approximates the natural, uncompelled harmony which binds father to child and brother to brother.

Schiller misses no opportunity to drive home the point that the *family* is the archetype of just social order. The Austrians' crimes—the blinding of Melchtal, the attempted violation of Baumgarten's wife—are presented, dramatically, as crimes against the family: the "one great happy family" (to use a cliché not altogether unjust here) which the Swiss are, or would be if they were left alone. Gessler is inhuman because he is not a father:

Herr, ihr habt keine Kinder—wisset nicht,
Was sich bewegt in eines Vaters Herzen

[My lord, you have no children—you do not know the stirrings of a father's heart];

whereas the Swiss are, almost without exception, fathers, mothers, grand-parents, uncles, sons, brothers—"ein einig Volk von Brüdern." The play's "problem" figure—corresponding to Thusnelda—is Rudenz, who spurns paternal tradition and to whom Attinghausen appeals in the name of "Vater" and all its derivatives. And at the very end, to make assurance doubly sure, Schiller takes the utmost care to draw a sharp line between the tyrannicide and the parricide: Tell properly a hero and Parricida an abject criminal almost beyond the pale of human fellow-ship.[7]

In this way the family serves Schiller to evade the specifically *political* problem he is ostensibly dealing with. Even if we assume that families cohere in natural concord, we have said and settled nothing yet about the law and the state. Schiller's patriotic idyll about the invaded and restored family not only lacks relevance for the divided and endangered Germany of 1804 (let alone of 1808); it lacks genuine political relevance altogether. His Swiss are, without exception, nature's noblemen: not all equally brave, wise, and enterprising, but all in their various degrees act-ing on impulses which, if they could be assumed to govern all men, would make laws and governments practically superfluous. Class distinc-tions, aristocratic privilege, and serfdom are glanced at, to be sure; but they dissolve in the warmth of fraternal feeling.

Questions that have plagued political theorists for centuries, Schiller glides over with sublime reliance on the rhetoric of human solidarity. Within fifty lines Stauffacher says, on the one hand:

> Denn herrenlos ist auch der Freiste nicht.
> Ein Oberhaupt muss sein, ein höchster Richter,
> Wo man das Recht mag schöpfen in dem Streit.
> Drum haben unsre Väter . . .
> Die Ehr gegönnt dem Kaiser. . . .

> [For even the most free is not without master. There must be a head, a highest judge, from whom one can obtain justice in a dispute. For that reason our fathers . . . granted the Emperor the honor. . . .]

(how odd that this absolutely essential supreme authority should then be described as no more than an "Ehre," a ceremonial dignity which the Swiss were content to bestow on the emperor!)—but exclaims, on the other hand:

> Nein, eine Grenze hat Tyrannenmacht.
> Wenn der Gedrückte nirgends Recht kann finden,
> Wenn unerträglich wird die Last—greift er
> Hinauf getrosten Mutes in den Himmel,
> Und holt herunter seine ewgen Rechte,

Die droben hangen unveräusserlich
Und unzerbrechlich wie die Sterne selbst—
Der alte Urstand der Natur kehrt wieder,
Wo Mensch dem Menschen gegenübersteht—

[Nay, tyranny has a limit. When the man oppressed can find justice nowhere, when the burden becomes unbearable—he reaches confidently into the heavens and fetches down his eternal rights, which hang there on high inalienable and indestructible as the stars themselves—the primordial state of nature returns in which man is confronted with man—]

"Welcher Mensch welchem Menschen?," we might interrupt to ask, if we were not swept along by the magnificent flow of language. Gessler and Parricida? Robespierre and Danton? Or perhaps only Stauffacher and Attinghausen? And if the former, just what is the state of nature like? What would Tell answer Parricida if the latter, instead of grovelling for compassion, asked him to define, in precise terms, the point "wenn unerträglich wird die Last"—a point Parricida evidently thought he had reached? *That* is the question the inalienable stars need to answer; but they are silent. Schiller's answer is always the same:

Wir stehn für unsre Weiber, unsre Kinder!

[We are responsible for our wives and children!]

or:

Hast du der Kinder liebes Haupt verteidigt?
Des Herdes Heiligtum beschützt? das Schrecklichste,
Das Letzte von den Deinen abgewendet?

[Have you defended precious children? Protected the sanctuary of your hearth? Turned aside what is most frightful and final from your own ones?]

Thus the genuinely political question—of law and the last court of appeal—is persistently begged; in placing the rulers outside all human fellowship and the subjects within the sacred and harmonious precincts of the family, Schiller solves the problem of order—of the destruction of an old legitimacy and the founding of a new one—by circular definition.

Schiller took pains, we know, to provide his play with an authentically Swiss setting. But the fact is that the fatherland which his Swiss love and defend is every true man's fatherland; it appeals not to those indissoluble ties into which, for good or ill, we happen to be born, but to moral sentiments we all approve of. This "Volk von Brüdern" is not the ordinary kind of family—the kind one is stuck with. Except that (or rather *because*) it lives in the mountains by hunting, herding and fishing, untainted by the vices of civilization, it is the family of MAN. The prodigious leap—

Tell, Tell, ein sichtbar Wunder hat der Herr
An euch getan, kaum glaub ich meinen Sinnen—

[Tell, Tell, the Lord performed a visible miracle upon you, I hardly believe my senses—]

has been taken; beneath the guise of specificity and particularity we discover the grand abstraction. Indeed, we discover that the leap was hardly necessary; for properly considered, the most particular and the most universal are one and the same. The stars inalienably suspended in the heavens and the flame of my hearth are identical, ultimate referents of justice. The true patriot is also the true citizen of the world.

It was, of course, no accident that Schiller chose Switzerland for his locale and the "Eidgenossen" for his nation. Switzerland had become the living embodiment of what I will call the Tell illusion. Small, pastoral, federative, republican and sturdily independent, it was the *pièce de résistance* of those who felt the need to find an actuality answering to the seductive dream of a "natural society." Rousseau had been a great shaper of the illusion; and the famous Johannes von Müller (whose *Geschichten schweizerischer Eidgenossenschaft* was Schiller's main source)[8] had put it on what was considered a sound historical basis. This was the illusion that drew the young Kleist to Switzerland; for there, it seemed, one could not only lead the simple, natural life but also be a citizen without having to be political. The reality, though not quite so idyllic, still looked attractive enough at first; on January 12, 1802, Kleist, having decided to invest his remaining fortune in a Swiss farm, writes Ulrike:

Die Güter sind jetzt im Durchschnitt alle im Preise ein
wenig gesunken, weil mancher, seiner politischen Meinungen
wegen, entweder verdrängt wird oder freiwillig weicht.
Ich selbst aber, der ich gar keine politischen Meinungen
habe, brauche nichts zu fürchten und nichts zu fliehen.

[On an average, farms have all dropped a bit in price now, since many a person, because of his political opinions, is either being ousted or is withdrawing voluntarily. I myself, however, having no political opinions, do not need to fear or flee anything.]

But within a month the prospect was clouding over:

Wenn du [das Geld] noch nicht abgeschickt hast, so
schicke es *nicht* ab. . . . Es hatte allen Anschein, dass die
Schweiz sowie Cisalpinien französich werden wird, und mich
ekelt vor dem blossen Gedanken.—So leicht indessen
wird es dem Allerwelts-Konsul mit der Schweiz nicht
gelingen. . . . Wenn er sich deutlich erklärt, vereinigt
sich alles gegen den allgemeinen Wolf.   (to Ulrike, Feb. 19)

[If you have not sent off [the money], then do *not* forward it. . . . There is
every indication that Switzerland as well as the Cisalpine Republic will
become French, and the very thought disgusts me.—In the meantime, this
busybody of a Consul will not succeed so easily with Switzerland. . . . If he
makes a clear declaration, everybody will unite against the universal wolf.]

And by March 2, the dream was ended; Switzerland was becoming, *de
facto* if not *de jure*, a province of the "Allerwelts-Konsul":

Mich erschreckt die blosse Möglichkeit, statt eines
Schweizer Bürgers durch einen Taschenspielerkunst-
griff ein Franzose zu werden. . . . Es sind bereits
Franzosen hier eingerückt, und nicht ohne Bitterkeit
habe ich ihrem Einzuge beigewohnt. . . . Unter diesen Um-
ständen denke ich nicht einmal daran, mich in der
Schweiz anzusiedeln.   (to Zschokke)

[I am frightened by the mere possibility of becoming a Frenchman, instead
of a Swiss citizen, by sleight-of-hand. . . . French have already moved in
here, and I attended their entry not without bitterness. . . . In these circumstances I would not so much as think of settling in Switzerland.]

Kleist, then, had had direct experience of the Tell illusion;[9] he had,
moreover, experience of its proponents. As for Schiller, there were the
two "Xenien" (nos. 85 and 86) entitled "Das deutsche Reich" and
"Deutscher Nationalcharakter":

Deutschland? Aber wo liegt es? Ich weiss das Land nicht zu finden.
   Wo das gelehrte beginnt, hört das politische auf.
Zur Nation euch zu bilden, ihr hoffet es, Deutsche, vergebens;
   Bildet, ihr könnt es, dafür freier zu Menschen euch aus.

[Germany? But where is it located? I am not able to find the country.
Where learned Germany begins, political Germany stops. Germans, you
hope in vain to constitute a nation; instead, develop yourselves—you can—
into human beings with greater freedom.]

To this view, *Die Hermannsschlacht* was the bitter and specific reply:

Ich weiss, Aristan. Diese Denkart kenn ich
Du bist imstand und treibst mich in die Enge,
Fragst, wo und wann Germanien gewesen? . . .
Doch jetzo, ich versichre dich, jetzt wirst du
Mich schnell begreifen, wie ich es gemeint:
Führt ihn hinweg and werft das Haupt ihm nieder.[10]   (ll. 2611–18)

[I know, Aristan. I am familiar with this mode of thinking. You are in a position to press me hard, asking where and when there has been a Germany. . . . But now, I assure you, now you will understand right away what I meant: lead him away and strike off his head!]

If Schiller was (in Kleist's eyes) criminally wrong, Johannes von Müller must have seemed contemptible. Until the collapse of Prussia, the great historian (who was living in Berlin on a handsome stipend from Frederick William III) was a passionate anti-Bonapartist; as of February 28, 1806, these were the Swiss sentiments:

Die Zeit ist jetzt schändlich, aber aus der Verwesung scheint sich ein Phönix zu bilden. Sehr viel erhoffe ich von dem Er-
wachen Oesterreichs. . . . Eine Vereinigung [against the French] zu gewissen Sätzen muss notwendig verabredet werden, und man muss alle Gleichgesinnten auffordern, mit Wort und Schrift auf die hinauszuarbeiten. Eine Zeit wird kommen, vielleicht schnell: Dass die [uns?] nicht unbereitet finde, das Joch zu brechen, das der finstere Tyrann den entarteten Grössen so höhnisch auflegt, und herzustellen die in eine stinkende Pfütze von ihm zusammengegossene Selbständigkeit, für welche der Sinn verloren ist.

[The times are now disgraceful, but a phoenix seems to be rising from the decay. I am expecting a great deal from the awakening of Austria. . . . An alliance [against the French] for certain principles must necessarily be agreed upon, and all like-minded persons must be called upon to work toward it in word and writing. A time will come, perhaps quickly: Let it not find [us?] unprepared to break the yoke that the sinister tyrant is so cynically imposing on the degenerate powers, and to restore that inde-pendence, the feeling for which has been lost, he has dumped into a stinking pool.]

Though the syntax is already opaque and the rhetoric strained, the resolve seems unambiguous. But on November 20, 1806, J. von Müller met with the "finstere Tyrann" himself, the first to be so summoned in Napoleon's effort to court the intellectual leaders of Germany. (Goethe's turn came on October 2, 1808, in Erfurt: "Voilà un homme!") Within ninety minutes, the historian's independence melted in the illustrious presence, readily dissolving into what half a year earlier he had called a stinking pool. Adam Müller cites J. von Müller as writing to Boettiger:

> Er habe anderthalb Stunden mit dem grossen Mann gesprochen, über alle grossen Stellen in der Politik . . ., er habe ihn in allem so stark, tief and unergründlich gefunden, dass er unter allen Gesprächen, die er je abgehalten, nur das mit Friedrich II. mit diesem vergleichen könne: indes habe an Schärfe des Blickes und Umfang der genialischen Idee der gegenwärtige Held den der Jahre 1760–70 weit übertroffen. . . . Was aus Preussen werden würde, sei nicht zu sagen: er, Johannes, sei über das Schicksal dieser Monarchie . . . zu seiner Tagesordnung übergegangen. . . . Die an das morsch gewordene Alte nutzlos verschwendeten Kräfte müssten auf das Neue übertragen werden: Gott sei es ja, der die Regierungen einsetze. Man müsse sich *umdenken*. . . .

[He said he talked with the great man an hour and a half, about all important political topics, . . . and had found him so well informed, profound and unfathomable in every respect that he could compare with this conversation, among all the other conversations he had ever held, only that with Frederick II: for all that, the present hero surpassed by far the one of the years 1760–70 in sharpness of vision and in breadth of inspired thought. . . . What would become of Prussia could not be said: he, Johannes, had passed by way of the fate of this monarchy . . . to his own agenda. . . . The energies vainly wasted on the old become rotten would have to be transferred to the new: after all, it was God who constituted governments. One would have *to change one's views*. . . .][11]

Which he promptly did. He transferred his energies to the divinely instituted puppet kingdom of Westphalia, which he served as minister of education until he died (1809). His new appointment was not hindered, we may assume, by an address he gave in French to commemorate, in French-occupied Berlin, the anniversary of the Great Frederick's birth. The title of the address was "La gloire de Frédéric," and Goethe translated and published it with hearty approval. Here is a sample:

> Ein solcher Mann [Frederick] gehört, wie die unsterblichen Götter, nicht einem gewissen Lande, einem gewissen Volke— diese können veränderliche Schicksale haben—, der ganzen Menschheit gehört er an, die so edler Vorbilder bedarf, um ihre Würde aufrecht zu erhalten.

[Such a man [Frederick] belongs, like the immortal gods, not to a certain country, a certain people—these can have changeable fortunes—he is a member of all mankind, which has need of such noble examples in order to maintain its dignity.]

"Der ganzen Menschheit!" In its name the great historian of Swiss independence—his dignity sustained by so great a "Vorbild" and his position by the still greater protection of his new paymaster—severed his connection with "a certain country" which had proved to have so "changeable" a fate. God evidently meant him to belong where Frederick also belonged, the whole of mankind being presently embodied in King Jerome. If Kleist needed a case history of what, concretely, the Swiss metaphor could be made to mean, Johannes von Müller furnished it nicely.[12]

VII

My implicit argument has been that Kleist avoided—or rather throttled—the family metaphor because it offered an altogether specious escape from the problems it was meant to solve. Under the guise of particularity it concealed an image of man, and of the nation, featureless in its universality; on the fluid of natural affection and harmony it pretended to construct a firm social order. And perhaps worst of all: by its easy perfection it invited an equally easy devotion—an allegiance that could hardly withstand the shock of reality. Who would not be a patriot if his fatherland were Schiller's Switzerland? But who *would* be a patriot if his fatherland was Prussia after Jena or the Germany of the *Rheinbund*?

Those who know how to read Kleist will have noticed, in the "key" passage quoted above, a significant because seemingly odd and wilful substitution for the term "Schlüssel":

Reiss ihr das Werkzeug weg!

[Snatch the tool away from her!]

and again:

Reiss ihr das Werkzeug, Childerich, hinweg!

[Childerich, snatch the tool away from her!]

This is not the first time "Werkzeug" is used in the play; it occurs twice before, once when Thusnelda tells Hermann of Ventidius' theft:

... löst er
Mit welchem Werkzeug weiss ich nicht, bis jetzt,
Mir eine Locke heimlich von der Scheitel (ll. 631–33)

[... he secretly removed a lock of hair from the top of my head, with what tool I don't know even now.]

and again when Hermann tells her of other such Roman outrages:

Nun ja! Und ihr nicht bloss, vom Haupt hinweg,
Das Haar, das goldene, die Zähne auch,
Die elfenbeinernen, mit einem Werkzeug
Auf offner Strasse aus dem Mund genommen.   (ll. 1026–29)

[Indeed so! And not just the golden hair from her head, but took also with a tool her ivorylike teeth from her mouth, on the public road.]

The Romans possess tools of which the primitive Germans do not even know the names; and those tools are in the most literal sense tools of abstraction and ex-traction. By their means the most personal and seemingly "inalienable" things can be removed from their organic context, be turned into bits of mere, transferable stuff—ornamental matter that will adorn whoever has the power to obtain it. It turns out that man are not "brothers under the skin"; the barriers between men go deeper—witness Toni. Our bodies, our hair and teeth, the noises we make when we speak, are constitutively ours; but they are alienable. Our very selves, it seems, can be expropriated by the sleight-of-hand of abstraction.

But one tool *is* available to the Germans: the key, the tool not of abstraction but of *inclusion*, of locking in, of trapping the abstractors into the most fearful of confrontations. We now begin to see the honesty of Kleist's dramatic scheme—that is to say, the merciless rigor with which he locks his characters, his play, himself and us into the sheer corporeality of his "key" metaphor. *No one* is left free to abstract himself, to stand aside or above; as Thusnelda is locked in with Ventidius, as her plot is locked in with the main plot, so is Hermann with Varus and the legions, so are we with this frightful *drame à clef*. Do we want to know what it means to be a poet, more specifically a German poet in the year of disgrace 1808? It means to be so utterly responsible for the physicality of one's metaphors that if one is compelled to write *à clef*, one must do so in the most literal and corporeal sense. It means that one has to pay the bitter price of one's necessity.

In Germany after 1806, patriotism was not the last refuge of scoundrels; there were many genuine patriots. But even genuine patriotism may be had on relatively easy terms. By a simple process of abstraction one can construe, as the object of one's love and allegiance, the "true" nation, the "real" fatherland. Schiller again furnishes the best illustration of how the thing is done. In a fragment which Suphan later entitled "Deutsche Grösse," we read:

Deutsches Reich und deutsche Nation sind zweierlei Dinge. . . . Abgeson-
dert von dem politischen hat der Deutsche sich seinen eigenen Wert
gegründet. . . . Die deutsche Würde ist eine sittliche Grösse, sie wohnt in
der Kultur und im Charakter der Nation, der von ihren politischen
Schicksalen unabhängig ist. . . . Dem, der den Geist bildet, beherrscht,
muss zuletzt die Herrschaft werden, wenn anders die Welt einen Plan,
wenn des Menschen Leben irgend nur Bedeutung hat; endlich muss die
Sitte und Vernunft siegen, die rohe Gewalt der Form erliegen. . . . Unsere
Sprache wird die Welt beherrschen. Die Sprache ist der Spiegel einer
Nation; wenn wir in diesen Spiegel schauen, so kommt uns ein grosses,
köstliches Bild von uns selbst daraus entgegen. . . . [Der Deutsche] ist
erwählt von dem Weltgeist, während des Zeitkampfes an dem ewigen Bau
der Menschheit zu arbeiten. . . . Jedes Volk hat seinen Tag in der
Geschichte, doch der Tag des Deutschen ist die Ernte der Zeit.

[German Empire and German nation are two different things. . . . Isolated
from the political, the German has established his peculiar worth. . . .
German dignity is a moral quantity, it dwells in the culture of the nation
and in its character which is independent of its political fortunes. . . .
Sovereignty must at last come to him who cultivates and controls the
mind, if the world has any plan and man's life has in any way meaning;
morality and reason must finally triumph, raw force succumb to form. . . .
Our language will dominate the world. Language is the mirror of a nation;
when we gaze into this mirror, a great, priceless image of ourselves confronts us. . . . (The German) has been chosen by the Weltgeist to work
(during the struggle of the age) at the eternal structuring of mankind. . . .
Every people has its day in history, but the day of the German is the har-
vest of time.][13]

These ideas are echoed over and over again by other patriots. They
inform Fichte's *Reden an die deutsche Nation* as well as Adam Müller's
Dresden lectures on German literature and thought (1806); we find
them expressed by the men around Stein who were founding the
"Tugendbund" and working for Prussia's and Germany's regeneration.
Of course there were differences—particularly in the degree of political
activism, in the impatience with which the German's accession to his
rightful "world-historical" role was being awaited and prepared for. But
common to much of this patriotic rhetoric is what we can only call cultural imperialism, not to say chauvinism: the conviction that Germany
was somehow "chosen." Her very deficiencies as a political entity were
chalked up as assets; in contrast to the closed and "inorganic" perfection
of France, she was "universal," growing, many-sided. Her lack of definition was her strength.

In the absence of the normal defining characteristics of nationhood,
it was inevitable that the patriots fell back on the German *language* as
the essence of Germany's national identity. Fichte rests his case for

German superiority largely on linguistic, philological grounds. Rahel Levin speaks of the language as

> der eigentliche Rhein . . . , welcher jene vorstürmenden Tempelräuber zurückhält von dem heiligen Gebiet unserer geistigen, sittlichen und religiösen Besitztümer

> [the true Rhine . . . , which holds back those charging desecrators of the temple from the holy territory of our spiritual, moral and religious possessions].

Carl Gustav von Brinckmann, a Swedish diplomat who spent the dark months of 1807 in Memel in intimate contact with the men around Stein, writes to Friedrich von Gentz:

> Das edlere *Denken, Sprechen* und *Schreiben* sichert uns eine noch unbesiegte *Sprache,* die glücklicherweise, ihrer höheren Eigentümlichkeit nach, von den Fremdlingen nicht begriffen wird

> [Our more noble *thinking, speaking* and *writing* assure us an as yet unconquered *language,* which fortunately, in its superior peculiarity, is not understood by outlanders].[14]

The italics are Brinckmann's; he is also the source of the quote from Rahel.

The patriots' party line (as we may almost call it) shares with Schiller also a reliance on a kind of historical or even metaphysical destiny which—"wenn anders die Welt einen Plan hat"—must inevitably provide for Germany's ultimate, universal predominance. The passivism resulting from this faith is sometimes startling; even Brinckmann cites Schiller's "herrliche Zeilen":

> Die fremden Eroberer kommen und gehen,
> Wir gehorchen, aber wir bleiben stehen

> [Foreign conquerors come and go, we obey but we remain].

And why not? If the "Weltgeist" in person guaranteed—if the very scheme of things depended on—the final triumph of German speech and thought, there was no occasion for undue alarm and desparate measures. Adam Müller states the true faith:

> Deine . . . Sprache blüht kräftiger und reiner unter allen Erschütterungen deines Bodens: wer ihre innerlichen Töne zu vernehmen weiss, muss das Vaterland . . . kommen hören. Den Glauben an die Zukunft, wie ihn diese Sprache auszudrücken weiss, lasst uns bewahren. . . . Bleibt Ihr der Erkenntnis, der Wissenschaft treu, so wird sie *von selbst* [my italics] zur Kraft und Handlung, die jede einseitige Macht beugen und zu ihrer Zeit die wilde Tyrannei, die euch jetzt zu Boden wirft, bezähmen wird.

[Your . . . language flourishes more vigorously and purely amid all the convulsions of your soil: he who can perceive its intimate tones cannot help hearing . . . the fatherland coming. Let us preserve our belief in the future as this language can express it. . . . If you remain true to knowledge and science, it will become *of itself* [my italics] strength and action, which will subdue any one-sided power and tame in its time the wild tyranny that now crushes you.][15]

What sets Kleist off from these patriots is not greater fanaticism but his inability to share either their confidence or their "Kulturstolz." For him Germany was not a metaphysical necessity; it was simply a nation, sadly perishable and—for lack of political definition—very much in danger of perishing utterly. This was his reply to the confident ones:

O du, der du so sprichst, du kömmst mir vor wie etwa ein Grieche aus dem Zeitalter das Sülla, oder, aus jenem des Titus, ein Israelit. Was! Dieser mächtige Staat der Juden soll untergehen? Jerusalem, diese Stadt Gottes, von seinen leibhaftigen Cherubimen beschützt, sie sollte, mit Zinnen und Mauern, zu Asche versinken? . . . Der Tod sollte die ganze Bevölkerung hinwegraffen, Weiber und Kinder in Fesseln weggeführt werden, und die Nachkommenschaft, in alle Länder der Welt zerstreut, durch Jahrtausende . . . elend, verworfen . . . das Leben der Sklaven führen?
Was!   (SW II, 377)

[O you who speak thus, you seem to me like a Greek from the age of Sulla, or an Israelite from that of Titus. What! This mighty Jewish state is to perish? Jerusalem, this city of God, protected by its cherubim in person, should sink with its battlements and walls to ashes? . . . Death should snatch away the whole population, women and children should be led off in chains, and their offspring, scattered into every country of the world, throughout millennia . . . wretched, . . . lead the life of abject slaves? Imagine!]

Nor is Germany uniquely endowed—worthy to be loved because she has a language, and thus a galaxy of "Dichter und Denker," much superior to other nations. As to the language itself, Kleist's comment might well have been: "Iphikon! Pfiffikon!"[16] As to cultural superiority, he made his point in the "Katechismus der Deutschen":

FRAGE: Warum liebst du es?
ANTWORT: Weil es mein Vaterland ist.
FRAGE: Du meinst, weil Gott es gesegnet hat . . . , weil viele schöne
             Werke der Kunst es schmücken, weil Helden, Staatsmänner
             und Weise . . . es verherrlicht haben?
ANTWORT: Nein, mein Vater, du verführst mich.

FRAGE: Ich verführe dich?
ANTWORT: —Denn Rom und das ägyptische Delta sind, wie du mich
            gelehrt hast, mit Früchten und Werken der Kunst und
            allem, was gross und herrlich sein mag, weit mehr gesegnet
            als Deutschland. . . .
FRAGE: Warum also liebst du Deutschland?
ANTWORT: Weil es mein Vaterland ist.   (SW II, 351)

[QUESTION: Why do you love it?
ANSWER: Because it is my fatherland.
QUESTION: You mean, because God has blessed it . . . , because many
            fair works of art adorn it, because heroes, statesmen and
            sages . . . have glorified it?
ANSWER: No, my father, you lead me astray.
QUESTION: I lead you astray?
ANSWER: For Rome and the Egyptian delta, as you have taught me,
            are far more blessed with the fruits and achievements of art
            and with everything great and splendid than is Germany. . . .
QUESTION: Why, then, do you love Germany?
ANSWER: Because it is my fatherland.]

And if we go on to read the other material which Kleist was then preparing for publication in the projected *Germania*, we get the impression
that a still better answer might have been: "*obwohl* es mein Vaterland
ist [*although* it is my fatherland]." For—with one exception: "Was gilt
es in diesem Kriege? [what is at stake in this war?]"—Kleist does not try
to praise the Germans into patriotism; he tries to shame and whip them
into the resolution of despair. He tries to persuade them that—
materially, culturally, even morally—they have nothing to lose. Their
officers are without honor (Satirical Letter No. 1), their women without
shame (No. 2), their civil servants scoundrels (No. 3), their journalists
servile liars (No. 4). Among his "Anekdoten" there are two which
Kleist singles out, by subtitles, as exemplary: "wert in Erz gegraben zu
werden [worthy of being engraved on metal]," and "das man nachahmen
sollte [that should be imitated]." Both of them show the French as men
of honor, courage and dignity; one of them is worthy quoting here:

Zu dem französischen General *Hulin* kam, während des Kriegs, ein . . .
Bürger, und gab, behufs einer kriegsrechtlichen Beschlagnehmung, zu des
Feindes Besten, eine Anzahl im Pontonhof liegender Stämme an. Der
General, der sich eben anzog, sagte: Nein, mein Freund, diese Stämme
können wir nicht annehmen.—"Warum nicht?" fragte der Bürger. "Es ist
königliches Eigentum."—Eben darum, sprach der General, indem er ihn
flüchtig ansah. Der König von Preussen braucht dergleichen Stämme, um
solche Schurken daran hängen zu lassen, wie er.   (SW II, 262)

[During the war a ... citizen came to the French general *Hulin*, and reported in the interest of the enemy, for purposes of requisition under martial law, a quantity of tree-trunks lying in the shipyard. The general, who was just getting dressed, said: No, my friend, we cannot take these trunks—"Why not?" asked the citizen. "It is royal property."—Just for that reason, said the general, giving him a cursory glance. The king of Prussia needs such trunks in order to hang on them rascals like you.]

Kleist's intention, here as in *Die Hermannsschlacht*, is unmistakable—and in deliberate contrast to the patriotic "party line." A German has shamefully small cause to be proud of his nation; he must learn to love it because he is *stuck* with it. Germans must be taught, not the disembodied patriotism of abstraction, but the patriotism of inclusion—of being locked in. It is not for nothing, nor a mere external misfortune, that Germany is a country in which the patriot has to lie or speak "verschlüsselt"; it is a condition of her being, moral as well as political. The shifty stratagems—the flattery and servility real or pretended—of slaves are demeaning and repulsive. But they constitute the reality of slavery. Truth, dignity, and manly self-respect are the privileges of freedom. In an enslaved country, the true patriot is not he who tries to intoxicate himself and others with the rare essence, the "Geist" of idealized national virtues. The true patriot is he who immerses himself, a fermenting agent, in the ill-smelling brew of his country's political and moral realities—hoping that ultimately it can be distilled into a clear and noble liquor.

We are now in the position to understand fully the moral and aesthetic inversions we observed in *Die Hermannsschlacht*. The anecdote about General Hulin compresses them into capsule form. Down here crawls the servile German, while up there the victorious French general pronounces his contemptuous "Schurke!" Deserved? Of course it is deserved, but at the same time it is so hatefully and despicably *unearned*. That is the true meaning of "Die Guten! Das sind die schlechtesten!" For if they were truly good, they would have to feel a deep and personal shame at having a part in reducing other human beings to such meanness. Their moral superiority—displayed with such style, such pithy and devastating wit—who is furnishing them with the moral means for it if not that cringing creature at their feet? In morals as in economics, the labor theory of value applies; the crucial question is not: who *has* it? but: has he *earned* it? Take the "generosity" of Septimius:

CHERUSKER: Septimius Nerva kommt, den du gerufen....
WINFRIED: Wo war er?
HERMANN: Bei dem Brand in Arkon, nicht?
          Beschäftiget zu retten und zu helfen?

CHERUSKER: In Arkon, ja, mein Fürst; bei einer Hütte,
Die durch den Römerzug in Feuer aufgegangen.
Er schüttete gerührt dem Eigner
Zwei volle Säckel Geldes aus!...
HERMANN: Das gute Herz!
WINFRIED: Wo stahl er doch die Säckel?
HERMANN: Dem Nachbar auf der Rechten oder Linken?

                                   (ll. 2174–87)

[CHERUSKER: Septimius Nerva is coming, whom you have summoned. . . .
WINFRIED: Where was he?
HERMANN: Was he not at the fire in Arkon, busy rescuing and helping?
CHERUSKER: Yes, in Arkon, my liege, at a cottage that went up in flames in consequence of the Roman advance. He was moved to pour out two full purses of money for the owner! . . .
HERMANN: What a kind heart!
WINFRIED: But where did he steal the purses?
HERMANN: From the neighbor on the right or left?]

To put it differently: the conqueror is able to throw his sword into the *moral* balance; his being the representative of a powerful, proud and victorious nation gives him not only a physical but a moral advantage over the conquered. What is despicable is that he then proceeds to abstract this superiority from its very concrete physical base and to think, talk and act as though it were morally earned, as though his confrontation with the oppressed were, or ever could be, one of MAN to MAN. Not only this: he tries, and only too often manages, to persuade his victim of the truth and justice of this abstraction and thereby gains a still greater *physical* advantage; for he thus robs him of his inner defenses after previously having robbed him of his outer ones. The most insidious Roman weapon is this: that on the point of her sword Rome carries the doctrine of "universal" laws and "natural" rights and duties. This is the meaning of the final encounter between Hermann and Septimius:

SEPTIMIUS: Wie, du Barbar? Mein Blut? Das wirst du nicht—!
HERMANN: Warum nicht?
SEPTIMIUS (*mit Würde*):   Weil ich dein Gefangner bin!
An deine Siegerpflicht erinnr' ich dich!
HERMANN (*auf sein Schwert gestützt*):
An Pflicht und Recht! Sieh da, so wahr ich lebe!
Er hat das Buch vom Cicero gelesen.
Was müsst ich tun, sag an, nach diesem Werk?
SEPTIMIUS: Nach diesem Werk? Armsel'ger Spötter, du!
Mein Haupt, das wehrlos vor dir steht,
Soll deiner Rache heilig sein;

> Also gebeut dir das Gefühl des Rechts
> In deines Busens Blättern aufgeschrieben!
> HERMANN (*indem er auf ihn einschreitet*):
> Du weisst, was Recht ist, du verfluchter Bube,
> Und kamst nach Deutschland, unbeleidigt,
> Um uns zu unterdrücken?
> Nehmt eine Keule doppelten Gewichts
> Und schlagt ihn tot![17]   (ll. 2205–20)
>
> [SEPTIMIUS: What, you barbarian? My blood? That you will not—!
> HERMANN: Why not?
> SEPTIMIUS (*with dignity*): Because I am your prisoner! I remind you of
> your obligation as victor!
> HERMANN (*leaning on his sword*): Obligation and justice! Behold, verily
> he has read Cicero's book! Tell me, what should I do accord-
> ing to this work?
> SEPTIMIUS: According to this work? You miserable scoffer! My head,
> defenseless before you, should be sacred from your revenge;
> the feeling of justice, inscribed upon the pages of your heart,
> commands you thus!
> HERMANN (*stepping over to confront him*): You know what justice is, you
> cursed villain, and came to Germany, without provocation,
> in order to oppress us? Take a club of double weight and
> strike him dead!]

The Roman abstraction—the sleight-of-hand by which, *after* the conquest, "man" is made to appear as the primary and essential constituent
of both Ro-man and Ger-man—is in truth no more than a tool of rape.
The Roman does not strip himself of his Roman-ness to confront the
German nakedly; on the contrary, he comes to the encounter in full
political and cultural panoply. Having taken the utmost advantage of
his belonging to a powerful and self-aware state, he then makes light
of that advantage so as to deny it to the people he enslaves. He is like
the white supremacist (of the genteel sort), who—after centuries of
depriving, exploiting and humiliating the Negro—stands proudly before
the world and adopts the posture of human superiority. There is no
hatred bitter enough for such pride—not because it is false, but on the
contrary, because it has and employs the means to create its own intol-
erably unjust reality.

VIII

Kleist's nationalism, then, amounts to this: that "German," "Roman,"
etc. are not composite nouns consisting of a common stem and readily
abstractable prefixes, but are integral substantives. There is, of course, a

common substratum "man" which is prior to nationality, indeed to any
social grouping, but it is biological only; having no social content, it has
no moral force. As "man" in this sense I am no more than a member
of a certain animal species.

Nevertheless we misunderstand Kleist radically if we assume that for
him the nation is a *non plus ultra* absolute, a value transcending and
transvaluing all other values. For him the nation—clearly and strongly
defined as a political entity, a state—is a *sine qua non*. It represents no
absolute but a step in the process of abstraction and ordering—a step
which must not be skipped. Those who try to skip it will find themselves
not in the republic of MAN, but lapsed into slavish subjection to
nations who did not make so foolish a mistake.

Some of the commentators on *Die Hermannsschlacht*—particularly
Meyer-Benfey and H. M. Wolff—have been a good deal puzzled by a
speech in which Hermann holds out the vision of a future universal
monarchy:

WOLF: Es scheint, du hältst das Volk des fruchtumblühten Latiens
    Für ein Geschlecht von höhrer Art,
    Bestimmt, uns rohe Käuze zu beherrschen?
HERMANN: Hm! In gewissem Sinne sag ich: ja.
    Ich glaub, der Deutsch' erfreut sich einer grössern
    Anlage, der Italier doch hat seine mindre
    In diesem Augenblicke mehr entwickelt.
    Wenn sich der Barden Lied erfüllt,
    Und, unter *einem* Königsszepter,
    Jemals die ganze Menschheit sich vereint,
    So lässt, dass es ein Deutscher führt, sich denken,
    Ein Britt', ein Gallier, oder wer ihr wollt;
    Doch nimmer jener Latier, beim Himmel!
    Der keine andre Volksnatur
    Verstehen kann und ehren, als nur seine.
    Dazu am Schluss der Ding' auch kommt es noch;
    Doch bis die Völker sich, die diese Erd umwogen,
    Noch jetzt vom Sturm der Zeit gepeitscht,
    Gleich einer See, ins Gleichgewicht gestellt,
    Kann es leicht sein, der Habicht rupft
    Die Brut des Aars, die, noch nicht flügge,
    Im stillen Wipfel einer Eiche ruht.[18]   (ll. 300–321)

[WOLF: It seems you consider the people of blossoming Latium as a
    race of superior nature, destined to rule us crude fellows?
HERMANN: Hm! In a certain sense I would say yes. I believe the German
    enjoys the greater potential but the Latin has developed his
    lesser potential more fully at this point. If the song of the
    bards is fulfilled, and if all mankind is ever united under *one*

> royal scepter, it is possible that a German will hold it, a
> Briton, a Gaul, or what you will; but never by heaven that
> Latin, who can understand and honor no other people's
> character than just his own! Eventually it will even come to
> this; but until the peoples whom this earth cradles, now
> still lashed by the storm of time like a sea, find equilibrium,
> it can easily be that the hawk will pluck the brood of the
> eagle, which, not yet fledged, rests in the quiet top of an
> oak.]

H. M. Wolff, assuming with most critics that Kleist posits the nation
as a *non plus ultra,* has no recourse but to discount these lines:

> These lines can not contain the poet's true meaning; for if the Britons or
> Gauls should really attempt to rule all mankind and thus Germany too,
> from the German point of view the same situation would result as vis-à-vis
> Rome. . . . Only then would there be no impairment of the freedom of the
> Germans if they themselves were the ones who ruled the world. . . . Here
> it is probably a question of a concession to visionary ideas of certain
> romanticists.[19]

But if Kleist had felt the need to make concessions of this sort, he had
vastly more telling occasions for doing so; the entire play is, as we have
seen, a slap in the face of Romantic notions. Moreover, Kleist evokes
(and Wolff duly notes) exactly the same vision in "Was gilt es in
diesem Kriege" as one of the peculiar glories of German thought:

> Eine Gemeinschaft [gilt es], die, unbekannt mit dem Geist der Herrsch-
> sucht und der Eroberung, des Daseins und der Duldung so würdig ist wie
> irgendeine; die ihren Ruhm nicht einmal denken kann, sie müsste denn
> den Ruhm zugleich und das Heil aller übrigen denken, die den Erdkreis
> bewohnen; deren ausgelassenster und ungeheuerster Gedanke noch, von
> Dichtern und Weisen auf Flügeln der Einbildung erschwungen. Unterwer-
> fung unter eine Weltregierung ist, die, in freier Wahl, von der Gesamtheit
> der Brüdernationen gesetzt wäre.   (SW II, 378)

> [(At stake is) a community which, unfamiliar with the spirit of domina-
> tion and conquest, is as worthy of existence and of sufferance as any other;
> which cannot even imagine its own glory without imagining at the same
> time the glory and welfare of all others who inhabit the globe; whose most
> liberated and prodigious thought, reached by poets and philosophers on
> wings of the imagination, is subjection to a world government that would
> be voluntarily constituted by the totality of fraternal nations.]

Kleist and Hermann are thinking of a world government resting not on
conquest (like that of Rome or France) but on the free and balanced
consent of all "Brüdernationen." The same federative principle would

operate by which, in fact, the various German tribes are to be united into a national state:

MARBOD: Das Vaterland muss einen Herrscher haben. . . .
HERMANN: Lass diese Sach, beim nächsten Mondlicht, uns. . . .
           In der gesamten Fürsten Rat, entscheiden!
MARBOD: Es sei! Man soll im Rat die Stimmen sammeln.

(ll. 2581–92)

[MARBOD: The fatherland has to have a ruler. . . .
HERMANN: Let us. . . . decide this matter, at the next moon, in the council of all the princes.
MARBOD: So be it! The votes shall be polled at the council.]

Unlike most nationalists, even of his day,[20] Kleist realizes that the very logic and the very need that generate the demand for national unification—for a higher and more encompassing order—must ultimately lead to the still higher order of world government.

So we are back, after all, to Schiller's family of man? Not at all. Kleist speaks, with considered precision, of "Brüder*nationen.*" He fears, not the abstraction as such (for without it there can be no order), but the leap. His nationalism is both more modest and more demanding than Schiller's. He does not foresee an "Ernte der Zeit" when German speech and "Geist" will rule the world; but he does demand statehood for Germany. Schiller's concept is sharply dualistic; it assumes that by sacrificing the body of political union and power, the Germans can liberate their spirit, so that in the end *it* will conquer the world. (To put it linguistically: Schiller's concept is anti-metaphoric; it seeks universality by dropping the ballast of corporeality.) Kleist has as little use for the imperialism of the spirit as for that of brute force. More precisely, he sees that the first is almost sure to become a victim and a tool of the second.

The nation, for Kleist, is necessary but not sufficient. Moreover, we need to be very careful even in defining his nationalism as "organic." As always when we deal with such abstractions, their meaning is defined by their metaphors. Goethe was an "organicist" surely; but just as surely he was, in this, poles removed from Kleist—as far removed, to be more precise, as plants are from beast. Both of these are "organic" and "natural"; but the social philosophies they embody may be as different as Rousseau's and Hobbes'. When we talk about Kleist, we must rid "organic" of all the vegetative connotations it usually carries. Order, for him, is something willed and imposed rather than a spontaneous growth; in his social philosophy, exactly as in his writing, he is no lyricist. (That his

one signal failure, the forcedly lyrical *Käthchen von Heilbronn,* has been
such a favorite with German audiences testifies only to the invincible
sentimentality of these audiences.)

The Germans of *Die Hermannsschlacht* are not an "organic" community rising in spontaneous solidarity against their oppressors. Their
national—not to mention political—awareness is vestigial, quite unlike
that of Schiller's Swiss, whose sense of communal identity needs only to
be given outward, institutional shape. Almost singly, Hermann must
devise the means of forging a conglomerate of tribes into statehood;
"Nationalgeist" is not something he can count on and enlist but something he must try to create. "Geist" is possessed by the Romans, by the
"gegliederte Kohorte,"

> Die, wo sie geht und steht, des Geistes sich erfreut.

> [High morale is possessed by the Romans, by the well-ranked cohort that
> rejoices in morale wherever it may be.]

The "Haufen" whom *he* commands can be stirred to common outrage
and fury; but that is a far cry still from the clear sense of unity and
common purpose, the *esprit de corps,* which distinguishes a nation from
a "horde."

Here, as almost everywhere in Kleist, the body of act and fact must
first exist to give birth to the spirit; the spirit is *ex post facto.* In
Wilhelm Tell the Rütli scene takes place in Act II; in *Die Hermannsschlacht* the corresponding "Mondnacht" meeting, where the new state
is to be formally constituted, is a promise on which the play ends. Nor
is that state the product of a harmonious consensus; Kleist points with
the utmost harshness to the fact that it is a legal structure and thus, like
every new state or jurisdiction, caught in the paradox of *ex post facto*
law. Its founding is signalized by an act of law—the execution of
Aristan:

HERMANN: Weh mir! Womit muss ich mein *Amt* beginnen?

[HERMANN: Woe unto me! With what act must I begin my *office?*]

We may feel, as Aristan does, that this is not law but *ex post facto*
violence, since obviously there can be no treason against a not yet existing state, no violation of not yet existing laws. But the very inception of
a new state or jurisdiction is *ex post facto* (witness the Nuremberg
trials); the first and most basic law, being constitutive of a new sovereignty, is an act of force, a naked assertion of authority.

Schiller touches on the same problem—but lightly. The first law passed on the Rütli is a proscription:

MELCHTAL: So sei's. Wer von Ergebung spricht an Oestreich,
                Soll rechtlos sein and aller Ehren bar,
                Kein Landmann nehm ihn auf an seinem Feuer.
ALLE: Wir wollen es, das sei Gesetz!

[MELCHTAL: So be it. If someone speaks of capitulation to Austria, he shall be outlawed and devoid of all honors; let no countryman receive him at his hearth.
ALLE: We will it, let that be the law!]

"Alle" does not yet include Rudenz, who in the preceding scene (with Attinghausen) has strongly urged submission to Austria and thus seems destined to become the new law's first victim. But Schiller does not allow the issue to come to a point; instead, he dissolves it in lyrical harmonies. Here as elsewhere, the family metaphor takes over; Rudenz is won over by Bertha:

Da seh ich dich, du Krone aller Frauen,
In weiblich reizender Geschäftigkeit,
In meinem Haus den Himmel mir erbauen
Und, wie der Frühling seine Blumen streut,
Mit schöner Anmut mir das Leben schmücken
Und Alles rings beleben und beglücken!

[O glory of all women, I see you there in my house, in charming womanly activity, creating heaven for me, and, like spring scattering its flowers, adorning my life with lovely grace and quickening and blessing everything round about!]

Where Kleist dismisses us with the bitter truth that a state is a structure of laws claiming a capital jurisdiction, Schiller lulls us with rhymes.

One question raised by both plays is: What is the state of nature, and how does the state of law arise from it? Schiller, we noticed, takes it up explicitly:

Der alte Urstand der Natur kehrt wieder,
Wo Mensch dem Menschen gegenüber steht.

[The primordial state of nature returns in which man is pitted against man.]

The return to the state of nature is symbolized in the first "Tell-Schuss," when the previously existing state of law is shattered by Gessler's lawless and cruel abuse of his authority. The inception of the new state of law is symbolized in the second "Tell-Schuss," when Tell, claiming and exercizing his inalienable human rights, rids himself and the Swiss of Gessler. The process is expressed in the metaphor of the hunt:

> Jetzt geht er einem andern Waidwerk nach. . . .
> Ich laure auf ein edles Wild. . . .
>   Aber heute will ich
> Den *Meisterschuss* tun und das Beste mir
> Im ganzen Umkreis des Gebirgs gewinnen.

[He now pursues another quarry. . . . I lie in wait for noble game. . . . But today I intend to make a *master-shot* and win the highest prize in all this mountain region.]

Tell's marksmanship remains undisputed—and has become legendary. He is acclaimed at the end as "der Schütze und Erretter"—the man who made the "saving shot."

Now at the beginning of *Die Hermannsschlacht* there *is* a dispute over who made the saving shot, who is the true "Sieger des Urs." (And we will not be wrong, I believe, if we identify this "Ur" with the "Ur-stand" which Schiller thought he had returned to.) Ventidius, with more gallantry than sincerity, pretends to yield the honor to Thusnelda, though he lets it be understood that the truly saving shot was his after all. But we and the Germans know that he is deluding himself; he has hit the beast only after it was already mortally wounded and could do no further harm.

Kleist's point, I suggest, is this: Schiller had no conception of what the human animal is like in the "Ur-stand." The animal *he* thinks he has vanquished has already lost most of its savage and destructive force. The state of law he founds presupposes man as a peaceable being, normally curbed by an "inner" or "higher" law, gentled by the milk of human kindness. It is Gessler and his crew who are bestial: "Wütriche," "Horden," "Tiger" or, by insistent association, "Drachen," "Bären" and "Wölfe." Switzerland itself is " die sel'ge Insel," "der Unschuld Land"; the threats to it, whether from untamed nature or from a species of animal called "böse Menschen," are morally external to it.

In *Die Hermannsschlacht* it is generally the Germans who are linked to wild animals—most signally in Thusnelda's metamorphosis into the "she-bear of Cherusca." The fact is that "die deutschen Uren," as Herman calls them, are very much closer to the "Ur-stand" than the Romans are, and that the Romans, in depriving them of what statehood they have and preventing their ascent to higher and more articulate levels of it, reduce them to the state of nature—pre-social, pre-moral, ferocious.

IX

We have come back to the Thusnelda plot—with, I hope, the key to it and to the play as a whole. Thusnelda represents a concept of art and (for Kleist it is the same thing) of morality which has become false by living vastly beyond its social means—by unearned abstraction. (This is also a kind of betrayal, because abstraction is the enemy's most powerful and insidious tool.) Her generous and humane feelings are not ignoble in themselves; they are "unworthy" because they are purchased at the expense of those who know themselves bound to far less noble realities, locked in by brutally concrete metaphors. What makes Thusnelda the ultimate heroine of the play—

Mein schönes Thuschen, Heldin grüss ich dich!

[My lovely Thuschen, I hail you heroine!]—

is her determination to start again at the very bottom, the real and literal state of nature.

For she does not just return to Hermann's level; she plunges below it. Kleist knows, and tries to make us see, that even "Vaterland" is an abstraction (though a vitally necessary one). In man's slow climb toward universal order, truth and justice, the nation-state is a step up from a more savage, tribal state. But even that state is already at a level where moral terms are available and meaningful. Hermann can appeal to values such as freedom; he operates in a moral space, however paradoxical. He can act "in the name of" something higher; and the "embrace" he plots is already metaphoric—given meaning as a step toward a greater order, a higher form of humanity. Thusnelda is made to re-enact man's rise from the beginning. Nothing redeems her embrace from the horror of sheer physicality. She must *earn* her title as "Siegerin des Urs."

As must Kleist himself. I have been critical of *Wilhelm Tell*, but I hope I have made clear, through the term "unearned," the nature and limits of my criticism (which I believe is a reflection of Kleist's). Kleist was as open as the most confirmed classicist to the powerful appeal of classical nobility, simplicity, universality—in short, *beauty*. His "Satz aus der höheren Kritik" might have issued from Weimar itself:

Es gehört mehr Genie dazu, ein mittelmässiges Kunstwerk zu würdigen als ein vortreffliches. Schönheit und Wahrheit leuchten der menschlichen

Natur in der aller ersten Instanz ein; und so wie die erhabensten Sätze am
leichtesten zu verstehen sind (nur das Minutiöse ist schwer zu begreifen),
so gefällt das Schöne leicht; nur das Mangelhafte und Manirierte geniesst
sich mit Mühe. In einem trefflichen Kunstwerk ist das Schöne so rein
enthalten, dass es jedem gesunden Auffassungsvermögen, als solchem, in
die Sinne springt. . . . Wer also Schiller und Goethe lobt, der gibt mir
dadurch noch gar nicht . . . den Beweis eines vorzüglichen und ausseror-
dentlichen Schönheitssinnes; wer aber mit Gellert und Cronegk hie und
da zufrieden ist, der lässt mich . . . vermuten, dass er Verstand und Emp-
findungen, und zwar beides in einem seltenen Grade, besitzt.

(*SW* II, 346 f.)

[It takes more genius to evaluate a mediocre work of art than a superior
one. Beauty and truth are immediately apparent to the human mind;
and just as the most sublime principles are easiest to understand (only the
detailed is hard to comprehend), so the beautiful pleases easily; only the
imperfect and mannered can be enjoyed with difficulty. The beautiful is
so purely contained in an excellent work of art that any healthy perceptive
faculty, as such, immediately recognizes it. . . . If someone praises Schiller
and Goethe therefore, by this he still doesn't demonstrate to me at all an
outstanding and extraordinary sense of beauty; but if he is occasionally
satisfied with Gellert and Cronegk, he makes me . . . suppose that he possesses understanding and sensitivities, and indeed both to a rare degree.]

Can we suppose that even for a moment of bitter hostility Kleist was
not fully and painfully aware of the distance that separates Thusnelda
the she-bear from Tell the noble marksman?

Komm du hervor, du Bringer bittrer Schmerzen,
Mein teures Kleinod jetzt, mein höchster Schatz—
Ein Ziel will ich dir geben, das bis jetzt
Der frommen Bitte undurchdringlich war—
Doch *dir* soll es nicht widerstehn—Und du,
Vertraute Bogensehne, die so oft
Mir treu gedient hat in der Freude Spielen,
Verlass mich nicht im fürchterlichen Ernst!
Nur jetzt noch halte fest, du treuer Strang,
Der mir so oft den herben Pfeil beflügelt—
Entränn' er jetzo kraftlos meinen Händen,
Ich habe keinen zweiten zu versenden.

[Come forth, bringer of bitter sorrows, now my dear jewel and my
supreme treasure—I will give you a target that till now was impervious to
any gentle plea—But *you* it shall not withstand—And you, familiar bow-
string, who have served me faithfully in games of joy, do not desert me in
this moment of terrible earnestness! Hold firm just once again, faithful
cord, that gave wings so often to my bitter arrow—if it should now feebly
leave my hands, I have no second to dispatch.]

"Wie die erhabensten Sätze leicht zu verstehen sind [just as the most sublime principles are easiest to understand]"—especially if we put them next to such as these:

Thusnelda, bist du klug, die Fürstin ists,
Von deren Haupt, der Livia zur Probe,
Du jüngst die seidne Locke abgelöst!
Lass den Moment, dir günstig, nicht entschlüpfen,
Und ganz die Stirn jetzt schmeichelnd scher ihr ab!   (ll. 2393–97)

[If you are shrewd, it is Thusnelda, the princess, from whose head you removed of late a silken lock as a sample for Livia! Don't let the moment favorable to you be lost—now with blandishment crop her whole brow!]

But have Schiller's lines the *right* to be so nobly simple? Tell has just finished saying that his milk of human kindness has turned into "gährend Drachengift"; the difficulty is that neither his speech nor his feelings show any sign of the transformation. No sooner has he said it than the children are "brought in" to step between him and the monster within:

Die armen Kindlein, die unschuldigen,
Das treue Weib muss ich vor deiner Wut
Beschützen, Landvogt!

[Governor, I must protect these poor, innocent little children and this good woman from your fury!]

Repeatedly he calls his plan "Mord," but it is a figure of speech only:

—Und doch an *euch* nur denkt er, liebe Kinder,
Auch jetzt—euch zu verteidigen, eure holde Unschuld
Zu schützen vor der Rache des Tyrannen,
Will er zum Morde jetzt den Bogen spannen.

[—And yet he is only thinking of *you*, dear children, even now—to defend you and protect your sweet innocence from the tyrant's revenge, he intends to draw his bow now for murder.]

He is no murderer, only the executioner of a higher law: "Es lebt ein Gott, zu strafen und zu rächen. [A God exists, to punish and avenge.]" And in just the same way, Schiller here is no true "Stifter" or "Anstifter"; he is the authorized spokesman of a pre-established order and truth. By Kleist's much more exacting measure, he has not earned the praise he claims:

Wo ist der Tell? Soll er allein uns fehlen,
Der unsrer Freiheit Stifter ist? Das Grösste

Hat *er* getan, das Härteste erduldet.

[Where is our Tell? Shall he who is the author of our freedom be the only one missing? *He* did the most and suffered the most cruelly.]

There are depths of greatness undreamed of in Schiller's noble philosophy and rhetoric.

W. B. Yeats, at a turning point in his development as a poet, felt the need his language had of the "baptism of the gutter." The phrase describes Kleist's need and intention more tellingly than all my pages of commentary. It is exactly this baptism which Thusnelda suffers: this purification and redemption by immersion—in mud. In fact, Kleist anticipates Yeats' metaphor. Directly after Thusnelda's call for her children—and in their place—we get a song:

Ein Knabe sah den Mondenschein
    In eines Teiches Becken;
Er fasste mit der Hand hinein,
    Den Schimmer einzustecken;
Da trübte sich des Wassers Rand,
Das glänz'ge Mondesbild verschwand,
    Und seine Hand war——

[A boy saw the moonlight in the basin of a pond; he reached in with his hand to pocket the glimmering; the water's rim clouded and the gleaming image of the moon disappeared, and his hand was——]

"Drecken" is, I suggest, the only conclusion that would fit the stanza's sense, meter and rhyme scheme. It points to Ventidius' final reward for his theft (which he commits during the singing); but more threateningly it points to Thusnelda herself.[21] As this point everything still seems playful, manageable within the easy harmonies of the Age of Sensibility; but there is the first clear hint of what is to come. We may read the elision not only as standing for the throttled word "drecken," but also as a gesture of attempted, terrified withdrawal—"Schrecken!"—from that word as soon as it rises muddily into view. But there is no withdrawing now; "Reimzwang" holds Thusnelda and Ventidius as inescapably locked in as the "Zwinger" will hold them at play's end. The birth of a nation cannot be celebrated within the aesthetics of "schöner Schein"; a very different kind of baptism is required—a total immersion into the unredeemed physicality of man's origins.

We may well wonder if Kleist did not concede too much to the *sine qua non*—if the cause of humanity, justice and truth is not better served by the celebration of its fragile hopes than the exposure of its "sullied" beginnings (to borrow Shakespeare's profound word-play: "Oh, that this too too sullied [solid] flesh would melt!"). Kleist himself must have wondered; as we have seen, the price he had to pay for not leaving his art out of this cruel play was bitter. It would have been so easy; he could have been a poet—and a patriot too. He could have conspired, written pamphlets and perhaps even a straight propaganda play—but kept his muse pure. Or he could have followed Weimar's example and Friedrich Schlegel's principle:

> Man könnte zwar hier behaupten, dass im Falle des
> Krieges jeder die Vertheidigung des Vaterlandes übernehmen
> müsse. Ein Princip, welches man sehr oft praktisch zu
> realisiren gesucht hat. . . . Allein als allgemeines Princip
> ist es durchaus zu verwerfen. . . . Der Geistliche-, Ge-
> lehrte- und der Stand der Künstler müssen in Ruhe
> und Frieden ihren grossen Zweck verfolgen, und von
> dem stürmischen, rohen Handwerk des Krieges verschont
> bleiben.[22]

[Of course, it might here be maintained that in the event of war everyone must assume the defence of the fatherland. A principle to which one has often tried to give practical realization. . . . Yet as a general principle it is completely unacceptable. . . .Ecclesiastics, scholars, and artists have to pursue their great purpose in peace and quiet and be spared the turbulent, coarse trade of war.]

But of course Kleist had no real choice. His passion for integrity—for doing and being *wholly* whatever he did and was—forced him to make his art serve political ends when these ends seemed the most urgent; and his suspicion of disembodied and unearned beauty and truth forced him to the baptism of the gutter. He knew, far better than Schlegel, how rude and turbulent the craft of war is—in fact, how treacherous and cruel. But he did not think an art either beautiful or true which maintained its purity by parasitic reliance on the dirty work of others.

Kleist had perhaps more than his share of what Coleridge considered the main German failing: nimiety, "too-muchness." As he knew only too well, nothing in him was naturally well-tempered. Like the unfortunate brothers in "Die Heilige Cäcilie," he was condemned to howl his *Gloria in Excelsis* like a wolf. But he did not deceive himself that what came out was the music of the spheres. When he went down, he knew he was going *down*, and why; unlike too many nationalists of a later time, he did not try to persuade himself and others that down was up.

Korff calls *Die Hermannsschlacht* "ein tief fragwürdiges Gebilde." It is truly that—provided we take "frag-würdig" literally (as Korff does not). Kleist compels us to ask questions—some seemingly minute and almost physical in their insistent textuality, other encompassing and of broad import. He compels us to *ask* them, not to beg them. If we do, we find that the questions very much need asking—not only of Kleist and of Germany in 1809, but of a much more recent past, in fact of the present and of ourselves.

Notes

1. Language as Form in Goethe's *Prometheus* and *Pandora*

1. Hans Gerhard Gräf, *Goethe über seine Dichtungen*, Part II, Vol. IV, No. 3612.

2. Gräf, No. 3661.

3. Cf. Julius Richter, "Zur Deutung der Goetheschen Prometheus-Dichtung," *Jahrbuch des Freien Deutschen Hochstifts*, 1928, pp. 64–104. Richter is certainly right in his view that a more mature conception of God underlay the plan of the fragment than that expressed in the ode. Still, it must be kept in mind that the fragment did not grow beyond the vital consciousness established in the ode.

4. Quoted here, as elsewhere in this essay, according to the "Weimarer Ausgabe," Vols. XXXIX and L, Weimar, 1897 and 1900.

5. Gräf, No. 3664.

6. Friedrich Gundolf (*Goethe*, Berlin, 1920, pp. 579–602) treats *Pandora* in the main generically, as allegory and pageant; that in doing so he repeatedly makes valid observations, needs no mention. But in emphasizing in the language only the conceptual and decorative intention (the lyrical "interpolations" of course excepted), he seems to me to fail to recognize the really figurative function of the language as such.

7. What a monstrosity in this dramatic situation is even the ornamental epithet "geflochtnes"!

8. This is also why Wilamowitz' objection to the outcry of Epimeleia ("Goethes Pandora," *Goethe-Jahrbuch*, XIX, 1898, 1–21)—that no Greek would have done it thus and that here the "exaggeration of the imitator" becomes noticeable—completely misses the point. That Epimeleia exactly fills a line of twelve syllables with monosyllabic cries, again leads away from all realistic participation in her fright by giving the latter an almost abnormal stylization. The line is really no cry of woe, either Greek or German, but its formal verbal symbol.

9. Gräf, No. 3661.

10. Robert Petsch's essay, "Über die Kunstform von Goethes Pandora" (*Die Antike*, VI, 1930, 15–40) may serve as warning example for the errors to which an "empathetic" exegesis of the play necessarily must lead. It is doubtless possible to show Goethe's virtuosity in the way he knows how to adjust even such a strange language to changing characters and feelings. But the strangeness of the verbal corpus and its repeatedly interrupted course are basic for the interpretation of the whole. They offer not the least suggestion of a "Fichtean constructive mood," however.

11. Gräf, No. 3620.

12. Ernst Cassirer, "Goethes Pandora," in *Idee und Gestalt*, Berlin, 1921, pp. 3–26.

13. Paul Hankamer, *Spiel der Mächte*, Tübingen und Stuttgart, 1948, esp. pp. 153–206.

14. According to the stage direction, to be sure, water could be meant as common background of the Promethean as well as of the Epimethean world. But the symmetry of the suicidal elements—after all, the lovers plunge into the elements at opposite ends of the stage—makes it certain that water belongs essentially to the Epimethean side, from which alone, moreover, it is visible and approachable. Nevertheless we do not deny that a close relationship exists between Epimeleia and the uniting third element—"the forces": Eos speaks at the end in her metre and announces the Dionysian re-birth from water; even Epimeleia herself ranks water as one of the manifestations of the divine (V, 501). But on the human level this counter-element continues to obtain.

15. Cf. Oskar Seidlin, "Zur Mignon-Ballade," *Euphorion*, XLV (1950), 83–99.

16. Thus I here diverge from Hankamer's interpretation of these lines (*Spiel der Mächte*, p. 163f.). Hankamer emphasizes the contemplative human spirit, which "between cosmos and microcosmos . . . playfully and knowledgeably brings about a relationship." However much this may apply to Goethe's late style in general, the essential in *this* passage seems to me to lie in the fact that speech as such is not in a position to bring about this relationship.

2. "The voice of truth and of humanity": Goethe's *Iphigenie*

1. *Goethe*, Berlin, 1930, p. 304f.

2. Quoted here, as elsewhere in this essay, unless otherwise noted, according to the "Jubiläums-Ausgabe" (Berlin-Stuttgart, 1902), vol. 12.

3. Compare Oskar Seidlin's in many ways pioneer interpretation, "Goethes Iphigenie—'verteufelt human'?," *Wirkendes Wort*, V (1955), 272–80, to which I owe also other suggestions, in spite of holding some divergent views.

4. James Boyd, "Four Prayers in Goethe's *Iphigenie*," *German Studies*, Oxford, 1938, pp. 33–61, has the merit of having examined this utterance separately, but in my opinion reaches wrong conclusions, just as his later complete interpretation (*Goethe's Iphigenie auf Tauris*, Oxford, 1949), which finds expressed in Faust's "feeling is all" also the central idea of our play, seems to me unsuccessful.

5. What she intended was of course a condition: "If you wish to save your image in my soul, then save me from the necessity of lying." But as almost always with Goethe, the decisive thing is not the "intention" but the word really spoken: the very fact that this prayer is *not* a conditional clause, *not* an explicit ultimatum, marks the as yet incomplete autonomy of the one praying, that is, incomplete because not yet become speech.

6. That this is not altogether conclusive, that Iphigenia in her first hymn still speaks with her own voice and weaves in a prayer, confirms this interpretation. Iphigenia's mingling of languages is the exact opposite of Orestes' con-

fusion of language. She is not yet autonomous and therefore does not yet have the sure feeling for language which forces her (in the later hymn) into blank verse, as soon as she speaks as an individual person and calls Pylades by name.

7. In my opinion the interpretation of Hans Wolff (*Goethes Weg zur Humanität*, Bern, 1951, pp. 211–27), which is diametrically opposed to what is attempted here in almost every regard, shows to what radically false interpretations the neglect of Goethe's language forms (languages) leads. Wolff observes of the "Song of the Fates" that it saves the image of the gods in Iphigenia's soul in "leading her back again to the god of anger and predestination, the god with whom man cannot argue and towards whom only mute submission is possible."

8. Ludwig Kahn's opinion that Iphigenia's decision is "made easy for her because she finds security in an impersonal, absolute system of morality" (*Monatshefte*, XXXIX [1947], 235) seems clearly contradicted by the text itself. The contrast between Goethe and Kleist is indeed great, but of an entirely different nature than such a Schillerian version of Goethe would indicate.

9. It is gratifying, though not necessary as a matter of method, that we can show that Goethe consciously worked this grouping—and the resultant "supplantation" of the word "sister"—into the last version of the play. The following chart, set up on the basis of J. Baechtold's synoptic edition (*Goethe Iphigenie auf Tauris in vierfacher Gestalt*, Freiburg, 1883), shows this (reference to lines according to the last version):

	A, B, C	D
V. 566	Schwester [sister]	Schwester
611	Diane [Diana]	Schwester
722	Diane-Schwester	Schwester
738	heiliges Bild [holy image]	——
840	Diane	Schwester
[Iphigenia reveals herself as Orestes' sister]		
1438	der Göttin Bild [the goddess' image]	der Göttin Bild
1563	der Göttin Bild	der Göttin Bild
1602	der Göttin Bild	heiliger Schatz [holy treasure]
1605	Schwester	——
1709	Schutzbild [guardian image]	Bild [image]
1923	Bild deiner Göttin [image of your goddess]	——
1929/31	Bild der Schwester [the sister's image]	Bild Dianens/Schwester [Diana's image/sister]

Through the two omissions (738; 1605) the as yet unclear distinction in the first three versions is finally cleared up; in the last version of the confession (1929–31) the two words are no longer joined by the genitive case but placed side by side tautologically (see below).

10. From which would result that they really did *not* exist. Since creation is the essence of their being, they cannot deny their creature without denying themselves. Read aloud, in this line "true" and "are" would have to be spoken with equal emphasis, since "true" is to be understood adverbially as well as predicatively.

11. How anyone, like Korff (*Geist der Goethezeit*, vol. 2, Leipzig, 1927, p. 167f.), can conceive the Tartarus-idyl as a moment of "inner illumination"—of insight "that only love can overcome hate"—I do not understand. To be sure, death too solves the curse and heals all human frailties; but hardly in Goethe's sense. And how does Korff explain the horror that this vision ends in:

> Ihr scheint zu zaudern, euch wegzuwenden?
> Was ist es? Leidet der Göttergleiche?
> Weh mir! es haben die Übermächt'gen
> Der Heldenbrust grausame Qualen
> Mit ehrnen Ketten fest aufgeschmiedet?

[You seem to hesitate, turn away? What is it? Does the god-like one suffer? Woe is me! The All-powerful have attached with iron chains dreadful torments to his heroic breast.]   (ll. 1305–09)

12. John N. Hritzu ("Reflections on stage directions . . . in *Iphigenie* . . . ," *Monatshefte*, XXXIX (1941), 17–23) shows how Goethe lets movements and acts of the characters be expressed in the text, rather than indicating them by means of stage directions. Characteristically, the stage directions suddenly pile up where the sword threatens to take over the word: in the scene of the meeting between Thaos and Orestes.

13. Professor Heinrich Henel has drawn my attention to a possible objection: since Orestes was not present at the confession he would hardly be in a position here to explain the new truth. The objection, it seems to me, loses validity if we understand—as Goethe repeatedly demands of us—the word once spoken as a really corporeal element of the world of the poetic work. What has once been said, stands so to speak on the stage, a tangible reality, which is plain at least to a sensitive human being (Orestes) even if he does not "hear" it physically. Just such an "Aha!"-reaction Goethe intended and had to avoid, since this would have given rise to the impression that the truth existed from the beginning and is only discovered, while it is conversely being created for the first time.

14. In another sense Orestes is right, however: in the one already mentioned, that in God word and object, thought and act of creation are the same. Human beings "interpret" the word of God and have to err in doing so; God however "intended you," that is, created Iphigenia, who now has the responsibility of transforming error into truth.

15. *Spiel der Mächte*, Tübingen-Stuttgart, 1938, p. 176.

16. And thereby in confuting the judgment of Heinrich Meyer, who does not recognize just this corporeal density of imagery and therefore criticizes in the play very improperly an "excess of form, [a] lack of vitality, [a] pure spiritualization which found no human symbols but at best humanistic ones" (*Goethe*, Hamburg, 1949, p. 228).

3. The Consistency of Goethe's *Tasso*

1. Wolfdietrich Rasch, *Goethes "Torquato Tasso,"* Stuttgart, 1954; and Walter Silz, "Ambivalences in Goethe's *Tasso*," *Germanic Review*, XXI (1956), 243–68.

4. *Die natürliche Tochter*: Goethe's *Iphigenie in Aulis*?

1. Hans Egon Hass ("Goethe: Die natürliche Tochter," *Das deutsche Drama vom Barock bis zur Gegenwart*, hrsg. B. von Wiese, Düsseldorf, 1958, I, 215–47) shows convincingly why the work is to be understood as a completed whole despite Goethe's plans for continuation.

2. Goethe, II, Zürich, 1956, 378.

3. For this interpretation of *Iphigenie*, on which some further statements are also based, compare the author's "Die Stimme der Wahrheit und der Menschlichkeit: Goethes *Iphigenie*," translated in this volume.

4. Staiger, who feels fully the psychological inconsistency of this scene, explains it differently: "But Goethe does not remain too long with what is empty of meaning. If his people are caught in the fate of their time, he speaks over their heads, in his own name from their mouth, what a superior spirit has need of expressing" (*Goethe*, II, 379).

5. Compare Friedrich Gundolf, *Goethe*, Berlin, 1922 pp. 471–75; K. May, "Goethes 'Natürliche Tochter,'" *Goethe-Jahrbuch*, N. F., IV (1939), 147–63; B. von Wiese, *Die deutsche Tragödie von Lessing bis Hebbel*, Hamburg, 1948, I, 137–42.

6. Goethe II, 387.

7. Compare the excellent linguistic analysis of Verena Bänninger (*Goethes Natürliche Tochter*, Zürich, 1957, p. 93f.), which shows how in this work, entirely other than in the other works, verse and word "become absolute," are disengaged from the organic structure of the sentence and play an independent "role." I just cannot regard this without doubt correctly understood stylistic tendency as the solely determining one; it seems to me to become that only in *Pandora*.

8. H. G. Gräf, *Goethe über seine Dichtungen*, V, No. 3328.

9. Compare K. May's introduction to the Artemis-edition (VI, 1199). His assumption that the King's signature is to be found on a forged document finds no support in the text, indeed seems to me to be clearly refuted by it, especially by V, 5.

10. *Goethe*, I, 418f.

11. If I may interpret V. Bänninger's presentation of "appearance" as the central happening of the play in such a way that it culminates as form and becomes presence in the dressing-scene, yet I cannot go all the way with this fruitful insight. For we are at no moment unaware that this is an arbitrary, forbidden-premature and thus in the end a "mis"-appearance. True appearance and pure presence would have been Eugenie's admission to the royal circle; but this is thwarted.

12. A significant dramatic motif may be indicated here: that of fruitless speaking. Revealingly, it appears in its sharpest earlier form in Goethe's other tragedy, *Egmont*, that likewise can be interpreted as an interment of a dramatic form recognized as inadequate: the "discussion" between Egmont and Alba is empty sound, as we and Alba know from the beginning. And the great dialogue between Iphigenia and Thoas (V, 3) threatens to remain only a time-winning excuse behind which on both sides the "wary ambush" can be prepared; but at the last moment the battle of words turns into a true dialogue. In *Tasso*, the danger of fruitless speech is considerably intensified, but there is still the possibility of accommodation. In *Die natürliche Tochter*, as in *Egmont*, this possibility was eliminated at the outset. (For the Egmont-Alba-scene, compare Paul Böckmann, "Goethe: Egmont," in: *Das deutsche Drama vom Barock bis zur Gegenwart*, I, 155f.)

13. *Goethes Drama "Die Natürliche Tochter,"* Berlin, 1912.

14. This opinion is based on an as yet unpublished investigation by Professor Wolfgang Fleischhauer, who kindly made it available to me, which traces the antecedent history of this oxymoron so important for Goethe by way of the title of Gozzi's drama.

7. Kleist's *Hermannsschlacht*: The Lock and the Key

1. Friedrich Gundolf, *Heinrich von Kleist* (Berlin, 1922), p. 126ff.

2. No manuscript of the play is extant. Sembdner, in his invaluable edition of Kleist's works and letters (revised, Hanser, München 1961, 2 vols. hereinafter cited as SW), surmises that Tieck may have chosen the motto, slightly changing it from Kleist's distich "Die tiefste Erniedrigung" (*SW* I, 944). But this is mere surmise. Tieck did not supply mottos for any of the other plays; nor is it clear why he should have changed the distich (which reads: "... Das Lied, zum Ruhm dir, zu singen ...").

3. There is, however, what I consider strong internal evidence. Hally's father is "Teuthold, ein Waffenschmied"—and the archetypal "Waffenschmied" in Germanic mythology is Wieland. The name Teuthold may well express Kleist's gratitude for Wieland's generous encouragement of his "German" muse. Except for two short excerpts, Wieland's fragment remained unpublished until the end of the 19th century, when the sole extant manuscript of it was found among Bodmer's literary remains. But Kleist may well have seen another copy (now lost) during the months he spent as a guest in Ossmanstedt; or else he may have been told something of the epic's argument.

Text quoted here in taken from Wieland's *Gesammelte Schriften*, Berlin, 1909, p. 184f.

4. H. A. Korff, *Geist der Goethezeit* (Leipzig, 1953), p. 258f.

5. I am assuming—with the majority of critics—that "Die Verlobung in St. Domingo" was written, or at least drafted in considerable detail, before the composition of *Die Hermannsschlacht*. On thematic grounds, the story clearly belongs in the vicinity of *Penthesilea*, even though there is no mention of it prior to its first publication (1811) in *Der Freimüthige*.

6. For a comparable "key" passage, cf. *Käthchen von Heilbronn*, III. xii–xiii.

7. It is worth noting how rigorously Kleist denies himself the easy effects of the family metaphor. When Hermann sends his sons off to Marbod, there is not a sign of inner struggle, not a word about fatherly feelings; if two dogs were at stake, the business could not be transacted more matter-of-factly. With the sole exception of the Hally episode—and even it Kleist strips of its inherent pathos—there is no family scene in the entire play: no wives bidding their husbands a tender farewell, no fathers blessing or exhorting their sons, no children swearing vengeance for the suffering of their parents. The word "Brüder" is hardly ever used in the play; but the overblown form "Bruderherz" is used twice by Fust in the revolting scene alluded to above (ll. 2527 and 2533).

8. Schiller acknowledged the debt by working Müller's name into the text of the play:

> ein glaubenswerter Mann,
> Johannes Müller bracht' es [news of Albrecht's death]
> von Schaffhausen

[a reliable man, Johannes Müller, brought it (news of Albrecht's death) from Schaffhausen].

9. How much the experience was in his mind when he wrote *Die Hermannsschlacht* is evident from the many place names ending in –kon— Iphikon, Helakon, Thuiskon, Herthakon—which give the play's locale an oddly Swiss imprint.

10. Kleist's hymn of hatred, "Germania an ihre Kinder," must similarly be considered a reply to Schiller's "An die Freude," the metrical pattern of which it takes over.

11. *Briefe von und an F. v. Gentz*, ed. F. C. Wittichen, Berlin, 1910, II, 415.

12. I am aware that as late as December, 1807, Kleist mentions J. v. Müller among those from whom he and Adam Müller hoped to obtain contributions to *Phöbus*. It has been argued—especially by Hans M. Wolff (*H. v. Kleist als politischer Dichter*, Univ. of California Publications in Modern Philology, vol. 27, no. 6, 1947) and more recently by Richard Samuel ("Kleist's Hermannsschlacht und der Freiherr vom Stein," *Jahrbuch der dt. Schillergesellschaft*, 1961, 64–101)—that Kleist was happily apolitical until well into 1808. As prime evidence for this view the fact is adduced that Kleist hoped to obtain the German publication rights of the *Code Napoléon* and other French government releases. But in the letter to Ulrike in which

Kleist mentions these hopes, he adds an emphatic cautionary note: "Du wirst nicht voreilig sein, politische Folgerungen aus diesem Schritt zu ziehen über dessen eigentliche Bedeutung ich mich nicht weiter auslassen kann. [You will not be hasty in drawing political conclusions from this move, about the real meaning of which I cannot express myself further.]" That Kleist never was apolitical where Napoleon and the French were concerned, is clear from his letters of 1801/02; by the end of 1805 he was even more passionate (cf. SW II, 760 f.). His friends and associates in Dresden were mostly of the anti-French faction; they all testify to his strong political sentiments, and none of them as much as hints at a sudden shift toward political engagement. On the contrary, we hear of his being a contact man for the Lützows, who were then—with Schill, Graf Götzen and others—preparing a popular uprising against the French (cf. Sembdner, *Kleists Lebensspuren*, Bremen 1957, 220 ff.). In sum, everything speaks against Wolff's and Samuel's surmise—except the facade of *Phöbus*. But if we suspect Kleist of hoping to use Phöbus as a cover and to win French financial support for it even while he was secretly plotting against Napoleon, we suspect him precisely of what he has his hero Hermann do. In fact, is not the quadriga that is so oddly called attention to in the play—

THUISKOMAR: Schau, die Quadriga, die August dir schenkte!
SELGAR: Die Pferd aus Rom?
HERMANN (*zerstreut*):   Aus Rom, beim Jupiter!
  Ein Zug, wie der Pelid ihn nicht geführt!

[THUISKOMAR: Look, the quadriga that Augustus made you a present of!
SELGAR: The horses from Rome?
HERMANN (*distracted*): From Rome, by Jove, a team such as Achilles himself did
  not drive!]   (ll. 120–22)

is not this the very quadriga which adorned the cover of *Phöbus*? If so, Kleist was only hoping to steal from the French what the French had stolen in the first place. A patriotic legend current in 1808 went as follows:

Schill hatte bei Kolberg vier aussergewöhnlich schöne Pferde abgefangen, die für Napoleon bestimmt waren. Dieser bot ihm für jedes Pferd 1000 Taler, überschrieb den betreffenden Brief aber: "An den Räuberhauptmann von Schill." Schill antwortete: "Herr Bruder! . . . Gegen die angebotenen 1000 Taler kann ich sie Ihnen nicht zurückgeben. Wollen Sie aber die vier Pferde, die Sie von dem Brandenburger Tor in Berlin weggestohlen haben, wieder dort aufstellen lassen, so stehen Ihnen die von mir in Beschlag genommenen zu Diensten."

[Schill had intercepted near Kolberg four extraordinarily beautiful horses that were destined for Napoleon. The latter offered him 1000 thaler for each horse, but addressed the letter concerning the matter: "To Robber Captain von Schill." Schill answered: "Dear Sir My Brother! . . . I cannot give them back to you for the proffered 1000 thaler. But if you are willing to have put back on the Brandenburg Gate in Berlin the four horses you stole from it, those I seized are at your disposal."] (Cf. G. Vorwerk-Semler, *Ferdinand von Schill*, Braunschweig, 1941, p. 24.)

13. Säkular-Ausgabe, II, 386 ff.

14. Carl Gustav von Brinckmann, *Briefe von und an Gentz*, ed. cit., II, 309.

15. Adam Müller, *Vorlesungen über die deutsche Wissenschaft und Literatur*, ed. A. Salz, München, 1920, p. 168 f.

16. Not to mention its chances of survival, at least as a "Kultursprache." The time lay not far back when German had seemed in real danger of being submerged; under Napoleon the danger was hardly less acute than it had been in the days of Louis XIV. Johannes von Müller's much noted decision to give his address on Frederick in French may well have seemed symptomatic; it certainly was symptomatic for *him*. On January 28, 1805, he had written his publisher:

> Wenn Sie noch nicht angefangen haben, zu drucken, so tun Sie mir doch den Gefallen ... deutsche Lettern zu nehmen.... Es ist doch gar infam, dass wir uns unsrer Schrift zu schämen hätten. Ich bin von denen, welche die Deutschen nicht möchten zu Franzosen werden lassen. Ich will die Schmach der Deutschheit tragen. ... Wer mich lesen will, lerne deutsch.

> [If you have not yet begun to print, then please do me the favor ... of using German type.... It is really infamous that we should have to be ashamed of German characters. I belong to those who would not like to have the Germans become Frenchmen. I wish to bear the disgrace of being German.... If one wishes to read me, let him learn German.]

By November 8, 1806, he wrote his brother:

> "Das habe ich mir vorgenommen, künftig meine Bücher in beiden Sprachen zu schreiben.

> [I have resolved to write my books henceforth in both languages.]"

(J. v. Müller, *Briefe in Auswahl*, ed. E. Bonjour, Basel 1954, p. 296 and p. 329.)

17. Septimius is the prototype of the high German officers at the Nuremberg trials—as Varus is their prototype at or before the outbreak of World War II:

VARUS: Wieso? Meinst du vielleicht, die Absicht sei, Cheruska
Als ein erobertes Gebiet—?

VENT.: Quintilius,
Die Absicht, dünkt mich, lässt sich fast erraten.

VARUS: Seis! Was bekümmerts mich? Es ist nicht meines Amtes
Den Willen meines Kaisers zu erspähn.
Er sagt ihn, wenn er ihn vollführt will wissen. (ll. 1266–75)

[VARUS: In what way? Do you mean perhaps, the intention may be, Cheruska as a conquered territory—?
VENT.: Quintilius, the intention can almost be guessed, it seems to me.
VARUS: So be it! Why should it bother me? It is not my function to detect the will of my emperor. He will state it, if he wants to be sure it will be carried out.]

Since we can hardly avoid thinking uneasily of the Nazi era as we read Kleist's play, it is doubly important that we perceive the play's true moral structure and not bury its careful and subtle distinctions under such crude and blanket terms as "Nationalhass."

18. If, by the way, this passage offends us as a barbaric conglomerate of prosy argumentation and wildly mixed metaphors, that is precisely the offense Kleist means to give. No "Latier" would speak like this, nor would the most humble of Schiller's Swiss. The style is of a piece with such lines as: "Danach wird weder Hund noch Katze krähen [no dog or cat will care a straw about it]."

19. *Kleist als politischer Dichter*, p. 481.

20. The "Universalmonarchie" he envisages was anathema to men like Adam Müller, Gentz, and Friedrich Schlegel. To them it meant loss of national identity, cosmopolitanism, inorganic uniformity. Their idea of political order beyond the national level was one of "Gleichgewicht" (on which Gentz had written a treatise), somehow competitive but somehow also suffused with a common (read Catholic-Christian) "Geist," which would keep it from lapsing into international chaos.

21. It also fixes, I believe, the moment in Kleist's planning when he rejected the idea of "abstracting" the family subplot from the shining surface of *Wilhelm Tell*.

22. Friedrich Schlegel, *Philosophische Vorlesungen, 1800–1807, Werke*, ed. E. Behler, J. J. Austett, H. Eichner. (Zurich, 1964), XIII, 149–150.

Index

THE JOHNS HOPKINS PRESS

Designed by James C. Wageman

Composed in Electra text and display
by Monotype Composition Company
with Fraktur initials

Printed on 60 lb. Warren's "1854"
by Universal Lithographers, Inc.

Bound in Bancroft Kennett
by L. H. Jenkins, Inc.

Lightning Source UK Ltd.
Milton Keynes UK
UKHW041433150120
357004UK00001B/108/P